The Reputational Imperative

The ***Studies in Asian Security*** book series promotes analysis, understanding, and explanation of the dynamics of domestic, transnational, and international security challenges in Asia. The peer-reviewed publications in the series analyze contemporary security issues and problems to clarify debates in the scholarly community, provide new insights and perspectives, and identify new research and policy directions. Security is defined broadly to include the traditional political and military dimensions, as well as nontraditional dimensions that affect the survival and well-being of political communities. Asia too is defined broadly to include Northeast, Southeast, South, and Central Asia.

Designed to encourage original and rigorous scholarship, books in the Studies in Asian Security series seek to engage scholars, educators, and practitioners. Wide ranging in scope and method, the series is receptive to all paradigms, programs, and traditions and to an extensive array of methodologies now employed in the social sciences.

# The Reputational Imperative

NEHRU'S INDIA IN TERRITORIAL CONFLICT

Mahesh Shankar

Stanford University Press • Stanford, California

Stanford University Press
Stanford, California



Library of Congress Cataloging-in-Publication Data

Shankar, Mahesh.
  The Reputational Imperative : Nehru's India in territorial conflict / Mahesh Shankar.
Stanford, California : Stanford University Press, 2018. | Series: Studies in Asian security |
  Includes bibliographical references and index.
LCCN 2018001303 (print) | LCCN 2018001900 (ebook) |ISBN 9781503607200 (e-book) |
  ISBN 9781503605466 (cloth : alk. paper) | ISBN 9781503607200 (ebook)
LCSH: India—Boundaries—Pakistan—History—20th century. |
Pakistan—Boundaries—India—History—20th century. | India—Boundaries—China—
  History—20th century. | China—Boundaries—India—History—20th century. |
  India—Foreign relations—1947–1984. | Reputation—Political aspects—India—History—
  20th century. | Nehru, Jawaharlal, 1889–1964.
LCC DS450.P18 (ebook) | LCC DS450.P18 S525 2018 (print) | DDC
  954.04/2—DC23
LC record available at https://lccn.loc.gov/                              2018001303

Printed in the United States of America on acid-free, archival-quality paper

Cover photograph: Buddhist prayer flags near Pangong Pso, alpine lake in the Himalayas. Alexey Stiop | Alamy Stock Photo

Typeset at Stanford University Press in 10.5 / 13.5 Bembo

*For Archana*

# Contents

# Acknowledgments

Writing, as many will attest, is as solitary and lonely an experience as there can be. Yet very little of this book would have been possible without the support of numerous people over the past decade. This work is in large part a product of their generosity, and I owe them all a sincere debt of gratitude that I only inadequately express here.

I started research for this book at McGill University, and it would be no understatement to say that this work would not exist but for the exacting guidance of T. V. Paul during my time there. T. V. was incredibly generous with his time and attention, always willing (even demanding) to read and comment on multiple drafts and constantly encouraging me on at points when I saw no path forward in my research. In the years since then, T. V. showed more faith and interest in the project than perhaps even I did as he constantly prodded me to get this book written. His engagement has made this a better piece of scholarship than it would have been otherwise. T. V. has quite simply been the best champion a junior academic could hope for, and I will be eternally grateful to him.

Others in the Department of Political Science at McGill also deserve my profuse gratitude. Mark Brawley, Lorenz Lüthi, and Rex Brynen were gracious with their time and advice throughout. Lorenz in particular kindly shared some of his own research and archival finds with me early on, and he has remained interested in this project since then. He read the entire manuscript and offered valuable advice along the way. Vincent Pouliot and Erik Kuhonta provided characteristically trenchant feedback in the early stages of the project. Other friends and colleagues at McGill also helped me think through my research at various points. I specifically thank Theo McLauchlin, Harish Seshagirirao, Param Chopra, Jessica Trisko, Julie Moreau, Douglas Hanes, and Mohammed Sesay. In one way or another, feedback from all of these people has shaped this book.

I have received great support from several colleagues at other institutions over the years. Rajesh Basrur, a wonderful scholar and friend, gave me the opportunity to spend some time at the Rajaratnam School of International Studies in Singapore, where this book manuscript began really taking shape. Sumit Ganguly was incredibly generous with his time and encouragement, and thoroughly read and commented on earlier versions of the manuscript. Nabarun Roy and I went from India to Canada for our doctoral studies at the same time, and we have spent much time bouncing ideas off each other. At Skidmore College, where most of this work has been written and rewritten, Pushi Prasad, Ela Lepkowska-White, Aiwu Zhao, Beau Breslin, Paty Rubio, and Crystal Moore have ensured that I have lacked for nothing in personal and professional support. Jordana Dym and Kate Graney provided great advice on research and publication logistics. Steven Hoffman read early versions of the Sino-India chapters and offered superb advice.

In India, my archival research was made possible by the wonderful staff at the Nehru Memorial Museum and Library in New Delhi who guided me expertly as I pored through documents for dawn to dusk. Faculty at the School of International Studies at Jawaharlal Nehru University helped shape my research interests and were readily available to talk to and advise me during my visits to New Delhi. Happymon Jacob, Alka Acharya, Srikanth Kondapalli, Rajesh Rajagopalan, and P. R. Kumaraswamy deserve mention here.

I must also thank several people at Stanford University Press. The series editors, Amitav Acharya and David Leheny, have been generous in their advice and meticulously efficient in ensuring that the manuscript went through a swift but thorough vetting. At the press, Jenny Gavacs expressed early interest in the book, and Kate Wahl and Alan Harvey took over to shepherd the project through the peer review process and toward completion. Micah Siegel and Leah Pennywark provided exemplary editorial support, and Anne Fuzellier guided the book through production with consummate professionalism. Beverly Miller expertly copyedited this book. It has been a long road, but one that has felt significantly less so thanks to these individuals. I also owe my sincerest thanks to the two anonymous reviewers of the manuscript who provided wonderfully constructive and detailed suggestions to help make this book a better piece of scholarship. Thank you!

Portions of this book draw from two previously published pieces, "Showing Character: Nehru, Reputation, and the Sino-Indian Dispute, 1957–1962," *Asian Security* 11, no. 2 (2015): 99–115, © Taylor and Francis Ltd.; and "Nehru's Legacy in Kashmir: Why a Plebiscite Never Happened," *India Review* 15, no. 1 (2016): 1–21, © Taylor and Francis Ltd. They are reprinted here by permission of the publisher (Taylor & Francis Ltd., http://www.tandfonline.com), for which I am grateful.

I am lucky to have a wonderfully loving and supportive family. My mother has been an inspiration and supported my decision to study abroad without hesitation. My accomplishments here pale in comparison to what she has done, and continues to do, for our family. That I do what I do has everything to do with my father, who would have probably been the only one in the family I could trust to read this book cover to cover. I have also been fortunate to have a brother who has greater faith in my abilities than I have ever had and always inspires me to take life just that little bit easier. The same goes for my little daughter, Nayana, who finds it possible to compress more joy into each hour than I ever imagined possible. My parents-in-law have unquestioningly supported me as I pursued a perilously uncertain career and moved from one end of the world to another multiple times. Finally, Archana, my wife and best friend, helped me stay sane, healthy, and hopeful. She is hugely responsible for the fact that this work even exists and for any credit that it deserves. I dedicate this book to her.

# The Reputational Imperative

# 1

## Introduction

May 27, 2014, marked the fiftieth anniversary of the death of India's first prime minister, and global statesman, Jawaharlal Nehru. Along with the celebration of his exemplary legacy for independent India's domestic and international profile, the occasion also served as a barely needed reminder of what can be considered as the abiding challenge to, and puzzle of, Nehru's tenure: his failure to help find a satisfactory resolution to the Kashmir dispute with Pakistan and the territorial conflict with China.[1]

Several decades after his departure from the scene and with much ink having been spilled on the study of the two disputes, a complete picture and systematic understanding of the drivers of Nehruvian policy on territorial issues still largely eludes the scholarship. This gap is particularly glaring considering the nuanced and complex reality of India's approach to these conflicts in their formative years, involving instances of unexpected conciliation as well as puzzling intransigence; a willingness to compromise on clearly salient territory but also to provoke losing wars over seemingly worthless ones. It is with such puzzles in Indian policymaking that this book is primarily engaged.

In explaining the Indian government's conduct in territorial disputes in the first two decades after independence, much of the conventional wisdom emphasizes two considerations whose importance is both intuitively appealing and well established in the theoretical literature on international relations: security and nationalism. Security-driven explanations make two kinds of assertions. First, a view that has held sway for a long time contends that Nehru's approach to international politics was singularly naive and idealist and therefore put too little stock in ensuring security, a tendency that manifested in the country's lackadaisical approach to territorial issues. One scholar, for instance, has termed Nehru's China policy as "based more on what is called wishful thinking than on objective conditions."[2] A second view argues that elements of realpolitik, aimed at furthering the country's security and strategic interests within the material constraints the country faced, are basic to understanding Indian policy.[3] Maxwell offers the more extreme manifestation of this argument in contending that Nehru's government precipitated conflict in the Sino-Indian case by seeking to unilaterally impose a boundary on Beijing.[4] Raghavan provides a more nuanced recent expression of this perspective in suggesting that Nehruvian strategy was based on a blend of liberal and realist ideas that he terms "liberal realism," which "abhorred war" but "also held that conflict was an endemic feature of politics; for all national and social groups were inevitably motivated by self-interest."[5]

Another set of arguments contends, in contrast, that one cannot satisfactorily explain Indian policy during this period without factoring in nationalism and domestic politics. By this account, Indian attitudes on territorial issues with Pakistan and China were determined primarily by how much symbolic-nationalist significance the leaders attached to the disputed territories. Hoffman encapsulates this thinking when he suggests in the Sino-Indian context that Indian nationalism—defined as "beliefs, attitudes, and perceptions brought forth by India's struggle for independence . . . and shaped by the long history and culture of the Indian subcontinent"—played a "subtle and pervasive" role in shaping Nehru's attitudes on territorial issues.[6] This logic also postulates that decision making at crucial junctures was largely hostage to the pressures and constraints imposed on the prime minister by domestic public opinion, the political opposition, and from within Nehru's Congress Party itself. Domestic political imperatives, in other words, reign supreme in this telling of the story.

That both of these claims have found traction in accounts of Indian policy is not surprising. On Kashmir, a strong case can be made that the land holds great value for both contestants from security and nationalist standpoints. In security terms, the vital geostrategic position of state was always apparent, located as it is at the apex of the Indian subcontinent, historically buffering India from threats emanating from Russia, China, and Afghanistan.[7] Add to this the presence within the territory of the headwaters of three major rivers that constitute the lifeline of particularly Pakistan's agricultural economy, and it is clear why possession of the territory has seemed immensely advantageous to both sides. It is the symbolic-nationalist value of the state, however, that many argue is even more salient to understanding the conflict. Kashmir, in this view, embodies the clash of contested nationalisms that led to the partition of the subcontinent into India and Pakistan in the first place, with secular India pitted against Pakistan, the self-anointed home of the Muslims of the region.[8] As one scholar has put it, it is this ideational and ideological conflict that has been the "underlying issue" in the dispute because each state has been "keenly aware of the ideological significance of Kashmir and most unwilling to concede it to the other as this would undermine its own ideological legitimacy."[9] Another observer has neatly characterized Kashmir in the same vein as a "zero-sum test for each state's legitimizing ideology."[10]

In the Sino-Indian case, similarly, security and nationalism have seemed ready and persuasive explanations for India's conduct. While critics attribute the eventual outcome—India's ignominious defeat in the 1962 war—to Nehru's lack of strategic nous throughout the entire period, others see security motives as driving New Delhi's intransigent posture in the lead-up to war. Most accounts specifically attribute, for instance, India's interest in maintaining the McMahon Line frontier in the eastern sector to the crucial importance of holding the territory below that line to preserving the security of the entire Indian northeast from a potential Chinese threat. Other influential accounts have given privilege of place to nationalism and domestic politics in explaining Nehru's major decisions. These latter works have contended that a strong sense of nationalism, either in the form of the Indian leaders' own ideas and beliefs—for Hoffman about India's historical borders; for Miller the sense of postcolonial victimhood—or as a result of domestic political pressures due to an aggravated body politic, primarily determined Nehru's intransigence on the territorial issue.[11]

Important as these insights are to understanding Indian behavior during this period, they leave some crucial empirical puzzles underexplained. For example, if the salience or value of the territory was so central to the Nehru government's positions, it is not clear why, on the highly salient territory of Kashmir, leaders were willing to make significant concessions to Pakistan from even before partition and until late in 1953. Indeed, soon after the tribal invasion from Pakistan in 1947, the Indian government acquiesced to holding a plebiscite in the state, and it maintained that commitment even when it had become clear to Nehru himself that India was certain to lose such a vote. Only in 1954 did the Indian prime minister renege from that position to asserting that Kashmir's accession to India was complete and nonnegotiable with either Pakistan or the Kashmiri populace. A focus on salience alone misses out on these crucial nuances in the empirics of the case and provides little explanation for why Nehru was open to a plebiscite in the first place, why a plebiscite was then never held, and, finally, why New Delhi withdrew that offer in 1954.

Similar issues confront any explanation relying on salience to account for India's actions in the Sino-Indian dispute. In that case, it is amply apparent from internal documents that Nehru and his officials were very clear from early on that the disputed territory in the western sector was of little importance to India in strategic, economic, or nationalist terms. What is more, Indian officials were also persuaded for much of this period that even on legal grounds, the government's claims to territory in the region lacked any strong standing. It was the territory in the east that they viewed as crucial to the security of the entire Indian northeast and where India's legal claims were understood to be more ironclad.[12] Given these facts, it would be reasonable to expect the Indian government to have been open to making concessions in the western sector in exchange for the Chinese giving up their claims in the far more valuable eastern sector. Yet it was precisely such a solution that Nehru rejected in talks with Zhou Enlai in New Delhi in April 1960.

Other security- and power-based logics are similarly unsatisfactory. If it is true, on the one hand, that Nehru's idealism precluded strategic thought and made India unnecessarily accommodative, it is difficult to explain the many instances in these cases where the Indian government assumed uncharacteristically tough stances. On the other hand, to the extent that it has been argued that strategic thinking did indeed shape New Delhi's conduct, including its intransigence, it is unclear why the Nehru government, counterintuitive to standard bargaining expectations, seemed most open to concessions on clearly salient territory in Kashmir during times of its greatest relative military strength in relation to Pakistan. The realpolitik logic is arguably even more problematic when it comes to the Sino-Indian conflict. There, it bumps up against the puzzle of why India chose the path of intransigence in a context where it was amply clear to both military and political leaders in the country well before the war itself that the Indian army was woefully unprepared for any military confrontation with China.[13] That New Delhi chose to reject Zhou's offer of compromise and instead pursued a risky political path despite such obvious military debilities seems unfathomable from a security-seeking standpoint.

In each of these cases, then (as well as in the Chinese approach to the Sino-Indian dispute discussed as an extension to this work in chapter 7), not only are the conventional security and nationalist perspectives inadequate as an explanation, but we also see another theoretically puzzling phenomenon: of strong states being more conciliatory than necessary and weaker states adopting more intransigent positions than seems wise. This work seeks to fill these theoretical and empirical gaps in our understanding of the nuances of Indian policy in the country's major territorial disputes under its first prime minister.

## Reputation, Compromise, and Conflict in Territorial Disputes

This book makes a novel theoretical argument to account for the puzzling aspects of decisions such as those made by India under Nehru. It suggests that New Delhi's approach to territorial disputes during this period can be explained best by a reputational logic, termed the *reputational imperative*. This framework broadly suggests that when leaders are faced with the costs of territorial disputes, their decisions to compromise or be intransigent on their claims are in many cases driven by reputational considerations, that is, decision makers' assessments of what kind of reputations particular actions are likely to engender from immediate adversaries and interested third-party audiences. In essence, compromise or intransigence becomes less or more likely depending on the perceived reputational costs or benefits of either option.

That reputation matters is itself not a particularly new insight. The idea has a rich pedigree in both the scholarship on international relations[14] and recent work on territorial conflict.[15] It is, after all, as Schelling famously observed "one of the few things worth fighting over,"[16] a feeling seemingly shared by policymakers who have often resorted to just this logic to support monumental decisions. This book, however, offers what I suggest is a distinct and more nuanced take on reputation and how it matters to state conduct in territorial disputes. It assumes a more complex portfolio of reputations—reputations of not just resolve and weakness but also those of generosity and being a bully—that states seek to pursue and avoid and identifies a mechanism, the bargaining context, to help specify the reputational calculus driving state behavior.

Briefly, I argue that the reputational calculus of decision makers is shaped essentially by the *bargaining context*, which in turn is constituted of a leader's perceptions about the contestants' relative *bargaining strength* and the history of an adversary's *bargaining tactics*. The theoretical framework suggests, counterintuitively, that where bargaining context is favorable, state leaders are likely to find it easier to make concessions on their claims in the belief that compromise from a position of strength is more likely to carry reputational benefits (of appearing generous) rather than costs (of appearing weak), whereas intransigence, by conveying a tendency to bully and coerce, might generate unnecessary reputational costs. Similarly, the more unfavorable the bargaining context is, the more likely state leaders are to remain firm in the fear that compromise in the face of an adversary's strength or coercion (or both) will convey weakness rather than generosity, encouraging further challenges and threats, whereas intransigence in the same situation will serve to establish resolve and hence aid deterrence and compellence.

Using this theoretical framework, developed in the next chapter, the book demonstrates that Indian decision making on territorial disputes during the Nehru era was influenced to a significant degree by precisely such considerations. Where compromise was viewed as carrying reputational costs—of India appearing weak—and intransigence to convey the positive impression of resolve, Indian decision makers chose to remain firm regardless of the salience of the territory. This was most clearly the case in the Sino-Indian dispute where despite the low value attached to a significant portion of the disputed lands, but owing to weaker bargaining power, Nehru decided to stand firm for fear that any concessions would convey weakness and invite greater challenges from Beijing.

By contrast, to the extent that the Indian prime minister believed making concessions would not signal weakness but instead perhaps convey Indian generosity, and at the least preserve any reputation his government had for cooperation at the international level, New Delhi was willing to make concessions on even clearly salient territory. This was the case with Kashmir and the offer of the plebiscite. Only on the issue of the conditions under which the plebiscite could be conducted did Nehru's government adopt a firm stance, and that again was driven in major part by a fear that not imposing such conditions risked conveying weakness in the face of the fact that Pakistan's initial aggression had not been punished and reversed. By 1954, the entire bargaining context surrounding the dispute was perceived to have been radically transformed for India due to the signing of the US-Pakistan security pact, changing the reputational calculus in New Delhi, and leading Nehru to deepen Indian intransigence over Kashmir by withdrawing the plebiscite offer altogether.

None of this is to say that other considerations were unimportant in these cases. In Kashmir for instance, as the case study acknowledges, military-strategic considerations were equally central to the sorts of preconditions Nehru attached to the conduct of a plebiscite, conditions that proved unacceptable to Pakistan. Nevertheless, what this book does demonstrate is that reputational considerations are independently significant in understanding the Indian government's decisions at crucial junctures of these disputes, decisions that in some instances make little sense otherwise.

## Methodological Note and Overview

Because this book is driven primarily by empirical puzzles, the cases do pick themselves. Nevertheless, there are a few more reasons why this "small-*n*" research design focused on Indian decision making in the Kashmir and Sino-Indian dispute in the Nehru period recommends itself from a methodological perspective. First, it fills a significant lacuna in the literature on India's territorial disputes in that, barring the rare notable exception,[17] most works focus either on only one or the other dispute or address singular developments within them. This work, in contrast, offers a systematic explanation for variations in Indian policy over the most formative years of both disputes. In doing so, it offers a more general story and explanation for Indian conduct than almost any other previous work has done.

Second, the cases can be considered as hard ones for the theory I offer in this work. To the extent that there is a claim to be made that the territories in contention in both disputes held some undoubted importance for the postindependence Indian leadership, and considering the recurrent crises and wars that characterized the period, we can reasonably expect to see salience and military-strategic considerations dominating any explanation of Indian policy and thereby crowding out the reputational logic offered in this book. If, however, we see reputational concerns playing a significant and independent role in Indian decision making despite the presence of these other factors, and sometimes even outexplain the alternatives, that would suggest that the theory has passed a particularly demanding test. Finally, a brief exploratory study towards the end of the book of Chinese behavior in its territorial dispute with India (and others) during the same period allows for a plausibility probe of the generalizability of the argument beyond just Nehru's India.

In the following chapters, I test the theoretical argument and explain the empirical puzzles through in-depth case studies based on extensive use of primary sources gathered from both previously published work and till recently untapped archival material in India. The analysis of the Sino-Indian dispute, for instance, has benefited from access to the papers of Subimal Dutt and P. N. Haksar, both of which provide some new insight into Indian thinking leading to the war of 1962. In addition, this book exploits various other sources, including oral histories, memoirs of senior functionaries and participants in Indian decision making, and some excellent recent scholarship on Nehru era foreign policy.

Chapter 2 begins by detailing the reputational framework that undergirds this study. It makes a case for why such a logic should be considered independently important in thinking about state behavior, identifies gaps in the international relations literature on reputation, and offers a modified reputational imperative framework.

The following two chapters investigate Indian policymaking in the Kashmir dispute. Chapter 3 begins by providing background to the Kashmir dispute and then goes on to identify the prominent puzzles from this case. Empirically, it focuses on establishing the fact that Nehru was indeed willing to make significant concessions on Kashmir from very early on despite the high salience of the territory and was, contrary to the claims of critics, sincere about the plebiscite offer until 1954. This chapter details how while ideological and material-strategic factors do matter in accounting for India's early conciliatory policy, reputational considerations seemed to assume increasing importance in New Delhi's thinking with the passage of time, even as the other explanations become less persuasive.

Chapter 4 then uses the theoretical argument to explain two further puzzles. The first is why, having offered a plebiscite, Nehru insisted on strict preconditions regarding the military and administrative situation in the state prior to holding such a vote, preconditions that ultimately proved unacceptable to Pakistan. The second is why, in 1954, having been open to a plebiscite for so long, Nehru eventually withdrew the offer and adopted a significantly more intransigent position on Kashmir by asserting that the dispute could now be settled only in accordance with the status quo. As this chapter suggests again, military-strategic considerations were certainly not negligible in Nehru's calculus, yet reputational factors played an equally significant and independent role in Indian policy.

Chapters 5 and 6 turn to the Nehru government's policies in the territorial dispute with China. Chapter 5 provides an introduction and background to the dispute and a discussion of the early bases (from 1947 to around 1955) of Indian policymaking in this arena. It shows how, despite the dormancy of the dispute during this period, the underpinnings of India's later intransigence were present all along. While pursuing quintessentially accommodative policies with Beijing overall, Nehru made a conscious decision on the territorial issue from very early on to adopt a posture of firmness. He did this partly for strategic reasons but more clearly for fear of the reputational costs of making concessions to an already stronger China.

These reputational dynamics became even more pronounced after 1957 and, as chapter 6 elucidates, played out more crucially in two momentous decisions. This chapter therefore seeks to answer two major questions. First, why did the Nehru government reject Zhou Enlai's offer in 1960, which would have settled the border in a manner that would have left both sides with territory of greatest salience to them and involved India's giving up territory of ostensibly little value? The second is that having surprisingly rejected the package offer, why did the Indian government pursue a militarily risky policy in late 1961, despite being well aware that its army was little match for Chinese forces in the frontier regions?

Chapter 7 extends the logic of this book's argument beyond India by looking at Chinese decision making in its territorial dispute with India. The focus is on demonstrating the utility of the reputational argument offered here to explain, first, the surprisingly large concessions Beijing was willing to make as part of the 1960 offer by Zhou; and, second, having decided to be conciliatory, Beijing's equally surprising decision to then initiate war in 1962, only to unilaterally withdraw from most of the occupied territory after a brief and devastating offensive. In accounting for these decisions, this chapter also more briefly connects the Sino-Indian case to China's other compromises to its smaller neighbors in the region.

The conclusion in chapter 8 derives implications from this work for the study of the role of reputation in international relations, including the question that this work has been less concerned about: whether reputations actually form in the manner that states expect. It also assesses the importance of the findings for the broader literature on territorial disputes, as well as enduring rivalries. Finally, the chapter considers the lessons to be drawn for the contemporary state and future prospects of the Kashmir and Sino-Indian disputes, as well as in understanding India's conduct on other contentious security issues, including its internal territorial challenges of separatism and secessionism. It suggests that there may be great value in giving more attention to the reputational imperative in analyses of the foreign and security policies of countries such as India and China, especially as they develop greater prominence and interests on the global stage with their impending rise toward the role and status of global powers.

# 2

## The Reputational Imperative in Territorial Disputes

While territorial disputes have historically been one of the most prominent sources of conflict and war in international politics, even in the cases of the most intractable of them—such as the Kashmir and Sino-Indian disputes— the propensity of the contestants to pursue compromise or conflict on their territorial claims has varied over time. This is not surprising. Territory is often crucial to core state interests of security and survival, and therefore *the* issue over which states are most likely to go to war.[1] However, this very amenability of territorial disputes to military conflict makes them highly costly endeavors worth avoiding. Wars, and other military conflicts in general, not only have obvious material and human costs—which may often be prohibitively high, particularly for new and vulnerable states with scant resources—but also hold the prospect of major political punishment for leaders, especially in cases of long-drawn-out, costly, or unsuccessful wars.[2]

Since salience, the most common variable used to explain policy in territorial disputes, usually cannot account for such variations, this chapter offers an alternative framework to answer the question of what explains when and why state leaders seek to address their territorial disputes through concessions or intransigence and the extent to which they are willing to resort to either. I put forward a reputational framework, the *reputational imperative*, that will be used in later chapters to explain decisions by Nehru's India as well as Mao's China to pursue compromise or conflict at different junctures of their territorial disputes with neighboring states. The reputational imperative framework suggests that in many cases, the choice to fight or make concessions on territorial claims is determined to a significant degree, even if not exclusively, by considerations of the potential reputational costs and benefits likely to be associated with specific policy choices. By this account, where leaders expect compromise to carry significant reputational costs and firmness to be reputationally beneficial, they are more likely to pursue the path of intransigence and conflict. When they believe the reputational costs of intransigence are high and the benefits of conciliation more apparent, compromise becomes more palatable.

This reputational logic builds on the conventionally accepted underlying expectation that decision makers, inhabiting as they do an international environment plagued by uncertainty, base much of their decision making on their assessments about the potential long-term security implications of their actions. Yet contrary to the contentions of the more traditionally influential international relations perspectives, it argues that such thinking does not manifest itself in a concern for the material or strategic implications of compromise or conflict alone. Rather, it suggests that for the same reasons, decision makers are likely to be equally concerned about the reputational consequences of their actions and that there is little reason to theoretically privilege the material-strategic mechanism over the reputational one, as the latter may sometimes overwhelm the former.

The discussion in this chapter first highlights the basic assumptions that underlie the argument and justifies, in particular, why a reputational logic is worthy of attention. I then elaborate on how reputation has been conceptualized in the literature on international relations and territorial disputes and how this study both draws on and deviates from it. Following that, I develop the reputational imperative framework, offering expectations about the conditions under which state leaders are most and least likely to be concerned about reputation; how decision makers assess the probable reputational implications of their policy options; and, finally, how this calculus translates into the extent to which they are conciliatory or intransigent in their territorial disputes.

## States, Security, and Reputation

The basic simplifying assumption underlying this study is that states are unitary and rational actors. They are unitary in the sense that their leaders enjoy relative autonomy from societal forces within both the domestic context and the external systemic environment. The interests of the state are autonomous from those of the individuals and groups that lead them, to the extent that the private and corporate interests of the latter can be pursued only if the primary interests of the former have been secured first.[3] The fundamental interests of the state are survival, security, and the maintenance of autonomy, and, at the least, national leaders seek to create policies and undertake actions toward these ends in the face of challenges from external and internal sources.[4] This means that while domestic political pressures are not unimportant, policy preferences that state leaders develop and pursue with regard to national security issues cannot be reduced to the interests or preferences of particular individuals and groups within the state and society, even though policy outcomes may be shaped or filtered through domestic political mechanisms.[5] In effect, then, when it comes to security-related issues, state leaders develop independent policy preferences based on the external context, and rather than determining policy preferences, domestic political pressures only constrain, and sometimes reinforce, state leaders' preexisting proclivities.

State leaders are also assumed to be instrumentally rational, as defined in the limited sense.[6] That is, policymakers make basic cost-benefit calculations as to the consequences of their actions based on the limited information that they possess. This is meant to ensure at a minimum that any policies and actions pursued enhance rather than damage core state interests. In doing so, they assess not just the immediate consequences of their actions but also their long-term implications. This is the case for two contrary but related reasons. First, systemic anarchy, or the absence of an overarching authority to regulate state behavior in the international system, means that another state's future intentions can never be reliably divined due to the uncertainty enveloping those intentions.[7] As the formal literature on commitment problems has highlighted, this means that the possibility that an adversary will later renege on prior commitments can never be discounted, and indeed states can never credibly commit to adhering to those prior agreements even if they have every intention of doing so.[8] Given these uncertainties and fears, state leaders make decisions in the present with an eye on the future, and they are constantly wary about what developments in the present might mean for an adversary's intentions and behavior at a later point.[9] Second, the very conflictual dynamics—best captured in the concept of the security dilemma, where attempts by one state to improve its security often leads to an automatic decrease in the security of others, prompting spirals of insecurity—that such concerns generate between states mean that not only do wars become more probable, but the benefits of cooperation forgone in the long-term due to conflict are also far from negligible.[10] This again requires that leaders carefully assess the long-term implications, both positive and negative, of their decisions to either cooperate or persist in atomistic and conflictual behavior.

This focus on the long-term security prospects of their state means that decision makers are conscious, as the traditional international relations literature has pointed out, of the tangible material costs and benefits of their actions. For neorealists, for instance, "anarchy" results in a zero-sum focus by states on "relative gains," for fear that an adversary may exploit any material concessions made now, in the future.[11] At its extreme, this tendency leads to conscious expansionism on the part of states, within the bounds of minimal rationality.[12] Contests over territory are particularly likely to motivate such concerns, given that territory often possesses economic or strategic attributes that are easily fungible into military resources and advantage.[13] Indeed, commitment problems are particularly intense where territory with strategic value is concerned because they impart the holder with distinct offensive or defensive advantages that an adversary cannot credibly commit to not exploit later.[14]

While these tangible and material costs of concessions are no doubt significant to leaders cognizant of the long-term implications of their decisions, the central expectation motivating this work is that a concern for the future does not engender material concerns alone. Rather, logically speaking, in addition to these material-strategic considerations, state leaders also ought to, and do, care about what kinds of reputations others might attribute to them in response to specific decisions. Since another state's impression of oneself as resolute, weak, generous, or aggressive is just as likely to shape their behavior, there is reason to expect that decision makers are always aware of the reputational implications of their actions. Reputations, in other words, "not only supplement the more usual forms of power [military and economic resources], but are indispensable for reaching certain goals."[15] Indeed, as Snyder and Diesing comment on the centrality of uncertainty to reputational concerns, if "states were quite clear about the magnitude of each other's interests (other than resolve reputation) in any crisis, there would be no need for concern about preserving a reputation for firmness. One would be expected to be as firm in any crisis as 'justified' by one's known interests and capabilities."[16] Realist accounts often miss out on or underemphasize the importance of this reputational mechanism. Especially where territorial disputes are concerned, building in this reputational motivation also allows us to divorce choices of compromise or intransigence from the strategic value of the territory alone.

## The Reputational Imperative

*Reputation* refers to the dispositional attributions—of, for instance, being "weak," "resolved," "generous," or a "bully"—that people and states make about one another.[17] It is, in other words, an attribution based on judgments about someone's character based primarily on observations of that actor's past behavior.[18] In the context of international politics, such attributions often relate to one's commitment to certain values and interests, behavior when placed in specific situations and general tendency toward conflict or cooperation. Reputation therefore is founded in essence on "others' images of one's resolve, flexibility, trustworthiness, alliance reliability, predictability, etc."[19]

The reputational imperative alludes to the insight, in keeping with the previous discussion, that given their concerns about the future, state leaders care intensely about not only the long-term military-strategic implications of their actions but also the reputations that others attribute to them. Indeed, as work on the topic has pointed out, regardless of the fact that there is little evidence to suggest that reputation is actually attributed very often in international affairs,[20] there is in fact "massive evidence that decision makers think such inferences are made."[21] "If there is one feature of reputation . . . on which scholars agree," one work has noted, it is that "leaders, policy elites, and national populations are often concerned, even obsessed" with it.[22] In justifying intervention in Korea on reputational grounds, for instance, President Harold Truman contended that failure do so "would be an open invitation to new acts of aggression elsewhere," a view that Schelling unreservedly shared in his assessment that the costs of such a war were "undoubtedly worth it."[23]

States care (and are even obsessed) about such attributions because, from their perspective, a potential adversary's impression of one's type is bound to shape their expectations about one's conduct in the future and in turn influence their own short and long-term intentions and behavior. As Jervis articulates this logic, "Statesmen are often less concerned with the substance of the issue they are facing than they are with the inferences about them that others will draw from their behavior."[24] Such reputational inferences that others make ostensibly matter to decision makers because they deeply influence the very "psychological environment and policies of other decision-makers" and, thereby, their actions.[25]

In keeping with this reasoning, I argue that in cases such as that of India in the early years after independence, policy with regard to territorial disputes—especially the choice to pursue compromise or intransigence on territorial claims—is influenced significantly, even if not exclusively, by considerations of the perceived reputational consequences of such decisions. Where the reputational costs of concessions—and benefits of firmness—are perceived to be high, compromise becomes less likely; conversely, when being conciliatory is viewed to have reputational benefits—and intransigence is considered reputationally costly—compromise becomes more palatable to state leaders. I do, however, go beyond this basic insight. I also identify gaps in how the existing literature on international security and territorial disputes has understood the role of reputation and suggest an alternative framework that offers a more detailed and nuanced take on both the kinds of reputations leaders care for, as well as how they think about reputation building.

### Beyond Resolve: A Typology of Reputations

Intuitively appealing as the basic insight that reputations matter to states might be, it tells us very little about how decision makers think about reputation formation. In other words, what reputations do leaders care about, and how do they assess what reputations others will attribute to them, and under what conditions? On this, the conventional wisdom in the international relations literature is instructive—but also inadequate. "By a large margin," one set of scholars note, "the majority of attention of scholars and policymakers has focused" on reputations of resolve.[26] Underpinned by deterrence theory logic, this line of thought contends that on issues of national security, state leaders are—and ought to be—concerned almost exclusively with establishing resolve as a means of deterring adversaries, for fear that any wavering or concessions would engender a reputation for weakness, thereby inviting further challenges. By this logic, since states know little about each other's true interests—owing to informational asymmetries, which states have incentives to maintain—they draw inferences about the other's resolve from "*behavior* in previous encounters."[27] Consequently, the costs of not acting with resolve "can extend beyond the loss of position on the issue at stake and encompass the danger that others will see the state as unable to stand up for its interests. Losses then will tend to snowball."[28] Magnifying this problem for states is the fact that it is not only the immediate adversary in a crisis or conflict that is likely to make reputational inferences. Rather, other third-party audiences, especially potential rivals, are also constantly updating their beliefs in the course of these interactions.[29]

In territorial conflicts, this renders the land under dispute, especially for states engaged in multiple disputes, effectively indivisible, and intransigence the default policy stand.[30] Because commitments are viewed as interdependent— that is, actions on one issue are considered to have some nonnegligible implication for others' perception of one's commitment to all other values and interests—any compromise on territory becomes impossible because it risks conveying a strong signal of a lack of resolve and that future challenges will be similarly accommodated. Indeed, recent findings that "lessons from territorial disputes are more strongly associated with subsequent territorial challenges than are lessons from non-territorial disputes" suggest that decision makers may have valid reasons to emphasize such reputational concerns in cases of territorial disputes.[31]

This, however, is only a partial account of the reputational story. Empirically, the argument is difficult to sustain. States often do relent on at least some of their territorial claims even where they are conventionally expected to engage in communicating resolve. As later chapters demonstrate, South Asia provides ample evidence for this. In theoretical terms, missing from the reputational logic I have outlined is the fact that the intransigence involved in actions intended to convey resolve may also carry reputational costs; in reality, states have equally strong incentives to cultivate more benign reputations externally so as to reap the long-term benefits of peace and cooperation and avoid the devastating costs of war. A voluminous literature in international relations suggests that this is the case. Research on international organizations and law has found, for instance, that treaty compliance is attractive to policymakers because they recognize that "evidence of unreliability will damage their current cooperative relationships and lead other states to reduce their willingness to enter into future agreements."[32] Other work has highlighted the importance of being attributed a reputation of reliability in the context of alliance formation[33] or in the repayment of international sovereign debt,[34] to the prospects of long-term cooperation with other states and nonstate actors. Still others emphasize the importance of trust and a reputation of trustworthiness in the regulation of arms control in great power competition,[35] and of a record of honesty in international crisis management.[36] In territorial disputes, Huth has observed, such considerations mean that state leaders have strong incentives to adhere to, and not renege on, a territorial settlement once it is reached.[37]

Building on this intuition, this work proposes that states care about multiple forms of reputational benefits and costs that their actions, of intransigence or compromise, might potentially engender. It therefore offers an extended typology of reputations that state leaders engaged in addressing consequential foreign policy or national security issues such as territorial disputes are expected to be cognizant of. Resolve is clearly one of them, to the extent that leaders believe that demonstrating firmness on an issue at the risk of war carries the benefit of serving to discourage future challenges from the immediate adversary and other potential challengers. In so standing firm, state leaders also seek, at a minimum, to avoid the possible reputational risks that any concessions they make may carry—that of their being attributed to a weakness of disposition. Being viewed as weak in defending one's interests and commitments in one instance, deterrence logic would have us believe, risks communicating to others that one will similarly fail to do so in other instances in the future, thereby inviting more challenges.

Novel in the argument made here, however, is the contention that there are two other sets of contending reputational concerns that we ought to see prominently feature in the calculus of security-seeking decision makers. First, even as they are concerned with resolve, states will recognize that the same assertiveness that seeks to communicate it also carries the risk of being attributed by the adversary and other audiences to a more negative trait: that of being a bully, or a state that seeks to resolve any disagreements unilaterally and through coercive means involving the threat or use of force. For leaders who inhabit a strategic context often characterized by the security dilemma, such a reputation is clearly one that they have an equal incentive to avoid because it promises to animate greater fear and hostility in others, thereby further vitiating the state's security environment. This expectation is also in consonance with a growing body of theoretical work on provocation, dedicated to understanding how threats or actions that are aimed at communicating one's resolve—and consequently reducing that of others—often have the opposite effect of making the target state more resolute.[38] There is, in other words, a real reputational trade-off that we should see leaders confront when considering whether to adopt positions of intransigence in the interest of establishing resolve (and avoiding appearing weak), or assume more moderate and conciliatory attitudes so as to not be characterized as being of a bullying disposition.

Indeed, this dynamic further suggests that we should expect states to not only seek to avoid a negative reputation of bully, but also put some stock in acquiring a second, more positive reputation for generosity. Generosity here is similar to (and shares some overlap with), but is also conceptually distinct from, what others in the liberal institutional scholarship have identified as cooperation, a reputation for which states also clearly seek. Cooperation refers more precisely to the reputational incentives for states to adopt more rules, norms, and dialogue-based approaches to dealing with other states, as well as in complying with and adhering to any commitments thus made, in the interest of benefiting from the long-term mutual gains that may be achieved as a consequence. To the extent that a state is willing to negotiate, is agreeable to be somewhat accommodative of others' interests, and is committed to adhering to any agreements made either bilaterally or in multilateral fora, its leaders can reasonably expect to acquire a reputation for cooperation.[39] Cooperation therefore suggests a form of conduct that is in its essence conciliatory in nature. It does not, however, tell us much about the kind and degree of concessions that a state makes in the process of acquiring such a reputation.

A reputation for generosity certainly involves cooperation; it also requires being able to communicate to the target audience something more about the nature of concessions that one is willing to make. The crucial element in building such a reputation involves having others believe that the leaders of a state, in the interest of peace and friendly relations, are willing to make concessions much larger and consequential than they in fact need to, considering the terms they could clearly demand or impose in a standard bargaining situation. Being attributed such a reputation should clearly appeal to states, for several reasons. For one, given the potentially monumental risks and costs associated with security dilemmas, being viewed by others in such a manner has the benefit of mitigating spiral dynamics by reducing any fears and anxieties that might exist in a potential adversary or other audiences. A reputation for generosity (more than that for cooperation) can even help facilitate a more virtuous dynamic by helping to tailor more positive attitudes in both the immediate target of generosity and other third-party audiences. These others may respond by adopting more cooperative (and even generous) positions on other issues and arenas of potential contestation. As one example of such thinking highlighted later in this book, China sought to appear generous in its treatment of territorial issues with Burma and Nepal in the early 1960s so as to influence their attitudes toward the internal and external challenges the Chinese regime faced, but also to help shift India's stance on the Tibet and Sino-Indian border issues in more conciliatory directions.

States, in other words, think about reputation in more complex and nuanced ways than the scholarship would have us believe. They have a more diverse portfolio of international reputational goals, as illustrated in table 2.1. In addition, their leaders are cognizant of the fact that compromise does not always and necessarily convey weakness, and intransigence portray a positive impression of resolve. Rather, depending on the situation and context, com-

TABLE 2.1

*A typology of reputations and associated actions*

| Action | Reputation | |
|---|---|---|
| | **Positive** | **Negative** |
| Intransigence; use of threats or force | Resolved | Bully |
| Compromise | Generous; cooperative | Weak; irresolute |

promise may have the benefit of being attributed to one's generosity, while firmness may be viewed negatively as aggression. For leaders, then, reputational considerations cannot be diluted to the simple decision of establishing resolve through firmness or making concessions at the risk of appearing weak. They are, in contrast, always confronted by the task of having to address complicated trade-offs insofar as there is clear friction in pursuing both sets of reputational goals (for resolve as well as generosity) simultaneously.

Clearly, decision makers would like to appear both resolved and generous at the same time. Yet in most situations the pursuit of one of these reputations inescapably happens at the cost of the other. Intransigence in the pursuit of establishing resolve, for instance, eliminates the possibility of appearing generous and comes at the potential cost of making one look ungenerous or, worse, a bully. Concessions aimed at signaling generosity similarly risk communicating a lack of resolve, with all its attendant consequences. Snyder and Diesing have succinctly captured this dilemma as one of "whether to be firm and tough toward an adversary, in order to deter him, but at the risk of provoking his anger or fear, or to conciliate him in the hope of reducing sources of conflict, but at the risk of strengthening him and causing him to miscalculate one's own resolve."[40]

## Bargaining Context and the Reputational Calculus

How state leaders resolve this dilemma and address the trade-offs is crucial to understanding how the reputational imperative influences decision making on issues such as territorial disputes. In what follows, I argue that broader contextual factors and situational specifics, especially related to relative bargaining strength, are central to how policymakers assess of what kinds of reputation, if any, particular actions might breed. Building in context improves on the reputational argument in one crucial sense: it reduces expectations of indivisibility in territorial conflict, because context can mitigate reputational fears and thereby facilitate compromise just as much as it incentivizes building a reputation for resolve. It does so by allowing us to conceptualize how states think about reputation in a more complex, nuanced, and ultimately accurate manner. No longer are only two forms of reputation possible or important, a negative one of weakness and a positive one of resolve, making conflict endemic and cooperation all but impossible. States in this framework also equally value a reputation for generosity and seek to avoid appearing aggressive and overbearing to others.[41] As a consequence, decision makers are unlikely to consider compromise as necessarily conveying weakness, just because it involves a concession, or being firm and intransigent to always signal resolve. Rather, depending on context, policymakers in some situations may equally view firmness as more likely to signal aggression—a negative and costly reputation—and compromise to be processed by others as a manifestation of generosity. As Jervis has colorfully observed, state leaders likely recognize that "the [adversary's] appetite does not always grow with the eating. It partly depends on how one gains the meal and what suits one's taste."[42]

What is more, thinking about reputation in this manner also allows for more finely grained expectations about policy. For instance, an assessment by a government that compromise will be viewed as weakness may provoke intransigence; a belief of little or negligible reputational consequences may engender moderate concessions; and the expectation that compromise will be viewed as a manifestation of generosity may in fact lead to concessions that are extensive, and even beyond what might be necessary. Accordingly, this framework may help explain policy behavior that is puzzling on first look—cases where states stay firm on claims over territory with little symbolic or strategic importance at considerable risk to themselves; instances of compromise on territory of ostensibly great strategic or other value; and cases of extensive compromise by states on disputed territory, far in excess of what a favorable balance of military power would seemingly necessitate.

How then does context influence decision makers' assessments of the reputational consequences of their choice to pursue compromise or firmness? I suggest, as summarized in table 2.2, that whether a state's leaders view compromise or intransigence as reputationally benign or dangerous is influenced greatly by the bargaining context within which the territorial conflict is embedded. This bargaining context is a function of two factors: perceptions about the relative bargaining strength of the two sides, and the history of and perceptions about an adversary's bargaining behavior and tactics.

TABLE 2.2

*State expectations about reputation formation*

| Bargaining Context | Reputation | |
|---|---|---|
| | Compromise | Intransigence (including use of force) |
| **Favorable** (bargaining strength high; no adversary coercion) | Generosity (Positive) | Bully (Negative) |
| **Unfavorable** (bargaining strength low; adversary coercion) | Weakness (Negative) | Resolve (Positive) |

*Bargaining Strength*

Bargaining strength refers to the amount of control a state's leaders believe they can exercise over a disputed territory. This is based on actual physical possession of the land in question, because—assuming that defense is in general easier than offense[43]—the more of it a state occupies, the higher the costs of overturning the status quo are for an adversary. Bargaining strength is also a function of the contestants' relative capacity to project military power over the disputed territory. While the extent of territory a state holds obviously has an impact on power projection, much of this ability has to do with the balance of military capabilities between the disputants—mediated, of course, by other factors such as the availability of allies or geography—to the extent that even in the absence of any physical control over territory, the overall distribution of military capabilities between the two sides may be so in favor of one of them as to give it dominant bargaining strength in the theater of dispute.[44]

Conventional wisdom would suggest that the stronger a state's bargaining position is, the less inclined its leaders should be to compromise in their disputes. Greater bargaining power, after all, means fewer costs associated with using force, making war in effect much more attractive and compromise much less necessary as a means of fulfilling the entirety of a state's claims.[45] Given this, even when they agree to negotiate, stronger states arguably do so under the expectation that they will make only minimal concessions and that negotiated outcomes will reflect for the most part the relative bargaining strength of the contestants.[46] States with weaker bargaining strength, handicapped by their lack of capabilities, usually have little choice but to concede to the adversary's demands given the prohibitive costs of conflict.

Rational as it may be, this logic tells us little about instances where such expectations do not hold. In the Sino-Indian case, for instance, we are faced with the dual puzzle of why the stance of the stronger Chinese side—until the decision for war was made in 1962—was not more intransigent and maximalist, and even more puzzling, why India was unwilling to accept Zhou's 1960 compromise solution despite possessing very little bargaining strength and instead pursued a militarily risky policy. Counterintuitive to the conventional understanding, the reputational imperative suggests reasons that a stronger party may make generous concessions, while the weaker side may risk the costs of conflict through intransigence. From a reputational perspective, the very bargaining strength that can facilitate unilateralism also makes large concessions—and therefore a negotiated, compromise solution to a dispute—more viable. Because compromise in such a context is transparently not a result of succumbing to an adversary's greater strength, leaders are less fearful that it conveys weakness. Contrarily, these states can reasonably assume that the larger the concessions made, the more generous they will appear, a positive reputational outcome. At the least, decision makers will have reason to believe, a demonstrated willingness to compromise ought to embellish their credentials for cooperation. After all, the distribution of bargaining strength makes apparent in such a context that the stronger power could have reasonably assumed a firmer and less conciliatory stance on its claims and yet chose not to do so. Consequently, the larger and more obvious the gap in bargaining strength is in their favor, the more confident we can expect state leaders to be that compromise will carry with it more reputational benefits than drawbacks.

Such incentives for adopting a more conciliatory stance are encouraged by decision makers' likely recognition that firmness—let alone the forceful imposition of a solution on the weaker adversary—when occupying a position of significant bargaining strength may carry high reputational costs. Rather than necessarily serving as a demonstration of one's resolve alone, such actions also carry the potential of generating a negative impression in the adversary and relevant third-party audiences of a state as being of the bullying type; the reason is that the stronger state in this context had the option of being generous but chose instead to coercively bring to bear all of it bargaining advantages in the pursuit of a more maximalist outcome. Equally a casualty in this situation are any desires the state's leaders may have to establish other more positive reputations, such as that of cooperation, or to build a general image of benignity and benevolence at the regional or global levels. All of this in turn risks prompting only greater fear and hostility in others. These expectations in fact coincide with findings by Paul Huth and his coauthors that contrary to the conventional expectation that a willingness to engage in conflict always generates a positive reputation of resolve, in many cases assertive behavior was found to engender a negative reputation.[47]

This is, to be clear, not to say that a reputation for resolve is either unimportant or that states placed in an advantageous bargaining position will view it as unattainable in such a context. Rather, what I am suggesting here is that with lesser fears that concessions will be viewed as weakness, establishing resolve ought to be viewed as a less urgent imperative by states. With the reputational costs of compromise assumed to be low and to the extent that leaders have strong reasons to avoid vitiating their security environment by exacerbating fear and hostility in others, we should see them become more conscious of the need to establish and preserve more benign aspects of their reputation. Furthermore, the clear possibility that being conciliatory may help build an impression of generosity in target audiences should further incentivize decision makers in the direction of moderation and conciliation in resolving the fundamental tension involved in seeking to establish a reputation of resolve and that of generosity simultaneously.

In summary, then, by influencing the reputational calculus in unexpected ways, greater bargaining strength can make leaders of states not just more willing to enter negotiations in the first place, but also to make larger concessions than one would expect to be necessary in order to find a negotiated solution. As the French minister for war argued to the German ambassador to his country in 1894 in response to the latter's expressing reservations about the Franco-Russian alliance: "What makes us sensitive and touchy as you say, is mainly the idea that we are thought to be weak. . . . The stronger we shall be the less distrustful we shall be. Rest assured that our relations with you will become easier when we shall feel on a footing of equality."[48] Indeed even Winston Churchill, popularly viewed as fiercely resistant to making any concessions to Nazi Germany during World War II, is known to have given the impression during the famous War Cabinet meetings of May 26–28, 1940, that he would have been willing to make concessions to Hitler, but only after Britain had achieved some military successes and bolstered its bargaining strength. Without that, as one scholar has summarized Churchill's thinking, "even to inquire about German terms . . . would be a sign of weakness which would undermine Britain's fighting position at home and abroad."[49] "The position," the prime minister believed, "would be entirely different when Germany had made an unsuccessful attempt to invade [Britain]."[50]

By the same logic, state leaders who are clearly disadvantaged in bargaining strength can be expected to be wary not just of entering negotiations but, even more so, of making large and substantial concessions. Doing so in such a context, after all, is highly unlikely to be viewed by others as inspired by a spirit of generosity rather than a yielding to the force of structural circumstances. Compromise here more realistically risks conveying an impression to immediate and third-party audiences of a tendency to succumb to greater strength, spawning a reputation for weakness and a lack of resolve. Such a reputation will be feared to further encourage adversaries—particularly those who pose long-term threats and enjoy bargaining advantages in other arenas—to initiate additional territorial and other challenges.

It is reasonable to expect, then, that when dealing from a weaker bargaining position, decision makers are likely to believe that the more extensive the concessions they make, the more probable it is that they will be attributed a reputation of weakness by an adversary and others. Indeed, the same amount of concession that when made from a position of strength might signal generosity is likely to be viewed very differently—as conveying weakness of constitution—when state leaders find themselves dealing from a context of unfavorable bargaining strength. Churchill's case for war with Germany in the War Cabinet meetings again epitomizes this thinking. As he put it then, "Nations which went down fighting rise again, but that which surrendered tamely were finished." For British policy, he therefore concluded, the implications were very clear:

> At the moment our prestige in Europe was very low. The only way we could get it back was by showing the world that Germany had not beaten us. If, after two or three months, we could show that we were still unbeaten, our prestige would return. Even if we were beaten, we should be no worse off than we should be if we were now to abandon the struggle.[51]

In such a context of bargaining weakness, then, firmness and even the use of force will suggest itself as reputationally beneficial to states. Intransigence in fact, however symbolic it may prove to be, will be viewed by leaders in the weaker state as unlikely to signal gratuitous assertiveness given that it emerges from a position of disadvantage. Even to the extent that it may do so, however, such states ought to be willing to assume the reputational risks of appearing unbending, in the belief that establishing a positive reputation of resolve, and thereby deterring any current and future challengers, is a far more consequential reputational goal from their perspective. To put it another way, with little possibility that concessions they make will be viewed as acts of generosity and the comparatively greater urgency of establishing a reputation for resolve, security-seeking states finding themselves in a position of bargaining weakness will resolve the tension between seeking to communicate resolve or generosity by preferring the former.

Consequently, given the obvious risks of conflict when weak, such states will prefer, to the extent possible, to delay action, diplomatic or military, on the issue.[52] Nevertheless, the reputational logic also leads us to expect that when delay is not viable, decision makers may choose to display significantly more intransigence, to the extent of risking military conflict, than their weaker bargaining position would lead us to expect. We should, moreover, see compromise as being palatable to them only under conditions where a negotiated solution offers demonstrably more territory than the balance of bargaining strength would suggest beforehand; such an outcome is likely to be not only more viable strategically, but important for our purposes, more acceptable for reputational reasons. This is so because such an outcome can be viewed both by themselves and others to have served as a demonstration of the weaker state's resolve and willingness to bargain hard even when faced with a more capable adversary.

Counterintuitive as it is to conventional wisdom, then, the reputational logic offered here suggests that when dealing with territorial disputes, states in a weaker bargaining position may sometimes act in ways that are more intransigent and conflictual than might be wise, while states in more advantageous positions can be expected to be more conciliatory than they need to be. This helps account theoretically for the surprising finding in Huth's influential study that "powerful challengers . . . [often] did not exploit a decisive advantage in military capabilities to overturn the territorial status quo" and that weaker states often mount challenges despite the lack of military capabilities.[53] The expectation is also in keeping with what Zartman and Rubin have identified as the "structural paradox": the surprising fact that while logically,

> expecting to lose, a weaker party would want to avoid negotiation with a stronger party at all costs; a stronger party would have no need to negotiate since it could simply take what it wants. . . . Yet weak parties not only take on stronger ones in negotiation, they often emerge with sizable—even better than expected—results.[54]

Indeed, the reputational imperative framework offered here may even help explain a related finding in the same study, that "contrary to received knowledge and experimentation . . . perceived asymmetry is the more productive condition for negotiation."[55] Because, as discussed above, in asymmetric disputes a weaker state's incentives to remain firm for reputational reasons are matched by contrasting reputational incentives for a stronger power to demonstrate generosity, the discovery that asymmetry often generates more effective negotiation outcomes that are acceptable to all concerned, is perhaps not wholly surprising.

*Bargaining Tactics*

In addition to relative bargaining strength and especially as a supplement to it, an adversary's bargaining tactics can similarly influence the reputational calculus of decision makers. In particular, the perceived use of unilateral or coercive tactics on the part of the adversary can make concessions problematic. As one set of scholars note, whereas states often resort to coercive threats and violence in the belief that they will cow a target into compliance, "in practice coercion often results in provocation: coercive acts often increase the resolve of the target, in some cases leading to greater resistance and retaliation."[56] Coercion here is broadly understood as acts "asserting firmness, making threats and warnings, and exerting pressure in various ways to influence the other party to accept one's will."[57] In the specific context of territorial disputes, such acts most typically involve perceived change of or attempts at altering the status quo by an adversary through either occupying land previously not in their possession or extending or reinforcing political or physical control (or both) over territory already controlled by them.

Whatever the case, when an adversary is perceived to have resorted to unilateral or coercive means—especially when it involves explicit use of military force—it can lead to concerns among the provoked target leadership about not only the obvious material changes in the bargaining context that may result, but also about the reputational consequences of compromise in the face of such tactics. Much as in the case of dealing from a position of weaker bargaining strength, decision makers will fear that any concessions made in such a context will appear to the adversary and others as surrender to coercive means and generate an attendant reputation of weakness. As one scholar has observed, "Concessions that are wrenched from the state by dire threats are more apt to lead to an image of it as weak than are concessions that appear to be freely given."[58] To the extent that such a reputation can only embolden expansionist tendencies in one's challengers, leaders are likely to view any succumbing to coercive means as highly unwise.

As a consequence, compromise will be acceptable in such cases only under conditions that unambiguously reverse both the aggression and gains an adversary made through coercive means. Doing so ensures that any concessions are only pursuant on a demonstration of resolve, and thereby do not carry the troublesome reputational implications that they otherwise would. "To negotiate while an opponent's threat is outstanding," after all, "is to acquiesce in his assertion of superior power, which by its effect on the adversary's expectations actually does enhance his bargaining power . . . the target of threat [therefore] demands its removal as a condition for the continuance or initiation of substantive bargaining."[59] When unable to reverse or punish aggression, however, state leaders are likely to prefer intransigence, and even resort to the use of force, so as to both rectify any material losses in bargaining leverage, as well as firmly signal to the adversary that coercion will not be tolerated and must be reversed before any conciliatory actions can be contemplated. "Coercive acts," Dafoe and his coauthors emphasize, "are often perceived as tests of resolve. . . . By resisting coercion, agents signal to others that they will not allow themselves to be coerced. . . . Others will then be encouraged to substitute to more cooperative means of persuasion and to redirect their coercive ambitions."[60]

This is naturally likely to be most true of states that may come to a dispute with very little flexibility of stance owing to their low bargaining strength; they therefore find their reputational fears of appearing weak only more exacerbated by an adversary's resort to unilateral and coercive means. Even with states that are in a significantly stronger bargaining position, however, we should see any chance of generosity being clearly conditioned on the prior reversal of any threats of or gains from coercion so as to prevent any possibility of compromise being misperceived by others as less a sign of generosity and more as a lack of resolve in contesting threats or use of force. Crucial also to note here, in view of the broader discussion in this chapter, is the expectation that to the extent that a fear of appearing weak is activated due to a relative absence of bargaining strength or the coercive acts of the adversary, we should see states immediately show a greater willingness to sacrifice the quest for more benign forms of reputation or image in order to establish resolve. Considering the security perils, including to territorial integrity and even survival, attached to appearing weak under anarchy, the fact that states may make this choice is not surprising.

In the absence of resort to unilateral and coercive tactics by the adversary, and even more so with their adoption of explicitly cooperative approaches, conciliation becomes more reputationally palatable. Compromise here no longer risks conveying weakness in the face of coercion, and not reciprocating carries reputational costs of appearing, at the least, uncooperative, and potentially even looking dispositionally aggressive if a state adopts coercive bargaining means of its own. For weaker states, this may mean a willingness to budge from positions of absolute intransigence assumed for reputational reasons to one where some minimal concessions become viable so long as the stronger power is yielding substantively to the former's claims. On the more potent side, the adversary's more benign approach serves to reinforce the incentives for acting in ways that will be viewed as generous (see table 2.3).

TABLE 2.3

*State behavioral tendencies (reputational expectations)*

| Adversary Coercion | Bargaining Strength | |
| :---: | :---: | :---: |
| | **High** | **Low** |
| **High** | Compromise if coercion is reversed (conditional generosity) | Intransigence or minimal compromise if coercion is reversed (conditional resolve) |
| **Low** | Compromise (generosity) | Intransigence or minimal compromise (resolve) |

TABLE 2.4

*Hypotheses on the reputational imperative in territorial disputes*

| | |
|---|---|
| **Core hypotheses** | • States are more likely to compromise or be intransigent in territorial disputes depending on whether either act will benefit or harm their reputation.<br>• States seek to acquire (resolve; generosity; cooperation) and avoid (irresolution; bully) multiple reputations simultaneously. |
| **Hypotheses on compromise** | • States are more likely to believe that any concessions they make will lead to a reputation for generosity, the greater their bargaining strength in the dispute and in the absence of coercion from the adversary.<br>• States are more likely to believe that their intransigence will lead to a reputation for bullying, the greater their bargaining strength in the dispute and in the absence of coercion from the adversary.<br>• States are more likely to compromise and make larger concessions on their territorial claims, the greater their bargaining strength in the dispute and in the absence of coercion from the adversary. |
| **Hypotheses on intransigence** | • States are more likely to believe that any concessions they make will lead to a reputation for weakness the lower their bargaining strength in the dispute and greater the resort to coercion by the adversary.<br>• States are more likely to believe that their intransigence will lead to a reputation for resolve, the lower their bargaining strength in the dispute and the greater the resort to coercion by the adversary.<br>• States are more likely to be intransigent and prefer military conflict on their territorial claims the lower their bargaining strength in the dispute and the greater the resort to coercion by the adversary. |
| **Hypotheses on coercion** | • States are more likely to believe that any concessions they make will lead to a reputation for weakness, the greater the resort to coercion by an adversary.<br>• States that have been victim to coercion will be more intransigent on their territorial claims.<br>• States that have been victim to coercion will be more willing to compromise on their territorial claims conditional on the act of coercion being reversed and punished first. |

## Conceptual Clarity and Scope

Two basic clarifications need to be made here in order to impart more precision to the discussion in a conceptual sense and to be exact about the scope of the claims being made in this book for the importance of reputation in state decision making. First, while they are often used interchangeably in much of the international relations literature, this work distinguishes the concept of reputation from that of image.[61] That the two terms are often used as synonyms is not surprising; they are similar in many ways, not least in the essential fact that both denote attributions that people and states make about each other's characters. Nevertheless, the two concepts can also be viewed as different in at least one crucial sense: one of them (image) is often pursued by states as an end in itself, while the other (reputation) is more of a means to achieving other goals.[62] Reputation, in these terms, is an explicitly instrumental tool that states pursue so as to directly influence others to act—by either cooperating or capitulating—or desist from acting in a manner that is in accordance with one's security interests and preferences. Image building, while it may end up having similar effects in practice, is only indirectly aimed at shaping the conduct of others. It may be more fruitfully conceptualized as being driven by the psychological needs of decision makers to have their state be viewed as of a particular type for the purposes of confirming a particular perception of the self (self-image), maintaining ideological coherence, or as a means of status seeking.

This separation of concepts is not mere semantic game playing, and as the historical discussion in the book will show, it has some important empirical implications. In the case of India's treatment of the Kashmir dispute in the UN Security Council in 1947–1948, to take one example, it allows us to clearly distinguish drivers related to reputation building in order to influence the attitudes and actions of Pakistan and third parties, from those seeking to prop up India's image as a peaceful power for status reasons. This distinction is important where the two goals, reputation and image building, reinforce each other, such as where Nehru's commitment to a plebiscite sought to establish India's benign image and influence Pakistan's and others' behavior by communicating New Delhi's generosity and cooperation. It is even more vital to account for times when the motivations seemingly worked at cross-purposes, as in cases where the Indian government pursued a stance premised on firmness in the Kashmir and Sino-Indian disputes in order to establish a reputation of resolve, a course of action that was directly contradictory to, and came at a significant cost of, the antimilitarist image that Nehru sought for India globally at the same time.

The second point of clarification pertains to the scope of the argument. To be clear, in attaching the term *imperative* to it, I do not intend to suggest that reputation, as compared to factors such as military-strategic considerations or domestic politics, is *the* core determinant of foreign and security policies of all states at all times. Such a claim would be particularly indefensible in relation to the sort of states that this specific work is concerned with: India and China in the immediate postcolonial period. After all, logic would suggest that assuming some issue interdependence, reputation is likely to be of greatest concern to states with the most expansive and consequential of interests and commitments—in other words, the global powers.[63] Neither India nor China occupied such a position in the international system during the period under consideration, and it would therefore be unreasonable to expect that their foreign and security policymaking was always preoccupied with reputation.

Nevertheless, while it may not be the most important driver of their security policy, there are circumstances under which we can expect even states that are not global powers to care intensely about what others think of them. We should indeed see reputation matter to decision makers in these countries, if to a lesser degree than in global powers, to the extent that they expect significant future interactions with other states in their immediate neighborhood or globally. As Mercer puts it, "While some states may worry about reputation more than others, all states worry about their reputation."[64] This should be even more of the case, as Walter suggests, when they are engaged in or expect to be party to multiple territorial or other disputes, with behavior in one context understood to create expectations of future conduct in all others.[65] In fact, as long as leaders anticipate the possibility of being confronted with multiple axes of conflict and competition, including on territorial issues, with even one (as opposed to multiple) other states, we should see them care about how others view them. Regardless of whether the target audience is composed of one or several countries, then, there are some clear incentives for national security decision makers to care about reputation.

Indeed, newly formed states may display a deep concern for reputation building in their formative years. Prone as they are to feeling vulnerable to multiple threats—real and imagined, internal and external—to their immediate and long-term security and survival, such states are arguably uniquely sensitive to the reputational consequences of their actions. Indeed, for countries such as India and China that emerged from a traumatic experience such as colonial rule and carry with them a sense of uncertainty, bitterness, and victimhood—what Miller terms "scars of empire"—such concerns are likely to be especially salient.[66] Consequently, for the leaders of these new states, working as they are from something of a reputational tabula rasa, the need to tailor not only their strategic position but also the psychological environment will be particularly evident, most notably in the ultimate arena for the contest over security and survival: disputes over territory.

What I am suggesting, in short, is not that reputation is the sole or most important determinant of policy on issues of national security, such as territorial disputes, at all times. The claim, rather, is that there is reason to believe that it can be an important driver, independent of other no doubt significant factors, in the decision making of leaders, even in the cases of states that do not have interests and commitments as vast as those of the global powers. More precisely, as the empirical research in this book illustrates, the desire for a particular reputation may, in certain circumstances and under certain conditions, match or eclipse other considerations enough for it to be labeled as an imperative of policy in those specific cases.

## Alternative Hypotheses

The theory outlined suggests that a reputational imperative is often central to understanding when and why states choose to pursue either a conciliatory or an intransigent stance in their territorial disputes. In order to establish the validity of this argument through the case studies of Indian policymaking that follow, however, it will be important to show that reputation mattered to Nehru and his officials independent of, and often superseded other important considerations, which are summarized in table 2.5. One set of key alternative hypotheses emerges from the focus on salience in the theoretical literature on territorial disputes, which contends that the value of the territory at stake is central to understanding state decisions of compromise and conflict. What kind of value states attach to a territory, however, depends on the properties of the land in question.[67] Consequently, two distinct salience based logics can be put forward as potential competitors to the argument in this book.

TABLE 2.5

*Alterative hypotheses*

| Argument | Mechanisms | Hypotheses |
|---|---|---|
| Salience–Nationalism | Constructivist | Higher the nationalist attachment to territory, greater the intransigence; lower the attachment, greater the compromise |
| | Rationalist | Higher the perceived domestic political costs of compromise, greater the intransigence; lower the perceived domestic political costs, greater the compromise |
| Salience–Material-Strategic | Realism/commitment problem | Higher the strategic or economic value attached to territory, greater the intransigence; lower the strategic or economic value attached to territory, greater the compromise |
| Security Seeking | Power | Greater a state's bargaining power, greater the intransigence; weaker a state's bargaining power, greater the compromise |
| | Threat | Greater the intensity of the internal or external security threats a state confronts, greater the compromise; more benign a state's internal and external security environment, greater the intransigence |

The first emphasizes security in suggesting that salience is a function of material-strategic factors, when territory is viewed by state leaders as essential to the maintenance or enhancement of the physical well-being of the state. This may be because the land in question possesses specific geographic properties that directly influence the ease or difficulty of military offense or defense.[68] Land (or the seas) may also be seen as valuable from a security standpoint in a more indirect sense because of their economic value, either in terms of their own resource endowments or because they serve as crucial arteries for the vital transit of goods and resources. These territories are salient not only because they are essential to the economic prospects of the state, but also because the economic resources involved can contribute to physical security—or diminish it if possessed by an adversary—by being readily convertible into military capability. Such security-based considerations are inevitably prominent in a world characterized by—as realist scholars emphasize—an "anarchic" international system that engenders endemic mistrust and uncertainty in states about others. In such a context, making concessions over strategically valuable territory makes little sense to leaders because the other side simply cannot credibly commit—the commitment problem issue—to not exploit the advantages they gain from the current settlement toward further gains in the future.[69]

A second logic finds salience not in structural conditions, but inside states in domestic politics. The symbolic-nationalist strand of this argument highlights the psychological, ideational, and domestic political roots of attachment to territory that may sometimes render it effectively indivisible.[70] Certain pieces of land in this account acquire high salience because their possession is seen as central to the assertion of nationalism. This could be due to the ethnoreligious composition of the disputed territory's population or because it is perceived to have been part of the traditional historic borders of a homeland. From a constructivist perspective, because people and leaders are psychologically convinced that the state's and their own identities are intrinsically connected to the disputed lands, such territories are "not an object to be exchanged but an indivisible attribute of group identity."[71] An alternative, more rationalist thread of the domestic political argument makes the case that even when elites themselves may not be so psychologically invested in a territory, so long as the territory is viewed as being of some value to a large enough subset of the national population, the imperatives of political survival and opportunism can lead states to act in ways that eventually render the territory effectively indivisible.[72]

While premised on different guiding logics, both alternatives suggest that the more salient a piece of territory is to them, the less likely states are to compromise on it, and that they will prefer instead to assume the costs of conflict and war. When the value attached to that territory is low, however, we should see states being more open to making concessions on their claims. It follows that state policy on a particular dispute should remain fairly constant so long as the stakes remain the same and that any variation in policy over a specific claim can be accounted for only by a shift in the salience of the territory being contested. Intuitively persuasive as this logic is, the problem with the salience argument lies in the two difficulties it encounters when pitted against the empirical record. First, it cannot account for significant variations in state policies over time, even as there is little evidence that the actual salience attached to the territory has shifted in some consequential manner. Second, instances of leaders choosing to compromise on territory of high salience, or preferring conflict over lands that seem to be of ostensibly little value, are completely inexplicable by the terms of this argument. It is precisely these kinds of puzzles that the reputational imperative framework seeks to account for.

One other set of alternative explanations for decisions to compromise or remain intransigent on territorial claims merits our attention. These ones too see security seeking in the material sense (as opposed to the reputational mechanism offered here) as the driving impulse, but instead of focusing on salience, they emphasize the distribution of power and the strategic cost-benefit calculus of conflict as the crucial determinants of policy. The power-centric argument contends that structural constraints mean that weaker states have no choice but to compromise, regardless of the salience of the territory in question, because the costs of going to war are too high for them. Stronger powers, by contrast, have no need to concede anything because they can impose the solution of their preference on the other side, even using force if necessary at minimal cost to their security. A state's share of power, in other words, determines its choice of policy. A related threat-based logic would suggest that such decisions will be determined by costs that states anticipate from continuing to persist with a dispute. Where such costs become increasingly onerous, especially in the context of the domestic and international threat environment, this mode of thinking leads us to expect that decision makers in even strong states will be prone to compromise over all but the most salient territory.[73] Lower costs associated with a dispute should, conversely, encourage the assumption of more risk and more intransigent policy positions on the part of states.

These security-driven logics are persuasive in many cases, but they too leave open the riddle of accounting for outcomes where the opposite holds true. In the case of explanations that emphasize power, these are instances where stronger powers do not exploit their advantages, and rather make larger concessions than one would expect them to; or cases where the weak pursue intransigence and conflict in full awareness of the fact that if war were to result, they would undoubtedly have to bear tremendous costs. Arguments that emphasize threats, similarly, are theoretically indeterminate about policy, in that states are known just as well to respond to domestic and external dangers not with compromise but rather with greater assertiveness and even war making.[74] Why states choose one path over the other when confronting a threatening environment is a question that deserves further scrutiny. Indian (and Chinese) policymaking on territorial disputes is, in fact, replete with such puzzles that require explaining, and the theory offered in this book seeks to serve that purpose.

## Conclusion

This chapter has offered a reputational theory to explain state decisions to pursue compromise in some instances, and adopt intransigent postures at other times, in their territorial disputes. It proposes that the bargaining context—a combination of bargaining strength and adversary bargaining tactics—shapes these decisions. It does so by influencing the reputational calculus of policymakers. Where a favorable bargaining context is present, compromise is facilitated by the decision makers' expectations that concessions, by demonstrating generosity rather than weakness, will be reputationally beneficial. Conversely, the more unfavorable the bargaining context confronting a state is, the more problematic the reputational implications of territorial concessions become, with state leaders likely to fear that any concessions made will signal weakness, encouraging them to act in ways that convey resolve.

While the theory proposed tells us something about how leaders think about the reputational consequences of their actions, it bears making clear here that this is not an argument about reputation formation itself. In other words, this argument makes no claim as to whether states are in fact attributed reputations in keeping with their expectations. As other work has pointed out, it is quite possible that reputations do not in fact adhere in the way decision makers might believe. The calculus that states engage in may therefore be partly or wholly incorrect, in that others may end up either making no reputational attributions at all or making ones that are different from what leaders expect. If this was to be the case systematically, it has severe implications for the possibility of dangerous misperceptions among states. I address some of these issues in the concluding chapter.

# 3

## Kashmir

### *Independence, Accession, and the Plebiscite Option*

As the partition of undivided India and freedom from British rule approached in 1947, the fate of the more than five hundred princely states in the subcontinent became an immediate concern for the prospective leaders of India and Pakistan, as well as the British government. Given their unique status under colonial rule, a swift resolution was required to the question of what would happen to such states with the lapse of British paramountcy—whether they would join one or the other of the newly formed dominions of India and Pakistan or have the option of remaining independent. By the time of independence, fortuitously and thanks in large part to the insistence and persuasion of Lord Mountbatten, the last viceroy of India, and Sardar Vallabhbhai Patel, the new head of the Indian States Department responsible for managing relations with the princely states, nearly all of the latter had abandoned the prospect of remaining independent and agreed to accede to one or the other dominion.[1]

Jammu and Kashmir was one of three prominent states (Hyderabad and Junagadh being the other two) that had failed to have their futures resolved as the British left India for good on August 15, 1947.[2] This was in no small measure due to the fact that all three cases were complicated by the princely ruler's being of a religion different from that of the majority population. In Junagadh and Hyderabad, the ruler was Muslim with the majority population being Hindu, while in Kashmir, the opposite situation prevailed, with the majority Muslim population subject to the Hindu maharaja. Kashmir, however, became the crux of the territorial dispute between the two new states, in part due to its sheer size and salience but also because it met one important condition that the other two territories did not: Kashmir, in contrast to the other two states that shared no border with Pakistan, was geographically contiguous to both of the successor dominions. (See map 3.1.)

India's dispute with Pakistan over Kashmir has of course gone on to become one of the most intractable territorial conflicts in contemporary international politics. Since its eruption in the aftermath of partition, it has been the direct cause of at least three wars (in 1947, 1965, and 1999), a much larger number of crises, and, especially since the early 1990s, unconventional conflict

MAP 3.1   *The disputed area of Kashmir.*

and terrorism. The acquisition of nuclear weapons by the primary state protagonists in the conflict in the late 1990s has for many observers of the region increased the immense security risks the conflict presents, leading some to periodically label Kashmir as the most dangerous place in the world from a global security perspective.[3]

For much of the scholarly work and conventional wisdom on the dispute, this is hardly surprising.[4] Kashmir, after all, is understood to hold a great deal of salience for both contestants, and this fact naturally, it is often suggested, has generated a near-zero-sum contest between the two nations over the territory. In India and Nehru's case specifically—and the latter had an undeniable personal connection to the state as well, being of Kashmiri origin—this arguably led to a desire to acquire and hold the territory at significant cost, leaving very little room for any compromise that would in any way reconcile with Pakistan's own similarly expansive aims in Kashmir. Intractable conflict, it is argued, has therefore been the natural and unsurprising outcome of this set of circumstances.

Central to this salience has been the symbolic-nationalist value that both sides attach to the territory. As a Muslim majority state up for grabs in the immediate postindependence period, Kashmir represented in some sense an immediate test of the relative validity of the two contrasting conceptions of nationhood in India and Pakistan. For Nehru's India specifically, the successful and peaceful integration of Kashmir into the Indian union was viewed as crucial to the vindication of its professed secular national identity that was the antithesis of what Nehru and his associates believed to be an archaic and regressive religious nationalism underpinning the two-nation theory and the idea of Pakistan as the homeland of the subcontinent's Muslim people.[5] Moreover, beyond being violently contrary to the philosophical proclivities of Nehru, the acceptance of the two-nation theory in Kashmir also posed some practical dangers to the continued stability of the Indian body-politic. Were Kashmir to go to Pakistan, Nehru argued in late 1948, "the position of the Muslims in India would become more difficult. In fact, there would be a tendency of people to accept a purely communal Hindu viewpoint. That would mean an upheaval of the greatest magnitude in India."[6] This in a country that even after partition, was home to the third largest population of Muslims in the world, numbering then around 40 million. Indeed, Kashmir gave India "an example of communal unity and cooperation" that the Indian prime minister believed would be severely jeopardized by its loss.[7]

Beyond the undoubted symbolic-nationalist salience of Kashmir to the Indian leadership, the military-strategic importance of the territory was ostensibly no less of a concern. In geographic terms, it has been contended, the territory's proximity to two of the largest and most influential states in the international system, China and Russia, made its possession uniquely valuable to India in strategic terms, as well as to the country's contacts and position in regional and global geopolitics.[8] The British had acknowledged as much during their rule by identifying the state as a potentially crucial buffer against threats to their possessions in the subcontinent from the directions of Russia, China, and Afghanistan.[9] Consequently, the new Indian government explained the importance of Kashmir to the British in similar terms soon after the tribal invasion of Kashmir in October 1947 by noting that the state's location itself made it vital to Indian security, rendering assistance to Kashmir "an obligation of national interest to India."[10]

Indeed, at various other points, the Indian leadership betrayed the fear that Pakistan's possession of Kashmir posed potentially direct problems for the physical security of India. In the early months and years, such concerns were less about a direct threat from Pakistan and more in the nature of fears that a resource-strapped Karachi was likely to allow "foreign vested interests to exploit Kashmir directly for a substantial consideration," a development that threatened to immediately vitiate India's strategic environment.[11] However, as it survived the perilous early months and continued to contest India in Kashmir, it became clear to Nehru that Pakistan itself could pose a threat to northern India were it to be in possession of the disputed territory.[12]

Yet while the salience of the territory does tell a great deal about the conflict between the two countries, it proves inadequate in some important ways in accounting for the contours of India's attitudes and policies regarding Kashmir under Nehru. Importantly, were the intrinsic value of the territory to be the primary determinant of policy, compromise of any meaningful kind that alienated any significant portion of the territory ought to have been viewed by the Indian government as intolerable, with little to no variation in New Delhi's posture over time and changing circumstances. Rather, we should have seen an Indian leadership willing to assume great costs, and eager to embrace conflict, in order to acquire and hold the territory in dispute. Contrary to such expectations, however, as this chapter and the next demonstrate, the Indian government's thinking and policies on Kashmir during the first decade and a half of the dispute were far from being so zero sum. Rather, the Nehru administration's policies demonstrated more variation, flexibility, and potential for compromise than a purely salience-based account would allow for. Indeed, instead of treating the territory as practically indivisible, the Indian leadership in the early years was seemingly not averse to potential solutions that left open the possibility of a significant and quite crucial chunk of Kashmir, if not all of it, eventually becoming part of Pakistan.

The clearest manifestation of this Indian flexibility lay in the early offer of a formula to resolve the dispute that on the surface suggested an ostensibly fair path out of the imbroglio: a plebiscite through which the people of the state would decide whether to be part of India or Pakistan. The Indian leadership had committed itself to the idea soon after the accession of Kashmir to their country in October 1947, and both sides had officially provided their mutual acquiescence, in principle, to such a mechanism of resolving the dispute at the UN in the early years of the conflict. From that point on, despite apprehensions about the practicality of holding a plebiscite, Nehru was seemingly committed in principle to such a vote being held in the state under UN auspices. Crucially, as I demonstrate later in this chapter, this was so not only during periods when New Delhi was confident of a favorable verdict in a plebiscite, but also at times when Nehru and others had begun to entertain doubts about public support in the state and had become convinced that India would in fact lose such a vote were it to be held.

It was only in 1954 that the Indian government began to adopt a clearly intransigent position on Kashmir, backing out on a plebiscite formula that Nehru had pushed for in as late as 1953. Instead, Nehru now asserted that while a plebiscite was out of the question, the dispute could be resolved only in keeping with the existing status quo, which left India with some two-thirds of the disputed territory, including, importantly, the Kashmir valley. This is the policy stance that New Delhi has persisted with ever since, all the while unilaterally integrating Kashmir into the Indian union. Today both sides, begrudgingly and rarely officially in the case of Pakistan, recognize that the plebiscite option for resolving the status of Kashmir is all but dead.

This chapter and the next make the case that understanding such variations and nuances in Indian policy in relation to Kashmir and Pakistan during the Nehru period—and eventually making sense of India's part in the failure to resolve the dispute itself—requires taking into account factors beyond the salience of the territory alone. India's—and Nehru's—role in the failure to find a solution to the dispute had little to do with either some indivisibility that was imparted to the territory owing to its immense salience to India or due to a fundamental insincerity on the part of an intransigent Indian leadership. Rather, whether and under what conditions the Nehru government was willing to make concessions on Kashmir to Pakistan was shaped deeply and independently by the evolving bargaining context in the theater of conflict and beyond, and what leaders in New Delhi perceived to be the reputational implications of the choices available to them.

The next section offers a historical overview of the emergence of the dispute in the years immediately before and after partition, with a focus in particular on the evolution of India's policy positions during these years in order to emphasize the variation and room for flexibility present in New Delhi's approach to the dispute. The remainder of this chapter establishes Nehru's commitment to the plebiscite until as late as 1954, pointing to how the reputational imperative was already in play in these early years, not as the sole determinant of policy but certainly as an independent and key consideration that became increasingly important in Indian thinking with the passage of time.

## Independence, Accession, and Conciliation

The potential room for flexibility in the Indian leadership's stance on Kashmir, and the scope for accepting the possibility that the state would become part of Pakistan, particularly if the people of the state so wished, was clear well in the lead-up to partition and the eventual accession of Kashmir to India. As the lapse of British paramountcy approached, the 1946 Cabinet Mission Memorandum and, following that, the Indian Independence Act of 1947 had first addressed the issue of the constitutional future of the princely states such as Kashmir. In strict terms, it was acknowledged that once the British transferred power to the subcontinent, all rights that had been surrendered by the princely states in earlier years were to revert to them. Technically, this meant that the rulers of such states would have the freedom to accede to either India or Pakistan or remain independent.

The leadership of Indian National Congress party—soon to be the leadership of independent India—was quick to accept the right of the states to join one or the other dominion as undisputed. The only potential provision that seemed problematic and objectionable to them was that of allowing the princes the freedom to declare independence from both India and Pakistan. As Nehru made apparent, the only arrangement that would meet resistance by his party was one that offered the independence option to the states.[13] This position was hardly surprising. The prospect of several of these states located in the heart of the subcontinent remaining independent created the very real possibility of the balkanization of India. As one observer put it, "India could live if its Moslem limbs in the north, west and northeast were amputated, but could it live without its midriff?"[14] This was a concern that the departing colonial power recognized and shared equally. Indeed, for Mountbatten, the problem of islands of foreign territory being left within the newly independent dominions was of "far greater magnitude with the Dominion of India than it is with Pakistan."[15] The British prime minister, Clement Atlee, similarly expressed his government's hope "that all States will, in due course, find their appropriate place within one or the other of the new Dominions."[16]

In the case of Kashmir, this approach resulted in a concerted effort on the part of the Indian leadership to convince the ruler to desist from declaring independence. Nehru's advice to the maharaja was that independence for the state was unwise because "in the world today such small independent entities have no place, more especially in the frontier regions between two great states."[17] Barring this stipulation preventing independence, however, it was apparent that the Indian leadership was willing to countenance the possibility that the state would accede to Pakistan. In contrast to the situation in Junagadh, and particularly Hyderabad, balkanization was not a concern in the case of Kashmir given its contiguity to both India and Pakistan, which arguably made the prospect that the state would join the latter more practically feasible from an Indian perspective.

Indeed, the three stalwarts in the Indian government at the time—Nehru, Sardar Patel, and Mountbatten—all seemed to agree that an outcome where Kashmir acceded to Pakistan was preferable to one where the maharaja allowed paramountcy to lapse and consequently pushed the fate of the state into a dangerous limbo,[18] a situation that the Indian leadership feared would allow Pakistan to seek military conquest of the state. As the Indian prime minster wrote to Patel, if there was delay in accession "Pakistan will go ahead without much fear of consequences, specially when the winter isolates Kashmir."[19] He therefore sought to urge the maharaja to make a decision on accession, preferably to India, if he wished to avoid the potential that Pakistan would swallow the state with no regard for the wishes of Kashmir's ruler and its people. As it became increasingly apparent that the maharaja seemed to be leaning toward independence, Mountbatten clarified this position in trying to convince him otherwise, by conveying an assurance from the Indian government—and especially Patel—that "if Kashmir decided to accede to Pakistan, we will be perfectly friendly about it."[20]

That this was indeed New Delhi's position on the issue has received further corroboration from several other sources that were closely associated with the top leadership during that period. V. P. Menon, for instance, in confirming Mountbatten's account, notes that the latter "went so far as to tell the maharaja that, if he acceded to Pakistan, India would not take it amiss and that he had a firm assurance on this from Sardar Patel himself."[21] General Sir Roy Bucher, briefly the first commander-in-chief of the Indian army, has similarly said that in his understanding, India would have accepted the accession of Kashmir to Pakistan were that to have happened.[22] Indeed, for one scholar of the conflict, there is little reason to doubt the testimony of Mountbatten, Menon, and others because "Nehru, his compatriots and the Indian nation were far more idealistic then than the later events permitted them to be. Pressures to acquire the state were comparatively feeble within an India preoccupied with other problems."[23]

The prospect that Kashmir would accede to Pakistan was especially palatable to the Indian leadership were the act to reflect the wishes of the Kashmiri population. The Congress had always been discomfited by the idea implicit in the Indian Independence Act that with the lapse of paramountcy, the princes would have exclusive liberty to determine the future of their states. This concern was particularly salient with regard to cases such as Kashmir or Hyderabad where the religion of the ruler was different from that of the majority population.[24] Consequently, Mountbatten encouraged the maharaja in July 1947 to "ascertain the wishes of your people by any means and join whichever Dominion your people wish to join by August 14 this year."[25] Gandhi similarly, during his visit to Kashmir, reportedly made apparent his view that regardless of what the rulers may desire, in the case of states such as Kashmir, the wishes of the people ought to be paramount.[26]

Revealingly, this was a stance—that accession to India would be considered only if it was seen to emanate from the people of Kashmir—that the new Nehru government adhered to even as the state's ruler began to apparently gravitate toward acceding to India in the months following independence. By September 1947, in fact, the maharaja's repeated indications that he was willing to accede to India had been rebuffed by Nehru, who insisted that no such offer would be accepted unless it was accompanied by serious democratic reforms in the state.[27] The maharaja had no choice but to release from imprisonment the popular leader of Kashmir, Sheikh Abdullah, as well as other members of the state's National Conference (NC) party, and make serious and sincere political concessions to them before New Delhi was willing to consider accepting Kashmir into the Indian union's fold.[28] Around the same time, Nehru himself clearly reiterated the proposal that his government had been putting forward now for some months:

> We want an amicable settlement of this issue and we propose therefore, that wherever there is a dispute in regard to any territory, the matter should be decided by a referendum or plebiscite of the people concerned. We shall accept the result of this referendum whatever it may be as it is our desire that a decision should be made in accordance with the wishes of the people concerned.[29]

Adopting such a posture on Nehru's part carried with it the significant risk of infuriating the Kashmiri ruler, delaying the issue of accession, and leaving Kashmir exposed to the feared invasion from Pakistan. Such dangers were magnified, and the maharaja's requests to India turned to desperation as the state of limbo was shattered on October 22, 1947, by the tribal invasion of Kashmir from Pakistan with, according to the maharaja and the Indian government, the connivance and support of Karachi.[30] As the invaders first captured Muzaffarabad and then descended toward Srinagar, the maharaja sought immediate military assistance from India to repel the swiftly progressing offensive. Despite this, and in keeping with the above stance, however, the Indian government made clear that it would be unable to send Indian troops to Kashmir without possessing the legal authority to do so in the form of an official instrument of accession to India.[31] An instrument of accession in turn was acceptable only if it were seen to emanate from the people of the state. This required not only that the maharaja commit to undertaking the requisite political reforms, but also that Sheikh Abdullah be immediately integrated into the administration of the state and that the request for accession come from both the maharaja and Abdullah.[32] As Jha puts it, were it not for Nehru's obstinacy on this count, "Kashmir would have acceded to India well before the raiders invaded the State. . . . Nehru was prepared to lose the Valley and Srinagar to the raiders and take it back later if this was necessary to force the maharaja to take Abdullah into the government."[33]

## After Accession and at the UN

Given what we know about Nehru's—and other Indian leaders'—position on Kashmir in previous months, the stance of the Indian government immediately following the tribal invasion and the maharaja's decision to accede to India is hardly surprising. Even in accepting the instrument of accession on behalf of New Delhi, Mountbatten immediately informed the Kashmiri ruler that

> in consistence with their policy that in the case of any State where the issue of accession has been the subject of dispute, the question of accession should be decided in accordance with the wishes of the people of the state, it is my Government's wish that as soon as law and order have been restored in Kashmir and her soil cleared of the invader the question of the State's accession should be settled by a reference to the people.[34]

In the same vein, in late October and early November 1947, Nehru wrote to Liaquat Ali Khan, prime minister of Pakistan, confirming that despite the tribal invasion, believed in New Delhi to be carried out with the support of Karachi, his government was committed to adhering to its preinvasion policy.

Specifically, he called again for an acceptance by both governments of the principle that wherever a princely ruler belonged to a religious community different from the majority population, the decision of accession was to be determined by the will of the people of the state in question.[35] In a November 8 note to Liaquat, Nehru further clarified his proposals. He suggested that once Pakistan had ensured the withdrawal of the tribal raiders and law and order was restored in the state, India was willing to pull back its own troops and issue a joint request to the UN asking it to conduct a plebiscite as soon as possible.[36] In face-to-face meetings in late November, the two prime ministers explicitly discussed the possibility of having the UN administer a plebiscite in the state as well as recommend measures to be taken to ensure that such a vote was free and fair.[37] Within the state itself, Nehru was suggesting much the same to Abdullah: that a UN-supervised referendum be held once "troubles have subsided."[38] Although these early efforts amounted to little and incursions from Pakistan continued,[39] these proposals clearly recommitted Nehru and the Indian government to seeking out the people's opinion on the issue of accession.

On January 1, 1948, New Delhi formally referred the dispute to the UN Security Council, seeking the body's support against aggression from Pakistan. Even as it did so, however, the Indian government reiterated its position on the plebiscite. In doing so, India's representative again made it clear that despite Kashmir's importance his government had never sought to pressure the state into accession and in fact was committed to letting its future status be determined by its people.[40] The plebiscite option consequently acquired centrality in the UN as the Security Council began addressing the dispute, not least because India had voluntarily submitted itself to the mechanism.

Over the next several months, discussions at the UN quickly settled on debating and concretizing paths to a plebiscite in Kashmir. Three resolutions are of particular importance in this context. Resolution 47 of the Security Council, adopted on April 21, 1948, made the initial call for such a mechanism, noting the desire of both sides for the issue of accession to be "decided through the democratic method of a free and impartial plebiscite."[41] In order to bring this plan to fruition, the resolution recommended as a precursor the withdrawal of all tribesmen and Pakistani nationals from Kashmir and the almost simultaneous reduction of Indian forces in the state to the minimum required for law and order. Resolution 47 further provided for the establishment of a plebiscite administration and the appointment of a plebiscite administrator by the UN secretary general. Finally, in order to facilitate and expedite the entire process, the UN Commission on India and Pakistan (UNCIP) was expanded from three to five members and asked to immediately proceed to the subcontinent.

Two more resolutions followed, these issued by UNCIP after its visit to India and Pakistan. The first resolution, issued on August 13, 1948, stipulated that Pakistan, having recently been discovered to have introduced regular military troops into Kashmir, withdraw all nationals from the state before India progressively removed the bulk of its forces.[42] Once these truce arrangements were agreed on and adhered to, consultations over plebiscite arrangements could begin.

The second resolution, of January 5, 1949, reiterated the acceptance by both sides of the principle of holding a plebiscite in Kashmir and, in accordance with the first resolution, confirmed that such a vote would be held only when the demilitarization plan had been executed and plebiscite arrangements completed, with an administrator nominated by the UN secretary general to oversee the plebiscite.[43] While the Indian government rejected the first resolution primarily because it appeared to give Karachi parity and did not acknowledge Pakistan's aggression, it acquiesced to the second resolution after seeking some clarifications from the commission.[44]

## Nehru's Commitment to the Plebiscite

Much of the explanation that follows for this early evidence of conciliation, and even more so for the elements of firmness in India's approach, which meant that a plebiscite was never actually held, is valid only if the Indian government was in fact sincere in its promise to hold a plebiscite in Kashmir. It could, after all, be argued that the Indian government strategically feigned commitment to the formula as a way to put off the plebiscite. This view is in some ways intuitively appealing because it jells with the salience argument. In this account, Nehru—not surprisingly, given the value he attached to the state—had never truly accepted the possibility of allowing Kashmir to go to Pakistan. The offer of a plebiscite was therefore insincere and instead a delaying tactic allowing India to cement its military and political stranglehold of the state. At best, Nehru intended on following through with his promise only under conditions that ensured India's retention of the state.

Pakistan's leadership expressed such skepticism from very early on. Prime Minister Liaquat, for instance, accused the Nehru government of intending to "complete their occupation of Jammu and Kashmir and get entire control over its territory under superficial attractive slogan that ultimately the fate of Kashmir will be decided by people of Kashmir." He further anticipated that after India had established such control over the state, "the holding of a plebiscite or referendum will be purely a farce."[45] Such fears were arguably not purely in the realm of fantasy, and there is some historical evidence that arguably validates such claims. This evidence primarily revolves around Nehru's occasional expressions of doubt to his officials about both the wisdom of conducting a plebiscite and the practical possibility of holding such a vote. The most glaring of such communications came in an August 25, 1952, missive from Nehru to Sheikh Abdullah. In this note, Nehru admitted to having "ruled out the plebiscite for all practical purposes," a view he claimed to have held since 1948. In concluding the note, Nehru furthermore expressed the hope that as India grew in strength, "a time will come when, through sheer force of circumstance, it [Pakistan] will be in a mood to accept a settlement which we consider fair, whether in Kashmir or elsewhere."[46]

New Delhi's insistence on certain preconditions for the conduct of a plebiscite that in effect stipulated that India would continue to maintain some military and administrative presence in the disputed area is further evidence in this narrative of an attempt to either avoid a plebiscite altogether or at the least of strategically seeking to create conditions that would allow for manipulating a decision in India's favor. Indeed, if there was any sincerity in Nehru's plebiscite offer, this alternative story suggests, it was only until the point and under conditions that the prime minister felt would ensure India's acquisition of Kashmir—hence the early enthusiasm for a plebiscite and insistence on maintaining the Abdullah administration in the state, while Nehru was convinced that the Kashmiri population in general, and its leadership in particular, were favorably inclined toward India.

Abdullah and Nehru had indeed developed a deep personal regard for each other, in part owing to their shared commitment to secular and socialist ideas. The Kashmiri leader's political organization, the National Conference, had in turn moved closer to the Congress party.[47] As early as June 1947, Nehru had written to Mountbatten that "the normal and obvious course appears to be for Kashmir to join the Constituent Assembly of India" because it would fulfill what he considered to be the wishes of the Kashmiri population.[48] He believed this in part because of Abdullah's repeated "assurances of wishing to cooperate [with India] and of being opposed to Pakistan."[49]

By 1953, however, Nehru's reasons for such optimism had evaporated. By that point, support for India from both Abdullah and the general Kashmiri public had, even in Nehru's estimation, dropped precipitously.[50] Discontent in the state had progressively risen from 1951, primarily in response to the emergence late that year of the Praja Parishad movement—a mass protest in Jammu associated with the Hindu right Bharatiya Jan Sangh party led by Syama Prasad Mookerjee. By 1952, the movement was demanding removal of Kashmir's special status and the complete integration of the state with the Indian union.

These developments led to growing fears in Kashmir of a rising tide of Hindu communalism in India. Abdullah in particular gravitated increasingly toward more extreme positions. Within Kashmir, he cracked down ruthlessly on Praja Parishad protesters and began demanding the deposition of the Hindu maharaja. On the overall question of the status of Kashmir, he also began to move more certainly toward independence, which he had been exploring in previous years, a position that was unacceptable not only to India but also to his own colleagues in the state.[51]

This concatenation of tensions naturally exacerbated the large and obvious estrangement that had been emerging in Nehru's relations with Sheikh Abdullah around the same time. Already in 1951 the disagreement between the two leaders had become so obviously apparent that one of Nehru's top officials, G. S. Bajpai, secretary general of the Indian Ministry of External Affairs (MEA), had been forced to wonder why "we continue to pour out our treasure and risk war."[52]

By 1952, Nehru was complaining to colleagues such as Maulana Azad that Abdullah had "become very angry and, as a consequence, he has delivered and goes on delivering speeches which are most unfortunate."[53] The speeches betrayed an increasingly anti-India and pro-independence stance. Despite the signing of the New Delhi Agreement in July 1952 between the two leaders confirming that India would exercise control over only the three subjects (defense, foreign affairs, and communications) on which the state had acceded to India, relations had indeed degenerated to such an extent by mid-1953 that Abdullah had begun to refuse meeting with Nehru in New Delhi and even discouraged written correspondence. He had also, reportedly against the wishes of his colleagues in government, resorted to a "bitter campaign against India with the object of forcing India to revise her attitude of hostility to the idea of an independent Kashmir valley."[54] In this swiftly deteriorating context, anger with India in Kashmir's body politic reached fever pitch with Sheikh Abdullah's removal from power and imprisonment in August 1953. Not surprisingly for critics, as Nehru's faith in public support for India in Kashmir evaporated, so did his interest in a plebiscite.

A deeper look at the historical record, however, presents a contrary picture. It suggests that notwithstanding a strong desire that Kashmir be part of India, Nehru and the Indian government were indeed sincere about the plebiscite proposal until he abruptly withdrew the offer in 1954. This was certainly true in the earlier years when Nehru, convinced that public opinion in Kashmir was with India, welcomed "a plebiscite . . . as early as possible" in order to "put an end to this business of the doubt of others."[55] Indeed, as he suggested in an earlier letter to the maharaja soon after the tribal invasion, India had wished to arrive at "rapid and more or less final decisions about Kashmir with the Pakistan Government." Such a settlement could take various forms, including a plebiscite or some combination of partition and plebiscite. Whatever the case, though, and regardless of how much India desired the state, it was felt that a solution had to reflect the wishes of the people. As the Indian prime minister put it, while it was important that Kashmir remained part of India,

> however much we may want this, it cannot be done ultimately except through the goodwill of the mass of the population. Even if military forces held Kashmir for a while, a later consequence might be a strong reaction against this. . . . If the average Muslim feels that he has no safe or secure place in the Union, then obviously he will look elsewhere. Our basic policy must keep this in view, or else we fail.[56]

Nehru in fact backed the plebiscite option even as Abdullah and the maharaja had repeatedly insisted that as far as they were concerned, the issue of accession had already been settled. Rather, in late November 1947, as talks with Liaquat seemed to be moving in a somewhat positive direction, Nehru took pains to convince and reassure both that it was desirable for the government of India to adhere to its promises concerning a plebiscite and that the time was "propitious for a settlement on Kashmir."[57] Indeed, so seemingly wedded was Nehru to his word on this issue that he was initially disconcerted by the very proposition of a Constituent Assembly (CA) being formed in Kashmir in 1950. While the Indian prime minister did eventually relent to Abdullah on the matter, he simultaneously sought to ensure that the CA made no pronouncements on the issue of accession and publicly and privately reasserted that the act did not detract from any of India's prior promises with regard to a plebiscite.[58]

Nehru's apparent ruling out of a plebiscite as a practical option, as he did in the contentious 1952 missive to Abdullah, therefore had less to do with insincerity and more with his belief that the conditions under which a plebiscite was acceptable to India might never emerge. Indeed, in that same note, Nehru had made clear that he had not "mentioned the plebiscite, because it became clear . . . that we would never get the conditions which were necessary for a plebiscite. Neither side would give in on this vital issue, and so I ruled out the plebiscite for all practical purposes." He nevertheless went on to say:

> If the people of Kashmir clearly and definitely wish to part company from India, there the matter ends, however we may dislike it or however disadvantageous it may be to India. But, as I have stated above, I see no chance or whatever of any proper plebiscite determining this question, because the plebiscite itself raises highly controversial issues in regard to the conditions governing it and all that. . . . If the Constituent Assembly told us to get out of Kashmir, we would get out.[59]

The more striking evidence for the fact that the Indian government was indeed serious about the plebiscite offer came somewhat later, with Nehru's serious revival of the by then seemingly moribund option in late 1953. This was importantly at a time when, by Nehru's own admission, both Abdullah and public opinion in Kashmir had turned decidedly against India.[60] By June 1953, Nehru had acknowledged that were a plebiscite to be held in the state, India was sure to lose. New Delhi had lost all the goodwill of the Kashmiri people, and there were now public cries for the withdrawal of the Indian army in the state; it seemed to Nehru that Kashmir could be held indefinitely only "at the point of a bayonet."[61] In the circumstances, Nehru felt for the first time "very doubtful about the future."[62]

It was not just the Indian prime minister who held such a view. President Rajendra Prasad, for instance, informed Nehru at this time that Abdullah had told him that India was certain to lose a plebiscite in his state.[63] He went on to suggest that with India likely to lose all of the state in an overall plebiscite, a solution along the existing cease-fire line was ideal. Failing that, he recommended proposing zonal plebiscites or a plebiscite restricted to the valley, which likely meant losing the Kashmir valley, but at least left Jammu with India.[64]

In response to Prasad, Nehru made it clear that despite the unfavorable circumstances in Kashmir, his government's policy would remain the same as in the past.[65] In late July 1953, he began giving the plebiscite a new push in meetings with the Pakistani governor-general and prime minister. He explained the decision to Bakshi Ghulam Mohammad, soon to be head of the Kashmir administration, urging that while India's efforts in the state had seemingly been in vain, "even so we have to behave decently and honorably, adhering to what we have stood for."[66] Nehru even began to prepare Bakshi at this time for the potential outcome of a plebiscite, especially one to be held on a regional basis, by making clear that it was "obvious that some parts of the state will plump for India; other parts for Pakistan."[67]

Having begun to lay the ground domestically, Nehru raised the proposal officially with the Pakistani prime minister, Mohammad Ali Bogra, in talks in August 1953. He prefaced the offer to resuscitate the plebiscite option with the assertion that the "only way left was to cast the responsibility for the settlement on the people of Kashmir themselves." The Indian prime minister now also called for a "different approach" to the disposition of Indian and Pakistani forces in the state—an issue that we will see had so far plagued talks on the plebiscite—so as not to unnecessarily delay holding a vote.[68] He proposed that a plebiscite be held in all regions of the state, with the state to be partitioned according to the wishes of the people in each region. Once both sides had agreed, the expectation was that some two years might pass before the vote was held.[69] The Indian government's only demand during these talks was that the plebiscite administrator not be from one of the major powers so as to avoid delaying the process by embroiling it in great power politics.[70]

Important to note here is the fact that it was Nehru who initiated the proposal rather than having it imposed on him and that the offer was made despite initial opposition from the new leadership in Kashmir.[71] That he was willing to do so at this point, despite anticipating defeat, makes problematic the arguments that New Delhi had sought to avoid a plebiscite all along or desired it only under conditions where a positive outcome was assured. As Nehru had seemingly concluded and wrote to the Pakistani prime minister, "We are not going to settle this problem by mere cleverness or trying to overreach each other. We are also not going to settle it by coercive processes, whether they are of the nature of war or some other. Nor can it be settled by coercion exercised on the people of Kashmir or any large section thereof."[72]

## Explaining India's Early Flexibility

Despite the undoubted salience of Kashmir to India, prior to the tribal invasion and then immediately following the accession of the state until sometime in 1953, the Indian leadership was ostensibly open to the idea of losing the state to Pakistan, especially if it reflected the wishes of the leadership and people. That this was the case surely had something to do with the democratic proclivities of the Indian leadership and the ideational and idealistic elements of Nehru's worldview, allusions to which periodically featured in the prime minister's thinking, particularly in the period before the tribal invasion and then in the lead-up to the 1953 overtures to Pakistan.

The empirical evidence, however, arguably points even more clearly to the other material-strategic security-seeking motivations identified as alternatives in the previous chapter, especially those related to the threat and costs of conflict, as potentially important considerations explaining India's conciliatory position on Kashmir during this period. Even before the tribal invasion in October 1947, Indian leaders were acutely conscious of the high likelihood of war with Pakistan if the state had failed to accede to either dominion prior to the lapse of paramountcy. New Delhi recognized that Kashmir was as if not more salient for Pakistan, especially given the latter's "tottering" situation. The state's value to Karachi lay primarily in the fact that its loss would have irreparably damaged the ideological basis on which the Pakistani state had been created, leading to its potential crumbling.[73] In addition, however, as Nehru saw it, a new and vulnerable Pakistan was likely to be desperate to acquire Kashmir from an imperative of stability, with the strategically located state to serve as a potential avenue for raising resources "by giving special privileges, leases etc. for development" there to external powers, especially the United States.[74]

With war viewed as almost inevitable and the enemy expected to be highly resolved, the new Indian leadership was clearly concerned about the costs that would have naturally accompanied such a conflict; these costs were likely to be prohibitively high for a newly independent and resource-poor India. While Nehru had reasons to be confident that war would "undoubtedly end in the defeat and ruin of Pakistan," he also acknowledged that "it may well mean ruin of India also for a considerable time."[75] Even preparing for such a conflict and devoting the resources toward such an endeavor threatened to risk the country's longer-term economic and security prospects. "If we spend too much on maintaining an army and too little on the development of industry and science," Nehru had observed, "we do not add to the wealth of the nation and our resources shrivel up and we cannot even maintain that army."[76]

While the potential costs of war over possession of the state were undeniable, the military-strategic risks associated with compromise and even the loss of Kashmir were, in contrast, viewed as somewhat more manageable by the Indian leadership. This of course did not mean that there was any dearth of skepticism among them that the new Pakistani state was likely to persist with its pre-partition hostility and seek to undermine India's security when and where possible. Indeed, quite apart from the experience of partition itself, brewing disputes over the princely states (including Kashmir) and intense disagreements about the distribution of financial, military, and administrative resources had only reinforced this perception of inveterate Pakistani hostility in the Indian government. The tribal invasion did little to dampen these impressions. As one scholar has put it, Nehru's "perception of Pakistan was an extension of his image of the [Muslim] League: an entity with an inferiority complex, lacking a progressive platform but willing to stir mass emotion, and seeking parity of power and status through the imperial arbiter."[77]

Despite such fears about its immutable hostility, however, any concerns that Pakistan's possession of Kashmir would pose a strategic threat to India were moderated in New Delhi at this point by a recognition of the former's essential weakness in capability terms, especially in comparison to India. The bargaining context in the overall conflict, in other words, was heavily stacked in India's favor, which meant that there was only minimal risk that Karachi would be able to exploit any major Indian concessions in Kashmir to threaten other parts of the country later, considering that New Delhi was certain to prevail in any such war. Indeed, Pakistan's condition was assessed to be so frail in the early months after independence—given the financial, administrative, and other immense burdens that the country faced—that Nehru had strong doubts about whether it would "survive at all," let alone be able to challenge or threaten India significantly in the long term.[78]

Such an evaluation was far from unreasonable. Even prior to partition, British strategists had concluded that Pakistan's prospects in the postindependence period would be grim at best. After partition, the leadership of the new state shared such fears, acknowledging that the country was geographically "moth eaten," most obviously in its division into two wings separated by the vast Indian landmass. In resource terms, Pakistan was also handicapped enough that the very survival of the state was in doubt.[79]

In the military sphere, the gaps were stark. The armed forces personnel of undivided India were distributed between the two new states at a ratio of roughly 64:36 in India's favor. That left India with fourteen armored, forty artillery, and twenty-one infantry regiments as opposed to Pakistan's six armored, eight artillery, and eight infantry regiments. Pakistan's numerical disadvantages were compounded by the fact that none of the units it did receive were full strength as all non-Muslim troops were removed from them and many of the vital military logistical facilities and assets—such as bases, ordnance factories, and training institutions—had remained in postpartition India. Magnifying this massive military asymmetry between the two sides was Karachi's similarly fraught financial position, made worse by India's seeming intransigence in transferring even those limited financial assets that Pakistan was entitled to according to the partition plan.[80]

This meant that with or without Kashmir, Pakistan was viewed by the Indian leadership as too weak in the immediate aftermath of partition to pose anything like a substantial threat to India's physical security without in effect destroying itself. There was every reason, moreover, to expect that this would continue to be the case for the long term. The large mismatch in size, population, economic resources, and potential between the two countries to India's advantage more or less guaranteed this. In military-strategic terms, then, a case can be made that the high immediate costs of potential war, and the relative absence of fear that concessions (or even the loss of Kashmir) might provide some kind of exploitable strategic advantages that would allow Pakistan to fundamentally imperil Indian security in the future, made a conciliatory stance viable in New Delhi.

This thinking, that the costs of losing Kashmir were manageable, was ostensibly further facilitated by Nehru's stipulation that India was willing to see the state go to Pakistan only if the people of the territory wished it. A decision by the people of the state to reject India no doubt risked providing added legitimacy to the regressive ideas underlying partition. Yet as evidenced by the openness of the Indian leadership to the possibility of losing the state, such an eventuality was never viewed as imparting some indivisibility to Kashmir.[81] More to the point, however, that particular mechanism—a vote of the people—of determining the future of the state also jelled with the broader strategic motivations shaping Indian thinking. On that front, committing to the principle of referring the issue of accession to the people in princely states where the religion of the ruler and the majority population differed avoided the much greater risk of the balkanization of India by delegitimizing the desire of the rulers in states such as Hyderabad and Junagadh to unilaterally declare independence or accession to Pakistan.[82]

*The Emerging Importance of Reputation*

It is undeniable, then, that ideological factors and, even more so, material-strategic ones clearly mattered to India's adoption of a conciliatory approach to Kashmir, especially in the lead-up to the tribal invasion. To that extent, it must be acknowledged that a reputational imperative can hardly be the primary determinant of Indian policy in these years. Nevertheless, a case can be made for reputation serving an important and independent role in Nehru's thinking at this time. That it did so should be of no surprise given the theoretical expectations outlined in chapter 2. The very same circumstances of India's dominant bargaining position in the subcontinent that moderated India's fears on the military-strategic front also presented a context where Nehru and his associates could reasonably believe their willingness to be conciliatory and their openness to making large concessions on the disputed territory to Pakistan carried few reputational costs. In making such concessions from a position of undisputed strength, in other words, there was little risk that New Delhi would appear weak and lacking resolve. This was especially true prior to the tribal invasion, when there was no major instance of Pakistani aggression and coercion to complicate matters.

Even after the invasion and accession, however, as long as the tribal advances in the state were reversed—as Nehru demanded—the overall bargaining context meant that India was unlikely to convey weakness by being conciliatory. Rather, such compromise, if it was to have any reputational effects, was believed to only symbolize the generosity of spirit of the Indian leadership and its desire for peace with Pakistan. Nehru in fact made this dimension perfectly clear to the Pakistani leadership soon after the maharaja's accession to India and New Delhi's unilateral offer of plebiscite, noting that there had never been any need for his government to be as conciliatory as it had been, and continued to be, on the Kashmir issue. Indeed, if India had truly desired the territory at any cost, the Indian prime minister contended, it could have easily fulfilled such desires soon after independence, thanks presumably to its immense advantages over Pakistan in every domain of national power.[83] In early December 1947, in discussing the prerequisites to the conduct of the plebiscite with Mountbatten and Pakistani representatives, Nehru similarly protested that his government "had already gone far further than they need have done. They had gone out of their way to offer a plebiscite. There was no necessity for them to have done this."[84] In addition, as noted earlier, Nehru also claimed that as much as it was a generous concession to Pakistan, the offer of a plebiscite was also about being generous and accommodative to the people of the state itself. Without their goodwill, after all, it was neither right nor practically possible for India to acquire and keep Kashmir. In being so motivated, the Indian government's actions could hardly be construed as some kind of surrender to Pakistan or be read as a manifestation of weakness by the latter.

Of more crucial import to the discussion here is the fact that reputation appears to quickly become an increasingly important consideration in Indian decision making soon after Kashmir's accession to India. In many ways, only a reputational logic allows us to make sense of both the extent of compromise— the openness to the possibility of losing the crucial vale of Kashmir (if not the entire state) in a plebiscite—that the Indian government was willing to make in the dispute, as well the persistence with which Nehru adhered to that stance through the early years. Indeed, without reference to reputation, these crucial aspects of New Delhi's policy are inexplicable. Nehru's democratic instincts, for instance, might seem to offer a ready explanation, but it becomes increasingly unpersuasive with the passage of time. After all, if an ideological commitment to having the Kashmiri people decide their own future was truly of the utmost priority to Nehru, his government should have been willing to assume considerable risks to bring a plebiscite to fruition. Yet as the next chapter recounts in detail, significant evidence suggests that such a commitment was far from absolute. New Delhi had no compunctions in putting such an outcome in jeopardy by first imposing strict (and, to Pakistan, unacceptable) preconditions for a vote and eventually completely withdrawing the offer even as it had become amply clear that the people of the state were increasingly disenchanted with India. Such intransigence, and indeed the variance in Indian policy, is inexplicable solely on account of Nehru's supposed ideological predilections.

Similarly, were military-strategic concerns related to the high costs of war and the absence of a long-term threat posed by Pakistan alone important to New Delhi's early conciliatory stance, they should have dampened to a significant degree in the months after the invasion, for two reasons. First, as Kashmir acceded to India and the Indian armed forces progressively wrested control of a large part of the state, both the immediate prospect of war and its potential costs had undoubtedly dropped. Certainly India's physical presence in the state had never really translated into the sort of advantages that gave the government any confidence about actually expanding military operations to cover Pakistan-controlled areas. However, it was also true that the Indian presence in the border areas had increasingly become potent enough to maintain the status quo and effectively counter any future offensives from the direction of Pakistan. This was especially the case as India became able to gradually have its overall military superiority in relation to Pakistan bear on the theater of conflict, as developments elsewhere—particularly the military resolution of the Hyderabad problem in September 1948—allowed India to move forces previously engaged otherwise to Kashmir.[85] The coming into effect of a UN-sanctioned cease-fire on January 1, 1949, a development that itself indicated decreasing optimism in Pakistan about its military prospects, only increased the constraints on the possibility of war, and especially on Pakistan's initiation of one.

Second, while the prospects and anticipated costs of war had narrowed for India, even a year and half of conflict had confirmed that Pakistan was here to stay. Nehru's (and others') early prognostications that Pakistan's very survival was in doubt, and that even if it did survive, its ability to imperil Indian security in any meaningful way in the long term would be severely limited, had been categorically proven to be erroneous. To compound this, very early in the proceedings at the UN, Nehru had also become convinced that there was a perceptible anti-India and pro-Pakistan bias on display by the great powers. As he put it to Krishna Menon in February 1948, he "could never have imagined that this Council could possibly behave so irresponsibly as it has done."[86]

Such great power tendencies only fueled the impression in New Delhi that Karachi's inherent weaknesses could be compensated for somewhat by outside support. None of this meant at this point that there was any prospect of the immense disparity in capabilities between the two countries being bridged significantly. However, these developments also made the prospect of losing the entire state more problematic in military-strategic terms than before. In contrast to just a few years earlier, the Indian leadership now had reason to worry that Pakistan could strategically exploit its possession of Kashmir to threaten India. As Nehru himself later acknowledged to Abdullah in his 1952 letter, by the end of 1948, he had developed serious misapprehensions about the possibility of Kashmir going to Pakistan and personally preferred a settlement along the status quo. As he articulated these concerns:

> We are superior to Pakistan in military and industrial power. But that superiority is not so great as to produce results quickly either in war or by fear of war. . . . If the whole of the State went to Pakistan, it would be a danger to the north of India, and there would be continuous tension between us and the party controlling the State. Thus, purely from the point of view of India's national interest, we cannot agree, unless circumstances force us, to see this part of Kashmir go to Pakistan.[87]

As the threat and costs of war diminished with India's growing physical and political control of some three-fourths of the territory under dispute and as the military-strategic costs of losing the state itself swiftly became more apparent, the incentives for India to compromise on territory that was in any case of great salience to it for other reasons had fallen significantly. Indeed, given these circumstances, standard security-seeking explanations would lead us to expect New Delhi to exploit its advantages in military power and adopt a much less conciliatory position on Kashmir than in the past. Such a stance would have meant that India could have, at the least, refused to discuss any proposals aimed at resolving the dispute before its initial complaint about the tribal invasion was satisfactorily addressed by a hostile Security Council. Alternatively, Nehru could have moved to a firm insistence on what he certainly viewed as the ideal outcome: a settlement that reflected the status quo. Indeed, withdrawing the plebiscite offer altogether had become eminently viable in strategic terms as India's remaining balkanization concerns were assuaged with the military resolution of the Hyderabad issue in September 1948.

Instead, however, and despite his increasingly deep disenchantment with the proceedings at the UN, which he felt betrayed some hostility toward India,[88] Nehru not only continued India's engagement with the Security Council but also persisted with discussions focused on resolving the dispute through a plebiscite. Despite pressures at home to withdraw India's case from the UN as evidence emerged in early 1948 of the incursion of regular Pakistani troops into Kashmir, New Delhi welcomed the UNCIP delegation to India in the summer. Furthermore, while in London in October 1948, Nehru was pressing Liaquat Ali Khan to unconditionally accept the UNCIP resolution from August that had sought reaffirmation from both sides that the future of the state would be settled in accordance with the will of the people. If not, Liaquat was asked to consider partitioning the state as a solution.[89] And indeed, quite apart from the cease-fire agreement of January 1, 1949, it was Nehru's acquiescence to the UNCIP resolution of January 5 that concretized the Indian government's commitment to a plebiscite at the UN. Nehru seemed surprisingly willing to adhere to this commitment until as late as 1953, despite every indication by then that India would likely lose a plebiscite. Even domestically, the Indian prime minister had gone out of his way to ensure that neither Sheikh Abdullah nor the CA—once it was formed despite Nehru's reluctance—undertook any action that was seen to unilaterally confirm and finalize Kashmir's accession to India.

While such continued conciliation makes little sense in military-strategic terms, that is not the case from a reputational perspective. In proposing a plebiscite in the first place, the Indian government had reason to believe that there were few reputational costs to making generous concessions to Pakistan. Indeed, even after the tribal invasion, as long as India ensured that the fruits of Karachi's initial aggression in the state were reversed (an issue that will be discussed in the next chapter), there was little risk that compromise would convey some weakness of constitution. Rather, to the extent that Indian conciliation came from a position of undisputed strength, for Nehru, it could have only been read as a manifestation of Indian generosity by Pakistan, the Kashmiri people themselves, and an increasingly involved international community, with all the benefits attendant on such a reputation for benevolence. This basic context had changed very little over this period.

Adopting a more intransigent position, in contrast, quite obviously risked showing India to be ungenerous and aggressive and promised only to heighten fear and hostility in Pakistan and, consequently, the avoidable possibility of war. Similarly, to the extent that Nehru was also immensely sensitive to the importance of public opinion in Kashmir itself to India's long-term prospects in the state, he was conscious of the fact that backing away from a plebiscite was sure to have a negative impact on how India and its prime minister were viewed by the people of Kashmir. In other words, whereas its earlier willingness to hold a plebiscite might have been seen as evidence of a generosity of spirit, intransigence from a position of strength risked making India appear a truculent bully.

This opportunity and incentive to focus on creating an impression of benignity and benevolence concurrently alerted Nehru to the other dimensions of India's reputation that were at stake. Evidence suggests that quite apart from the possibility of looking generous, the Indian government's thinking was arguably even more impelled by the goal of establishing and preserving a reputation for cooperation in the international arena. As a result, once New Delhi had publicly declared its willingness to allow a plebiscite in the state and had reaffirmed that commitment repeatedly to Pakistan and at the UN, reneging on such a commitment threatened to impose serious reputational costs on India.

To not fall in the esteem of the international community had become greatly important to Nehru for very practical reasons. From this perspective, pulling back on the plebiscite commitment was sure to further imperil India's Kashmir case at the UN by legitimizing and encouraging Pakistani arguments about Indian high-handedness, as well as the already incessant pressure from the great powers, especially the British and Americans. Indeed, even as he became convinced that a plebiscite was beyond the reach of practicality and began contemplating other possible mechanisms of addressing the dispute, the Indian prime minister was clear that his government could not abandon the commitment because "this business of a plebiscite and the conditions governing it fills people's minds" and reneging on it would show India in poor light.[90] If India's aim had been to convince the international body of the correctness of India's view and elicit a condemnation of Pakistan, to be seen as both ungenerous and unwilling to keep one's word, was certain to hurt that cause.

Such fears were apparent in Nehru's unenthusiastic attitude toward the formation of the CA in Kashmir. While the development, especially if the CA planned to confirm the state's accession to India, promised to enhance India's stature in the state, the Indian prime minister himself appeared more concerned about the fact that the acceptance of such a significant change in the political status quo would be construed by others as a deliberate violation by India of its stated commitments.[91] Even as he eventually ceded to the Kashmiri leadership's demands on forming the CA, internally Nehru sought to prevent (contrary to Abdullah's desires) the new body from passing any resolutions that confirmed accession to India. As he intimated to Bajpai, Nehru had "repeatedly emphasized to Sheikh Abdullah and other Ministers in Kashmir that it would be a wrong approach for the constituent assembly even to discuss such subjects as accession."[92]

That this was indeed the case was confirmed later by one of Nehru's biggest detractors in India, Syama Prasad Mookerjee. The latter wrote in early 1953 that he "was told by Sheikh Abdullah that he and his colleagues were willing to adopt this procedure [passing a resolution in the CA in favor of accession to India]" but that Nehru had refused to approve of any such action.[93] As Nehru pithily observed in a communication to Abdullah during that period, his government was eager to avoid being accused of having reneged on a commitment made to the UN. "To be accused of a breach of faith with them [Pakistan and the UN] and some kind of underhand dealing," Nehru had concluded, "would be very bad" for India.[94]

The potential risks of failing to adhere to the plebiscite commitment extended beyond these direct reputational costs. In a more indirect manner, they threatened also to damage the very image that Nehru had been seeking to build for India in the global arena in these early years: that of a champion and leader of a movement away from the warmongering of Cold War politics. Reflecting the idealistic side of Nehru's international politics, India was to be in this view a force for global peace. Indeed, such an image was also central to establishing India's status as a great power, a role to which Nehru believed India was naturally destined. Khilnani has encapsulated this logic thus:

> The international profile of states depended on their economic and military prowess, and India obviously could not make its mark in these domains. A new state like India, weak by international standards, would have to pursue its interests by creating its own opportunities and chances. By speaking the language of morality and justice, it might just be able to surprise and unbalance the more powerful, extracting concessions through their sheer embarrassment.[95]

The UN itself was one of the important global mechanisms that Nehru hoped would facilitate this fundamental reshaping of global politics, one that India had to help legitimize and strengthen. As Nehru put it soon after the war in Kashmir had begun, the UN was "a very important organization," one that had "some element of hope in it of pulling this world out of the morass in which it has sunk."[96] Nehru's continued, even if hesitant, commitment to the plebiscite makes great sense given these broader goals and concerns about India's global image. To the extent that making such a concession from a position of strength was a manifestation of Indian generosity, and the continued adherence to the plebiscite commitment a testament to its cooperative tendencies, such acts also facilitated Nehru's attempts at building India up as a global moral force. Backing out on its word would have served to expose to the world that India's rhetoric on peace was purely instrumental and that Nehru had no compunctions in taking actions that delegitimized and weakened a global body created to serve the goals he professed. Nehru himself confessed at a public meeting in October 1948 that he "did not quite like the way the UN Council dealt with it [India's Kashmir referral], but we showed to the world how much we tried to depend" on it.[97] Even as the military-strategic incentives for compromise were progressively reducing, then, the reputational imperative kept Nehru committed to compromise on Kashmir, especially to the plebiscite option.

## Conclusion

In empirical terms, this chapter has used extensive primary documentation to add to the historiography of the Nehru government's treatment of the Kashmir dispute by establishing that despite its ostensibly high salience to India, the state was viewed as far from indivisible by the Indian leadership in the immediate aftermath of partition and the tribal invasion. To the Nehru government, a plebiscite in particular seemed an obvious and eminently suitable method for settling the Kashmir dispute. New Delhi was willing to publicly propose and repeatedly commit to the mechanism, unilaterally at first, and then bilaterally with Pakistan, and multilaterally at the UN, even at times when it had become plainly clear to Nehru himself that public opinion in the state had turned decisively against his country.

This chapter has also sought to theoretically explain these otherwise puzzling and counterintuitive aspects of Indian policymaking by contending that a favorable bargaining context in the early years of the Kashmir dispute created a situation within which it became eminently viable and preferable for New Delhi to adopt a conciliatory posture on the contested territory. Specifically, it has argued that the one important mechanism through which the bargaining context facilitated Indian concessions was a reputational one. By this account, to the extent that India considered the reputational cost-benefit calculus of compromise to fall on the positive side, and feared that intransigence carried significant reputational costs, such considerations incentivized India's more accommodative stance. New Delhi's expressed willingness, both before and after independence, to countenance the possibility of losing the state to Pakistan, especially if it reflected the wishes of the Muslim majority population of the state, was the centerpiece of this policy.

We see multiple reputations at play in Indian thinking at this time. The primary reputational consideration for compromise was quite certainly the fact that it was not expected to be viewed by others, especially Pakistan, as born out of weakness and that, if anything, concessions signified Indian generosity. Progressively, however, as the dispute became more embroiled at the UN, the more prominent reputational concerns animating Indian actions seemed to be less about establishing the country's generosity and more about not appearing as an intractable bully and preserving a reputation for cooperation. Once the commitment had been made to Pakistan and the UN, then, Nehru was acutely conscious of the irreversible damage to the benevolent strands of India's reputation that would result from a reneging on his word. To the extent that his global image-building aspirations jelled with these other reputational goals, it further encouraged the Indian government to adhere to a more conciliatory posture on the disputed territory.

This is not to suggest that other factors were unimportant. Nehru's ideological beliefs no doubt played a role, and military-strategic considerations arguably mattered even more, particularly as the impetus toward compromise prior to the tribal invasion. Yet each of these alternatives also has areas of explanatory weakness. Military-strategic incentives for compromise, for instance, had dampened swiftly within a year of the tribal invasion and therefore cannot explain Nehru's continued commitment to conciliation well into 1953. An explanation emphasizing ideology similarly struggles in light of the undoubted elements of intransigence in India's policy, suggesting that compromise was clearly not driven exclusively by some idealism or altruism on Nehru's part. Key aspects of India's initial offer of, and then even more its persistence in adhering to, a plebiscite commitment cannot therefore be understood without reference to the reputational factor. It is in this manner that reputation was an imperative of Indian policy—not in the sense that it was the sole or most important driver of it but in the independent and important role it played in facilitating and encouraging a posture that otherwise makes little sense. Presented in the form of a counterfactual, this suggests that were it not for reputational concerns, Nehru had little incentive by 1949 to continue to be conciliatory. By then, India had the official accession of a clearly salient Kashmir in hand, the support and willingness of the popular local leadership to confirm it, and, importantly, a more benign military-strategic context that allowed for taking up more intractable positions. Save for the reputational factor, in other words, we would have likely seen a less conciliatory Nehru government adopt the sort of unbending stance that it eventually assumed in 1954.

The discussion here, however, leads to more questions and puzzles. If Nehru was indeed sincere in his commitment to a plebiscite, why was it never held? What prevented the Indian side specifically from helping give effect to the process? And why did Nehru scrap the idea with some finality shortly after, in 1954? The next chapter turns to these questions and makes clear that reputational concerns of a very different kind had become even more explicit and pronounced in Indian thinking in the following years, reaching their apogee in the fateful year of 1954.

**4**

## The Failure of the Plebiscite Option

From 1947 through to Nehru's offer in 1953, two primary issues plagued the debate in the UN and outside over the prerequisites to a plebiscite: the disposition of the two sides' military forces (the "quantum-of-forces" issue) and the nature of the political dispensation in Kashmir in the lead-up to the plebiscite and during its conduct.[1] On both issues, it is undeniable that the government of India adopted a firm stance. Underlying India's demands lay the basic stipulation that Pakistan play no part in the administration and defense of the state or the organization and execution of the plebiscite.[2]

On the first question, New Delhi insisted, in keeping with UN resolutions, on a complete demilitarization by Pakistan (including the tribal and Azad Kashmir forces) of the territory under its control, to be accompanied by the withdrawal of the bulk of Indian forces in the state.[3] For Nehru, consideration of the Kashmir issue had to "proceed on the recognition of the sovereignty of Jammu and Kashmir over the entire territory of that State, of the fact that this state, by virtue of accession of India, became a part of the territory of the Indian Union." This meant, in essence, that what India was asking for was that "all armed forces should be removed from the Pakistan side of the ceasefire line and that Pakistan should exercise no authority over the area which it invaded."[4]

New Delhi's second precondition related to the political administration that would oversee a plebiscite. Following demilitarization, the government of India's representatives insisted, a vote was to be conducted under the authority of the existing administration in the state. It would not be held, as Pakistan and others demanded, under an "impartial" administration, ostensibly under the authority of a UN-appointed plebiscite administrator. To Nehru, for "any other administration to be imposed on Jammu and Kashmir" was unacceptable because it amounted to interference in India's and Kashmir's internal affairs. The state, after all, had legally become part of India with the maharaja's signing of the instrument of accession in 1947.[5]

To address concerns that such an arrangement would simply allow India and Abdullah to manufacture an outcome, however, Indian officials made it clear that any such vote would happen under the auspices of the UN. The Indian government was willing to undertake measures seeking to eliminate any undue influence that the Abdullah administration might have exercised in carrying out a plebiscite. Specifically, Indian representatives clarified, UN appointees could organize and conduct the plebiscite so long as their authority was seen to derive from the Kashmir administration. This meant, in practical terms, "that while Sheikh Abdullah will be Prime Minister in Jammu and Kashmir State and will run the ordinary administration of the State, the organizing, conduct and completion of the plebiscite will be in the hands of men who are nominees of the Secretary-General of the United Nations."[6] In other words, while the UN was welcome to supervise the plebiscite, it was unacceptable to Nehru to expect the administration in the state to hand over any governmental functions to an individual or body appointed by the Security Council.[7]

Throughout this period, New Delhi's position on these two issues constituted the primary Indian obstacle to a plebiscite. So strict were these terms, moreover, that it is possible to argue, as critics have done, that Nehru adopted them as a strategic ploy to create conditions in the state such that New Delhi could guarantee victory in a plebiscite by manufacturing an outcome if necessary. Alternatively, if the preconditions were rejected by Pakistan—as they were—it provided Nehru with a convenient excuse to avoid the plebiscite altogether, without having to officially renege on an international commitment that his government had perhaps misguidedly made in the early days of the dispute. Intuitively persuasive as this argument appears, especially considering the fact that there is no doubt that Nehru viewed Kashmir as highly salient territory that he would have dearly loved to have become part of India, the previous chapter has demonstrated in detail why it is unconvincing and shown that the preconditions do not point to a fundamental insincerity on Nehru's part.

I argue, in contrast, that India's imposition of such prerequisites was influenced to a significant degree by a concern in New Delhi that the failure to stipulate these conditions—ones that were viewed to be in accordance with both UN resolutions and what Indian officials saw as their legal rights in the state—would carry prohibitive costs. These costs were understood to be of both a strategic and reputational nature, which were liable to be exploited by a hostile Pakistan, the credibility of whose commitments was highly suspect in the aftermath of the tribal invasion.

## Bargaining Context in the Kashmir Theater

From very early on, Nehru and his officials viewed Pakistan, not without reason, as too weak to pose anything in the nature of an overarching threat to India's physical security. Although such optimism did dampen somewhat with the passage of time, it was in part due to this assessment that the overall distribution of power indisputably favored India—and that ostensibly even with Kashmir, Pakistan would have been significantly weaker—that New Delhi seemed to be quite open to the possibility of the state going to Pakistan. The immediate situation in the theater of conflict itself, however, was a little more complicated in these early years. Although it held much of the state, India's strategic advantages compared to those of the adversary were somewhat less obvious.[8] In Kashmir, Pakistan—despite lacking physical control of much of the territory or the overall military capability to match India—enjoyed the benefit of being able to project itself militarily with greater ease. The two major land routes that had connected Kashmir to undivided India passed through Pakistan, and, significantly, the only all-weather road linking the state to the outside world connected the capital, Srinagar, to the city of Rawalpindi in Pakistan.[9] Consequently, even before the tribal invasion, Nehru had noted with fear the ease with which Pakistani troops could enter the state when the winter isolated Kashmir from India.[10] "Conditions for carrying on military operations in Kashmir State," Nehru complained later, "are not favorable to us chiefly because our lines of communications are bad and limited, while Pakistan can just walk in whenever it likes."[11] Pakistan's logistical advantages in effect meant that, as Mountbatten would articulate, "For every crore that it [military conflict in Kashmir] cost India, undoubtedly Pakistan would hardly have to spend a lakh."[12]

While these strategic advantages Pakistan enjoyed in Kashmir were enough to make its leadership's protestations of benign intentions suspect to New Delhi, Pakistani commitments were made less credible by perceptions in India of Karachi's inveterate hostility. Soon after partition, fear that Pakistan was intent on balkanizing India had led Nehru to comment on the Muslim League's "utter lack of bona fides and its venom and enmity against India."[13] At a more immediate level, such suspicions were confirmed in what Nehru firmly believed to be the Pakistan government's active role in the planning and execution of the tribal assault on Kashmir.[14] India's case at the UN, for instance, contended that the tribal invaders had derived "all manner of help—men, arms, ammunition, other supplies, motor and other transport, bases of operation, transit facilities, gasoline—from or through Pakistan territory," in all of which the government of Pakistan was complicit.[15] These perceptions naturally made for a severe dearth of confidence in New Delhi that Pakistan would adhere to any of its stated commitments. As Bajpai put it, the Pakistanis' extreme hate for India meant that any settlement (on Kashmir or any other issue) was unlikely to be "sincere or enduring."[16]

In short, there were serious fears in New Delhi during this entire period that Pakistan possessed advantages in the theater of conflict itself, which in some ways negated the bargaining strength that India enjoyed owing to its control of the disputed territory. In view of such concerns, it was crucial to Indian leaders that no actions be taken in Kashmir, and no concessions be made to Karachi, that would create conditions and perceptions that an unscrupulous Pakistan could exploit before a plebiscite decided the ultimate future of the state. This meant avoiding creating situations that enhanced Pakistan's preexisting military-strategic advantages in the Kashmir theater. It also meant that Nehru was incredibly conscious of a reputational imperative that made him averse to making any sort of concessions that he felt might signal weakness of constitution to the adversary. These considerations are crucial to understanding the perplexing fact of Indian flexibility on the larger issue of resolving the Kashmir dispute and Nehru's intransigent firmness over the conditions under which a plebiscite could be held.

## The Military-Strategic Calculus

There is little doubt that the commitment problem–related military-strategic fears, identified as an alternative hypothesis in the theoretical discussion previously in this book, featured heavily in New Delhi's thinking about the conditions under which a plebiscite could be given effect. Such concerns were most pertinent to Indian demands on the quantum-of-forces issue. Underlying them was the preexisting conviction in New Delhi that Pakistan was likely to unscrupulously seek to exploit any strategic advantages in Kashmir militarily, a fear confirmed by Karachi's complicity in the tribal invasion of the state. For Nehru, even with an end to the fighting, there was "no surety of good behavior on the Pakistan side and even less on the part of the tribes."[17] With such little faith in Pakistani bona fides, a complete withdrawal of Indian troops, which Pakistan demanded, was out of the question.[18] Given Pakistan's logistical advantages and its "neurotic mood and hostile actions," "insurance against such recurrence of aggression" was viewed as imperative.[19] The prospect of Pakistani military presence in the plebiscite area was therefore even less acceptable.[20] Dixon later encapsulated Indian concerns best when he noted the "possibility either of incursions by marauders, a possibility which, with the experience that India had of what occurred in the autumn of 1947, cannot but be regarded as real, or of Pakistan, with her better lines of communications, herself staging another invasion."[21]

Such fears mounted over the years with two seemingly interrelated developments: the increasing anti-India bellicosity in Pakistan and the strengthening of a pro-Pakistani military presence and capabilities in Kashmir. On the first front, there was a strong sense in New Delhi by 1951 of a deepening mood of jihad within even the highest echelons in Pakistan. Tensions over the formation of the Kashmir Constituent Assembly (CA), as well as communal disturbances in Bengal, were viewed as central to what was perceived in India to be growing Pakistani hostility, a trend confirmed by increasing military provocations and skirmishes initiated by Pakistani and Azad forces in Kashmir.[22] In the midst of all this, the foiling of the Rawalpindi conspiracy, a failed coup in March 1951 by Pakistan army officers seeking, in part, more assertive policies in Kashmir was yet another disturbing indicator of the domestic churn in Pakistan. As tensions persisted over the next few months and domestic opinion pivoted to calls for war with India, the Pakistani prime minister made a combative speech on Defense Day in late July 1951, declaring that a clenched fist would be his country's national symbol from that point on.[23] So agitated in fact was public opinion that in August, Foreign Minister Zafarullah Khan believed that barring some drastic developments, war was inevitable by the end of the year.[24] Nehru was convinced that in this context, Karachi was likely to read the formation of the CA as "the final nail in the coffin as far as Kashmir was concerned," possibly prompting it to resort to force.[25]

The assassination of Liaquat Ali Khan in October 1951 only heighted fears among the Indian leadership that control of Pakistan might pass to, as Bajpai put it, "wild men" leading to "dangerous adventures, India being the first target," fears that turned out to be unfounded as Liaquat's death dampened the climate in Pakistan.[26] Nehru clearly viewed the change in the Pakistani mood following Liaquat's assassination as merely temporary, however. As he colorfully observed months later, the government in Pakistan was "like someone riding a bicycle. They feel the moment they return to normalcy the bicycle stops and they fall down."[27] The Indian prime minister therefore continued to fear that Pakistani leaders would soon look for opportunities to pursue more adventurist courses of action in Kashmir, in part to divert attention from the seemingly permanent domestic ferment.[28]

On the other front, the risks India faced in Kashmir were compounded by the progressive strengthening of the Pakistan-backed Azad Kashmir forces. Even by the time New Delhi and Karachi had agreed to a cease-fire at the UN in January 1949, these forces were some thirty-two battalions strong and being equipped by Pakistan.[29] This was a development that even the UN Commission on India and Pakistan had noted "makes the withdrawal of forces, particularly those of India, a far more difficult matter to arrange."[30] By early 1953, the Azad forces had become sufficiently stronger, better trained, and well equipped that Nehru considered them to be as effective as, and practically integrated with, Pakistan's regular army. For Nehru, the fact that these troops were backed up by regular Pakistani concentrations at a distance of around 20 to 25 miles from the cease-fire line only magnified the threat they posed. While none of these developments threatened to truly imperil India's strengthening military hold on the parts of Kashmir it controlled, it did mean that New Delhi was acutely conscious of the fact that the situation could dramatically change with any drawdown of its force strength in the state. Significant Indian military presence in Kashmir was therefore viewed as an absolute necessity in order to secure the state prior to and during a plebiscite. Any reduction of Indian troops was possible only "if all Pakistan troops were withdrawn from 'Azad' area and 'Azad' forces disarmed and disbanded."[31] Karachi, of course, had arguably been obligated to do precisely that by previous UN resolutions, a fact that added heft to the validity of India's demands. Given these fears, the Nehru government viewed it as highly unfeasible and dangerous to make any sort of substantive concessions on the quantum-of-forces issue that risked presenting a belligerent Pakistan with exploitable military-strategic advantages.

Similar political-strategic concerns extended to the issue of the political administration of the state, making concessions on that front seem equally dangerous. Any substantive concessions on political matters, such as, for instance, agreeing to an "impartial" administration, amounted in effect, in New Delhi's view, to a diminishing of Indian sovereignty in Kashmir. It also meant, importantly, an acquiescence to Pakistan's claims for parity in the state. That was unacceptable to Nehru because it risked equipping Pakistan with a legitimate vantage point that it had so far lacked from which to intensify its challenge and demands in Kashmir. Nehru and his officials even feared the acceptance of a cease-fire in 1949 to have "been interpreted to mean as if

Pakistan has not only acquired some kind of political right over the territory under its present control but had also a right to interfere in the other part of the Kashmir territory."[32] Even on the quantum-of-forces issue, Nehru was convinced that the Pakistani government's position was a devious ploy "to justify their occupation of that territory and to equate them with India on the other side of cease-fire line."[33] To acquiesce to any further Pakistani demands on this score was consequently viewed in India as facilitating the parity of status that the other side sought, a concession that was ripe to provide Karachi with the sort of political and legal standing from which to mount further challenges on the Kashmir issue.

This situation also explains India's insistence that Kashmir's accession was final and valid until a plebiscite was held; until that point, Pakistan had no constitutional position in the state. Karachi therefore could certainly not play any role in the preparations and conduct of a plebiscite; even more, any act that diminished Indian sovereignty over the state was similarly anathema to the Indian government.[34] What could be more advantageous to Pakistan, Nehru contended to Dixon, than to be able to say that they had "kicked out the Kashmir Government and the India Government from Kashmir"? That would have been "patently ninety per cent of victory for Pakistan then and there, quite apart from the plebiscite."[35] India's experience had, moreover, demonstrated that vague formulas and commitments were dangerous when dealing with the leaders of an "amazingly unscrupulous" Pakistan, with whom "sometimes it almost appears that unscrupulousness pays."[36]

The government of India consequently viewed setting and holding to firm preconditions as imperative to making the prospect of a plebiscite feasible. Any relaxation of those terms posed the danger of presenting Karachi with the sort of military-strategic or political position from which to make more extensive demands in Kashmir, which would have only undermined the prospects for a peaceful resolution of the conflict. As Mountbatten encapsulated the Nehru government's thinking on this matter, "the more concessions that we gave," the more the other side "would dig his toes in and insist on further concessions."[37]

## The Reputational Imperative in Indian Decision Making

Mountbatten's statement also hints at the fact that in addition to military-strategic concerns, there was a strong reputational element to how Nehru and his colleagues viewed the risks of making concessions to Pakistan on the issue of the logistics of organizing a plebiscite. Indeed, the reputational implications of their actions were a far from negligible consideration for the Indian leadership from early on. Even in dealing with the ruler of Junagadh's decision to accede to Pakistan,[38] Raghavan has noted that "reputational considerations played an important role" in New Delhi's decision making. As Nehru put it then:

> [If] Junagadh's aggression is tolerated, then the prestige of the Government of India suffers greatly with disastrous results in Kathiawar and in other states. This is likely to affect the position of Hyderabad also. It may be followed by other acts of aggression by Pakistan authorities. Each particular act might be relatively small. But it will help in breaking up the states acceding to the Union.[39]

With regard to Kashmir, such concerns influenced Nehru in interesting ways. Clearly, the fact that compromise in general—and even the loss of Kashmir if the people of the state so wished—was acceptable to the government of India suggests that it perceived few reputational costs to be attached to such an outcome. Indeed, given the fact that India was making such concessions from a position of being the indisputably stronger party in the dyad in overall capability, there were reasons for Indian leaders to believe initially that if there were any reputational consequences, they were likely to be positive. For Nehru in particular, the concessions that his government was willing to make were clearly more indicative of Indian generosity and benevolence rather than weakness. In keeping with this, he had emphasized to the Pakistani leadership that had his government really desired to gain Kashmir by any means, it could have done so easily without waiting until large chunks of the state had been invaded by the tribal raiders. In the process, it could have also avoided domestic criticism for being "dilatory."[40] In offering a plebiscite therefore, despite Kashmir's having legally acceded India, New Delhi "had already gone far further than they need have done . . . [even though] there was no necessity for them to have done this."[41]

On the narrower question of the prerequisites for the holding of a plebiscite, however, India's reputational calculus was diametrically different. This was in part due to the fact that Pakistan's bargaining position in the theater of conflict itself was significantly stronger owing to its better logistical position to project military power in the state. Perhaps more important, Karachi had also already demonstrated a willingness to exploit such advantages through coercive means by, for one, its complicity in the tribal invasion. The reputational stakes for New Delhi were therefore conceivably higher—and different—given the specific bargaining context in the territory under contention. Such concerns manifested in Indian fears that conceding to demands from Pakistan on the modalities of a plebiscite risked signaling weakness to the adversary, something that the latter was equipped to exploit. The terms and conditions under which compromise, and particularly a plebiscite, was to be given effect to were consequently of great reputational import to India's leaders. As one scholar has succinctly encapsulated the significance of this reputational imperative for the Nehru government, "The Indians could give up the state through plebiscite, but they could not be placed in the position of being forced out. New Delhi could not forget that the initial attacks had come largely from the area incorporated into Azad Kashmir."[42]

Essential to Nehru's concerns on this score from early on was the fear that whatever concessions India made beyond the basic offer of a plebiscite seemed to encourage Pakistan into making greater demands.[43] He articulated this thinking soon after the tribal invasion, observing that in his estimation, the mere desire for peace with Pakistan, and concessions to that end, ironically risked making war more likely. "Any *surrender*" by India, he felt, to "this kind of aggression would lead to continuing aggressions elsewhere . . . [and] war would become inevitable between India and Pakistan." Pakistan's initial failure to formally agree to a plebiscite two months after India had offered it reinforced this sense. As Nehru saw it, the failure to accept that offer and the fact that "war is being carried on" in the meantime "does not indicate either a desire for peace or for a plebiscite on the part of Pakistan."[44] It was viewed in New Delhi instead as a clear indication that Pakistan preferred to resolve the issue unilaterally, through force if possible. Peace was possible only if India resisted aggression firmly, since "that is the only way Pakistan seems to understand."[45] Undermining the prestige of the Indian government at a crucial time was viewed as a sure recipe to encourage the adversary to persist with aggression.[46]

In its legal and moral standing, Nehru considered his government's case in Kashmir to be strong, while Pakistan stood undisputedly condemned. This fact made succumbing on his preconditions—demands that were "consider[ed] on both moral and practical grounds to be perfectly justifiable"—even more reputationally damaging.[47] Peace, after all, Nehru contended, could not be achieved were it to be based on "untruth, immorality and acceptance of brutal aggression."[48] Pakistan's whole policy, as that of the Muslim League before it, had been premised on the efficacy of "threat and bullying," where "appeasement only leads to more bullying."[49]

From the Indian perspective, this perception necessitated a clear stance of not submitting to coercion because of the severe reputational costs of doing so. New Delhi's preconditions to a plebiscite— insisting on first rectifying Pakistani aggression and denying Karachi any standing in the state—sought to serve this very end. Relaxing these conditions was out of the question because that would mean that "aggression stands justified and will be repeated as in the past."[50] As the tone of the rhetoric emerging from Pakistan became shriller in the early 1950s, Nehru made it categorically clear to Liaquat that he could make few concessions to the latter's proposals because "peace is not offered with clenched fists nor with threatened aggressions and resounding cries of jehad."[51] Indeed, so intense was this reputational imperative that by late 1952, it had bled into Nehru's attitude on other issues concerning Pakistan. On the potential of common defense, for instance, the Indian prime minister cautioned his ambassador against raising the issue for fear that "Pakistan is likely to think that we are weakening and are afraid of them and the result might be a more aggressive attitude than now on the part of Pakistan."[52]

To the Indian prime minister, it was extraordinary that despite his government making what he felt were incredibly generous concessions given Pakistan's initial aggression, "gradually the aggressor wants equality with us in everything, and a step further, it wants predominance in everything."[53] Any further compromise in the face of such pressure, Nehru feared, risked confirming for Pakistan that it had succeeded in aggression "with all the psychological and other consequences that flow from it."[54] Given these considerations, the Indian approach to the Kashmir dispute, and specifically on the plebiscite issue, was, in effect, conceived of in New Delhi in this period as one "in which firmness is tempered by reason and restraint."[55]

This meant that India was open to some flexibility on the form the plebiscite would take. Dixon's proposal for a partition-cum-plebiscite approach to the dispute, for instance, was acceptable to Nehru in general and indeed central to his proposal to Karachi in 1953.[56] Similarly, in addition to being agreeable to UN auspices over the conduct of a plebiscite, the Indian leaders had also been open in the early exchanges at the UN to a reconfiguration of the Kashmir administration. As long as Abdullah remained its leader, Nehru was willing to accept a coalition government in the state incorporating members of the opposition Muslim Conference.[57] However, being overly accommodative on India's preconditions for a plebiscite was seen as unwise, as it would have amounted to surrendering some sovereignty to Pakistan in the face of aggression.[58] Even with regard to the possibility of a coalition government in Kashmir, G. S. Bajpai had made it clear to the British in February 1948 that any such proposal would not come directly from his government; it had to come from others. The logic, as Raghavan puts it, was that "if Delhi offered concessions Karachi would ask for more."[59]

Criticism of Indian firmness on these issues at the UN exacerbated Nehru's annoyance. Indeed, pressure from the major powers on India, demanding that it relent on its preconditions for a plebiscite, began intensifying soon after India had referred the issue to the UN. This was particularly true of the British, who had been frustrating New Delhi with their constant championing of Pakistan's case. The leader of the British delegation, Philip Noel-Baker, had been functioning under the premise that not backing Pakistan on the Kashmir issue risked antagonizing the wider Muslim world and Britain's already fragile position in the Middle East. He had consequently been pushing proposals on Kashmir that were viewed as highly hostile in New Delhi, sometimes without his own cabinet's acquiescence.[60] So biased was the UK's stance perceived to be that even Mountbatten was forced to write to London complaining about it, and Nehru feared that Britain was punishing India by blocking the transfer of arms and oil.[61] Furthermore, as Nehru wrote to Atlee in November 1948, he regretted that "these hostile forces [the invaders from Pakistan] are controlled and led by British officers who are thus participating in an invasion of the territory of the Indian dominion."[62] Later, in the crucial 1952 note to Abdullah, the Indian prime minister similarly noted that "there was always the question of what foreign powers might do either in interfering or in aiding Pakistan in other ways."[63]

In the UN's admonishing India thus and demanding that it be more conciliatory and generous, Nehru felt that critics at the world body had failed to acknowledge that the "acceptance of any aggression at any time and more especially in the present circumstances, means encouraging it for the future and has very far-reaching consequences."[64] Indeed, the appeal by others for "greatness" on New Delhi's part, beyond the already generous offer to hold a plebiscite in a state that had technically already acceded to India, was considered to be hardly appropriate because it was precisely such a logic that led in fact to appeasement, with all its negative implications.[65] Such pressures consequently made staying firm even more of an imperative for Nehru, not only to show Pakistan that "gangster tactics" would not work but also to signal to the great powers at the UN that India would not succumb to their "bullying."[66] Nehru consequently wrote to Mountbatten that he was becoming "a little tired of the advice being given to us from time to time in a minatory language from the U.S. and the U.K. They seem to forget that we are not some little Central American Republic or some Balkan country which can be cowed down. . . . Even if we were a small country, that has not been our past."[67]

## Taking the Plebiscite Option off the Table

The hopes for a concerted push toward a plebiscite in Kashmir, which the late 1953 bilateral talks had evoked, were soon crushed with India's abrupt withdrawal of the offer. The wishes of the people of Kashmir, which until recently had seemingly held priority for Nehru, were now sidelined. By late 1954, the

Indian prime minister had confessed that despite the fact that Karachi seemed "anxious to have a settlement and is prepared to go some distance for it," he saw "no way out except a recognition by both parties of the status quo, subject to minor modifications."[68] Indeed, by this point, Nehru was asking his envoys to delay the possibility of what were sure to be fruitless talks and, furthermore, that they make no reference to the plebiscite in any talks with their Pakistani interlocutors.[69]

Even as he eventually and reluctantly entered into talks with the Pakistani prime minister, Mohammad Ali Bogra, and the interior minister, Iskander Mirza, in May 1955, Nehru made it clear that despite his desire to stand by previous commitments, it had become progressively difficult to do so. The "only practical and safe way of dealing with it [Kashmir]," he said, "was to accept present conditions as they were, that is, the status quo, and then proceed on that basis."[70] The maximum that Nehru was willing to concede in these talks, and that reluctantly, was a transfer of Mirpur and parts of the Poonch area to Pakistan as part of a broader and final settlement along the status quo.[71] As Nehru himself concluded at the end of the expectedly fruitless talks, the two countries were now "apparently further away from each other than they had been at any time during the last seven or eight years."[72]

For New Delhi, speaking in terms of the old basis for resolving the Kashmir dispute had become impractical. As the home minister at the time, G. B. Pant, publicly stated in a July 1955 visit to Kashmir, the government of India now believed that the "tide cannot be turned."[73] In response to repeated calls from Pakistan for talks, Nehru made it unambiguously apparent to his officials that while his government was open to meeting Pakistani leaders, "we can no longer talk on the old basis."[74] In keeping with this new stance, the Indian prime minister once again ruled out a plebiscite during talks in 1956. This despite indications that Karachi, with a new prime minister at the helm in Chaudhry Mohammad Ali, was now amenable to accepting Nehru's 1953 terms, including that of holding a plebiscite along regional lines.[75] As Nehru saw it, his government was no longer bound by prior commitments,[76] regardless of what the people of Kashmir wished, where as one Indian leader, J. P. Narayan, asserted, 95 percent of the population had turned against India.[77]

The crucial development that triggered this drastic reversal of policy by India was the US-Pakistan Mutual Defense Assistance Agreement of May 1954, whereby Pakistan agreed to enter into a military relationship with the United States and become—in Ayub Khan's words—"America's most-allied ally in Asia."[78] In return, by October, Washington had promised Pakistani officials military aid to the tune of $171 million, to be disbursed over the next three and half years. Funds earmarked for economic assistance to Pakistan also saw a spike, with the United States promising, as McMahon details, "in excess of $105 million, including $5.5 million in flood relief for East Bengal, $5.5 million in technical assistance, $20 million in defense support funds that could be used for economic development, and $75.6 million in commodity assistance, targeted especially for consumer goods and industrial raw materials."[79]

The prospect of such a development had been of concern to New Delhi even before. As early as November 1952, in fact, there had been troubling reports in both the *New York Times* and the influential Pakistani daily *Dawn* about a potential agreement between the two sides that would involve American strengthening of Pakistani military capability in exchange for basing rights in the country and Pakistan's participation in the Middle East Defense Organization (MEDO).[80] Indeed, Karachi had been pushing for such an arrangement since the crisis period in 1950–1951 and had sent a military delegation to Washington soon after Liaquat's death with the specific goal of acquiring as much military equipment from the United States as possible and exploring the possibility of Pakistani participation in US arrangements for the defense of the Middle East.[81] By early 1953, Chester Bowles had confirmed this for New Delhi, conveying furthermore that Pakistani officials had on occasion been citing Kashmir explicitly as the reason for their requests to the United States.[82]

Consequently, soon after the 1953 talks, as the prospect of the US-Pakistan pact began to firm, Nehru warned Karachi that they had a choice between winning Kashmir through plebiscite or entering a military alliance with the United States.[83] He made it clear that the conclusion of a military pact, by significantly changing facts on the ground—especially in view of an already intractable demilitarization issue—would necessitate a reappraisal of India's attitude toward a plebiscite.[84] Prior discussions had taken place, the Indian prime minister pointed out, in "a particular context which existed then, and which exists, if you like even today." That context would change drastically "when one of the greatest powers of the world sponsors military aid to Pakistan,"[85] meaning that all "problems will be seen in a new light."[86]

It is important to note that until as late as March 1954, Nehru had been letting the Pakistani leadership know that he continued to remain bound to his government's commitment to a plebiscite. It was, he pointed out, Pakistan's continued failure to agree to India's preconditions and now, even more, the talk of a military pact with the United States that was inordinately delaying the actual carrying out of a vote in Kashmir.[87] Indeed, all the while that he was trying to convince Pakistan to put a stop to the momentum toward an alliance with Washington, Nehru was also internally restating his commitment to a plebiscite. In the hope and expectation that Karachi would react favorably to his warnings, the Indian prime minister instructed Bakshi Mohammad, now the new leader of the Kashmiri administration, that he continue to function on the understanding that the 1953 plebiscite plan was still on track.[88] In a February 14, 1954, letter to Bakshi, Nehru also let it be known that his government had no intention of unilaterally reneging on commitments made to the people of Kashmir, Pakistan, and the UN despite the fact that on February 6, the Constituent Assembly had ratified the state's accession to India.[89] Similarly, only four days before the US-Pakistan pact was officially confirmed, Nehru wrote to Ali Yavar Jung, India's ambassador to Egypt, that "so far as the Government of India are concerned, we hold on to those [plebiscite] assurances."[90]

Once the US-Pakistan agreement was officially concluded, therefore, New Delhi unsurprisingly reversed its position on the plebiscite. The Pakistani prime minister understood as much in acknowledging that the sole reason for the dramatic change in India's position appeared to be the introduction of American military aid to Pakistan rather than any other domestic developments or considerations.[91] For New Delhi, the pact, by fundamentally changing expectations about Pakistan's overall military capabilities and bargaining strength in Kashmir, had heightened the intensity of the potential military-strategic and reputational costs attendant on compromise along old lines. In response, the Indian leadership assumed a position of increasing firmness, key to which was a refusal to continue to contemplate a plebiscite in Kashmir. In the following years, Nehru began to insist instead on a solution along the lines of the prevailing status quo.

## Why Nehru Withdrew the Plebiscite Offer

From a military-strategic standpoint, in Indian perceptions the US-Pakistan pact promised to so change the military balance on the subcontinent that a plebiscite, and the prospect of losing Kashmir, both of which had so far been acceptable to the Indian leadership, became immediately problematic.[92] With regard to the plebiscite and the Kashmir theater specifically, the pact was seen in New Delhi as complicating the already contentious quantum-of-forces issue.[93] As Nehru saw it, with their progressively augmented military capabilities added to preexisting logistical advantages, even moving Pakistani troops 20 or 30 miles behind the cease-fire line would have done very little to mitigate the strategic quandary that India now faced.[94] It had consequently become "absurd to talk of demilitarization."[95] Rather, India needed to "retain full liberty to keep such forces and military equipment in Kashmir" as it saw fit.[96] Any major withdrawal from Kashmir, based on third-party assurances, was inconceivable given the ease with which an aggressive Pakistan, likely to be equipped with more potent military forces over time, could resort to an offensive in the state.[97] With a satisfactory demilitarization formula unlikely to be found, the pursuit of a plebiscite also lost any practical meaning for the Indian leadership. Indeed, so firm was Nehru's stance now that the Pakistani prime minister was forced to conclude that an agreement on the question of demilitarization had become impossible, requiring that the question revert once again to the UN.[98]

Beyond the specificities of the Kashmir theater and the plebiscite, moreover, the military pact also meant that the prospect of losing Kashmir itself, which had been reluctantly acceptable to the Indian leadership in earlier years, now became strategically unviable.[99] "It is not merely the Kashmir question that has become much more difficult," Nehru declared, "but a serious threat has arisen to India's security."[100] The military aid to Pakistan was expected to both "facilitate and encourage aggression."[101] Regardless of American assurances, Nehru felt that once advanced weapons were made available to Pakistan, they would be out of Washington's control.[102]

In an indication of how seriously he took this threat, Nehru began to raise concerns by early 1954 about military preparedness at home. For someone who had all along emphasized the importance of economic and industrial development as a foundation for military strength in the future, Nehru now concluded that security "cannot be provided for by some long distance programme of production." Moreover, it required serious consideration of rapid military acquisitions.[103] By March 1956, Nehru was complaining internationally that the flow of military aid to Pakistan had already ensured that the latter possessed better-quality military equipment than India did.[104] If such transfers continued, the Indian prime minister anticipated in an internal note to Krishna Menon in early 1957, Pakistan would soon acquire parity with India in numbers, backed by a definitive qualitative advantage in weaponry. That would have given Karachi, according to military opinion in India, enough of an advantage to be able to initiate war effectively.[105] Already, Nehru believed, both the Pakistan air force and its army's mechanized wing were superior in many ways to their Indian counterparts.[106] Furthermore, as he noted in a conversation with French Foreign Minister Christian Pineau, in discussions a few months earlier, John Foster Dulles, the US secretary of state, had reportedly acknowledged that the Pakistan army was on its way to parity with India.[107] This fact was seemingly not lost in Pakistan, where anti-India sentiment and talk of war had perceptibly spiraled as a result.[108] Finally, the introduction of the United States in a military way to its neighborhood was itself strategically troubling to New

Delhi. Nehru regarded the move as in part an attempt by Washington to "bring India to her knees" and force a reconsideration of nonalignment.[109]

Political developments in Pakistan only exacerbated fears in India that any concessions that presented Karachi with a strategic advantage, including the acquisition of Kashmir itself, would be exploited toward imperiling Indian security further. As the military acquired political supremacy across the border, Nehru felt that Pakistan's government "did not have a political or economic purpose or background, but was moved by a mentality which was adventurous and military."[110] A government, Nehru felt, that had used the bogey of an Indian threat to divert attention domestically from poor governance could only be expected to become even more adventurous with the generous military aid it was receiving.[111] "So far as the external danger to India is concerned," Nehru concluded, "the only possible danger is from Pakistan."[112] In essence, then, as the Indian prime minister put it, "US military aid to Pakistan and Pakistan's membership of military pacts . . . destroyed the roots and foundations of the plebiscite proposal in Kashmir."[113]

*The Reputational Dimension*

While military-strategic considerations were no doubt very important in Nehru's increasing intransigence on Kashmir in the aftermath of the signing of the US–Pakistan military pact, the drastically changed context on the subcontinent equally made reputational considerations independently salient to New Delhi's new thinking. So far, notwithstanding some of the specific strategic advantages Pakistan possessed in the Kashmir theater, an overall context wherein India enjoyed undisputed supremacy in bargaining strength over its adversary had allowed the country to be conciliatory, convinced that doing so from a position of strength carried few reputational costs and potentially promised gains associated with appearing benevolent and cooperative. To the extent that New Delhi's imposition of preconditions to a plebiscite emerged from fears of appearing weak, then, they were driven for the most part by Pakistan's previous coercion, which to Nehru had to be recognized and penalized before a plebiscite could be given effect to.

Karachi's entry into what amounted to a military alliance with the United States, however, portended the possibility of a transformation of the very balance of power in the subcontinent, and hence the distribution of bargaining strength in the conflict. This potentially dramatic shift in the bargaining context not surprisingly altered New Delhi's reputational calculus in a significant manner. In short, the prior experience of use of force by Pakistan, accompanied now by the very real prospect of that country's rapidly increasing military capabilities and improving bargaining strength, made greater intransigence with regard to Kashmir—including the rejection of a plebiscite—both necessary and a crucial means of demonstrating firmness and resolve on India's part.

For Nehru, it was apparent that the prevailing belief in Karachi was that following the conclusion of the pact, India would eventually have no choice but to relent on Kashmir when confronted with Pakistan's greater strength. Indeed, even as in practical terms the military balance of power had shifted very little in the year or so after the signing of the US-Pakistan agreement, the mere promise of such a shift had perceptibly transformed the psychological mood in Karachi. It had emboldened opinion there to such a degree as to force the Indian government into a reassessment of the merits of being conciliatory. To Nehru, Pakistan was seemingly engulfed in talk of war, with open boasts that having built up its military, it intended to speak to India from a position of strength.[114]

This increasing bravado in Pakistan had manifested itself in its leaders' extensive demands during the 1955 talks, which to Nehru were terms reminiscent of those dictated by a victor to the surrendering enemy.[115] Following the failure of those discussions, the Pakistani prime minister had also allegedly made clear, reflecting growing confidence that time was on his country's side, that he was no longer "going to seek interview with Nehru but if Nehru wants discussions on Kashmir" they could meet, provided they did so in Karachi.[116] Indeed, by 1957, the new Pakistani leader, Huseyn Suhrawardy, was publicly claiming that India's stranglehold over Kashmir was breaking and that Pakistan's involvement in the Western alliance had made "a favorable turn in the Kashmir dispute possible."[117]

Dangers of military adventurism were exacerbated by a sense in New Delhi that Pakistan "disintegrates also at a rapid pace, both in the West and in the East, politically and economically."[118] As Nehru noted, even responsible people in the neighboring country were now talking "with some glee of what they would do about a year hence."[119] Increasing border violations in this context suggested to him that the Pakistani leadership sought to "settle disputes with India from what is called a position of strength."[120]

India's response, Nehru now determined, was to demonstrate even greater firmness on Kashmir so as to leave no room for doubt in Pakistan that his government would not succumb in the face of military threats and the latter's increasing bargaining strength. Hence the insistence that the status quo was the maximum New Delhi was now willing to concede in Kashmir and the decision to withdraw even that offer once Karachi had rejected it.[121] Instead, Nehru instructed his officials that the "question of partition does not arise now and must not be raised."[122] India's leaders were determined not to weaken in any way or even suggest that they were willing to discuss or make alternative proposals.[123] In one revealing instance, after learning that the issue of a plebiscite had come up during former Indian army chief K. M. Cariappa's 1957 visit to Pakistan, Nehru expressed concern that even that meeting could be interpreted in Karachi as having happened at the instance of India's leaders, and therefore as a sign of flexibility in New Delhi, which patently was not the case.[124] Any such loosening of India's position was, given the reputational imperative, completely unacceptable to Nehru until India's "honor as a country" was vindicated.[125] Altogether absurd, he also felt, were calls to India to make "generous gestures" in the interest of peace, gestures that would smack more of surrender to Pakistan's threats and aggressions than anything else.[126] "I am quite sure," Nehru had by now concluded, "that if the Kashmir issue was settled even to the satisfaction of Pakistan, our troubles with Pakistan will continue. The issue is a much deeper one. Anyhow, we are rather tired of being cursed at and bullied and threatened."[127]

Indeed, Nehru now confessed that in hindsight, his government in previous years had been too "reasonable" and "decent" in the interest of peace.[128] "In the past we made a mistake in being too accommodating to Pakistan," Nehru wrote to his sister, and India's high commissioner to the United Kingdom, Vijayalakshmi Pandit, and those earlier concessions were now being held against India as commitments.[129] "It may well be" he now acknowledged "that if we had adopted a somewhat more rigid policy right from the beginning . . . we might have been in a better position to deal with this question now. . . . As usual, those who want a settlement are always at a slight disadvantage as compared to those who do not want it except on their own basis, that is, surrender by the other party."[130] With this recognition, Nehru concluded that the only viable response to Pakistan and its backers' attempts to bully and frighten India was to adopt an even firmer stance in order to communicate his government's resolve.[131] As Nehru explained to the UN secretary general, Gunnar Jarring, India's past experience meant that his government was no longer willing to try any methods that conveyed flexibility and could be exploited by an unscrupulous Pakistan yet again. The plebiscite proposal had been "picked up and misused by Pakistan as plebiscite commitment" and the Indian government was no longer willing to put itself in a similar position.[132] Indeed such firmness seemed to Nehru to be having a salutary effect even on hostile third parties in the Security Council. He believed that Washington, for instance, had seemingly realized that condemnation, rather than frightening the government of India, had only made it firmer.[133]

The essence of the matter, as Nehru saw it, was that as a strengthening Pakistan persisted with its hostility, India was "neither a small nor an ignoble country to submit to threats and bullying."[134] While peace with the neighbor was desirable, the Indian government could not concede on its basic demands because doing so "only encourages the other party to open its mouth wider, claim more and shout more." New Delhi could not, he asserted, risk having its generosity being mistaken for an expression of weakness or a prelude to capitulation. "Surrender," after all, "creates a position of future demands for surrender and so it goes on step by step."[135] New Delhi had no desire to humiliate Pakistan, but given these facts, there was simply no basis for any progress in Kashmir unless Pakistan admitted to both its initial aggression and the validity of the state's accession to India.[136] Peace, as the Indian prime minister clarified in 1958, and a resolution of the Kashmir problem that ignored "certain basic issues and which endeavors to put us on the same level as Pakistan—that is the aggressor and the aggressed continue on the same level" was unviable.[137] The military pact between Pakistan and the United States, by fundamentally transforming the bargaining context underlying the conflict in Kashmir, had exacerbated these reputational concerns to a degree that the sort of generous concessions Nehru was willing to make in 1947, and until as late as 1953, became progressively more impractical after 1954.

Within Kashmir, all this meant that the will of the people was no longer a concern for the Indian leadership. "By the middle of the 1950s," as one observer has noted, "any substantive autonomy Kashmir had managed to carry over from its earlier princely statehood had largely vanished—a victim of New Delhi's insistence that Kashmir's accession to India was final and irrevocable, not subject to negotiation with Pakistan or, by implication, with the Kashmiris."[138] Sheikh Abdullah was briefly released from imprisonment in early 1958 but was promptly returned to it soon after for adopting what Nehru termed "a wrong and dangerous path."[139]

Into the beginning of the 1960s, the last few years of Nehru's leadership in India, the country's firmness on Kashmir had only concretized. The ascent of a new military regime under General Ayub Khan in Pakistan led to the unexpected resolution of the contentious Indus water-sharing issue, but on Kashmir there was little movement. This owed itself in part to Nehru's distrust of a naked military dictatorship in Pakistan, one that he expected to be ever more prone to war.[140] Consequently, it was now "quite beyond any possibility for the government of India to agree to hand over any part of our territory to the Pakistan government or to agree to any process which might lead to this."[141] As Pakistan prepared to reignite the issue at the UN in 1962, Indian officials let it be known to their American counterparts that while they were willing to "go through the motions of negotiations,"[142] the status quo was the only solution that they were seriously prepared to discuss with Pakistan.[143] Indeed, it was made clear, even the offer based on the cease-fire line was unlikely to remain open forever.[144]

The increasing buildup of tensions at this time in Sino-Indian relations, and the related and simultaneously blooming relationship between Pakistan and China, reinforced these tendencies in New Delhi.[145] The initiation of Sino-Pakistan boundary negotiations in 1962 made even more unlikely "any kind of accommodation now as the two aggressors had already combined."[146] Events came to a head with the disastrous (for India) Sino-Indian war in late 1962, discussed in later chapters. The war left Nehru bitter not just about China but with Pakistan as well. He furiously complained that the country's new-found love for China had demonstrated that "hatred was at the very root of the creation of Pakistan." Rawalpindi, which had replaced Karachi as Pakistan's capital in 1958, had believed—mistakenly—that "it can intimidate us because we are facing this threat from the Chinese." For Nehru, though, the Chinese invasion had made it even more important that India make no concessions on Kashmir to Pakistan that would risk confirming such an impression.[147]

Not surprisingly, Nehru only reluctantly entered the 1963 talks with Pakistan—prodded by the United States and the United Kingdom—with little intention of budging on his government's previous position. This was so despite the fact that a failure to come to an agreement with Ayub threatened to jeopardize the prospect of substantial American and British military assistance that India so desperately required to deter any future threats from China.[148] The Indian prime minister had reason to believe that in this period of intense trauma, worsened by the finalization of the Sino-Pakistan boundary agreement in the midst of the India-Pakistan talks on March 2, 1963, a deal as part of which Indian officials believed that the Pakistanis had surrendered "a good chunk of the north-eastern frontier of Kashmir" to China[149], anything but firmness would have been reputationally disastrous for India. Concessions made at the country's lowest point, even if they led to a resolution of the Kashmir dispute, threatened to encourage further demands from the other side. Indications during the talks themselves that Pakistan's "appetite had grown in the changed circumstances" as "India seemed in a much weaker position than ever before"—Zulfikar Bhutto, the leader of the Pakistan delegation, had even chided the Indian side by noting, "You are a defeated nation, don't you see?"—served only to confirm such fears in India. In this context, talks for Nehru had little purpose but to prevent Pakistan from joining hands with

China in renewing military aggression on India.[150] Indeed, as even President John F. Kennedy seemed to have grasped midway through his efforts to cajole India into accommodating Pakistan, Nehru was "unlikely to settle Kashmir with too obvious a gun at his back."[151]

TABLE 4.1

*India in the Kashmir dispute: A summary*

| Period | Bargaining Strength | Adversary Coercion | Policy | Reputational Explanation |
|---|---|---|---|---|
| **1947 (preinvasion)** | **Strong** India was strong owing to the distribution of capabilities | **None** | **Compromise** Proposal that the future of Kashmir be resolved through plebiscite | Compromise would not make India appear weak to Pakistan; it would rather bolster India's reputation for generosity and cooperation |
| **October 1947–1953** | **Dominant** India was dominant owing to the distribution of capabilities and physical control of most of Kashmir | **High** Pakistan had facilitated the tribal invasion in 1947 and introduced regular troops soon after; it refused to vacate aggression | **Compromise– Conditional** Continued commitment to plebiscite provided Pakistan reversed/ was punished for aggression (preconditions to plebiscite) | Compromise was still reputationally viable because it was coming from a position of strength; doing so without preconditions risked signaling weakness in the face of coercion |
| **1954 onward** | **Declining** The US-Pakistan alliance weakened India's bargaining position in New Delhi's perception | **High** Aggression had yet to be reversed in Kashmir; Pakistan had introduced the United States into the region through the pact | **Intransigence** Withdrawal of plebiscite offer; status quo (favorable to India) the only acceptable solution now | Compromise was increasingly unviable because it risked conveying weakness in the face of Pakistan's growing strength and continued coercion; intransigence was necessary to demonstrate resolve and deter Pakistan |

## Conclusion

Indian policy with regard to Kashmir had moved in the space of less than two decades from a position open to significant compromise, in accordance with the wishes of the people of the state, to one willing to accept only the status quo favorable to New Delhi, in disregard of popular sentiment. Most prominent accounts of the Kashmir dispute attribute Nehru's role in the failure to achieve a settlement of the conflict to the immense nationalist, strategic, and even emotional value India's first prime minister attached to the territory. They consequently suggest that either New Delhi had not been serious about the offer of a plebiscite all along or that it logically reneged on the commitment as it became progressively clear over the years that large sections of the people of Kashmir had become disenchanted with India. Chapter 3 demonstrated, however, that as strong as the pull of Kashmir was for Nehru and the Indian government, it rendered neither the territory indivisible nor New Delhi's approach to it inflexible. Indeed, and no doubt with some reluctance, Nehru remained committed to compromise and to carrying out a plebiscite in Kashmir until 1954. This was true even during times when he and others in India were convinced that the people of the state would throw their lot in with Pakistan. This surprising position owed itself in significant part to Nehru's early assessment that given India's undoubted superiority in overall power terms in relation to Pakistan, concessions—including the prospect of losing Kashmir, if the people of the state so wished—carried tolerable costs, especially in comparison to the potential dangers of conflict. In military-strategic terms, even if it acquired Kashmir, there was little risk perceived of a tottering Pakistan being able to exploit such territorial gains in the future. On the reputational front, Nehru anticipated that a concession such as the plebiscite offer, made from a position of overwhelming strength, carried little risk of betraying weakness; if anything, it promised to buttress the more benign aspects of India's reputation.

This chapter has offered an explanation for the more intransigent aspects of Indian policy. I have argued that the Indian obstacles to the plebiscite—preconditions regarding demilitarization and the political dispensation in the state—were motivated not by a desire to stall the process altogether. Rather, they were driven by a very different Indian calculus in the theater of conflict itself: a response to Pakistan's initial act of aggression and consequent fears in New Delhi that making concessions on those specific preconditions could carry some very serious risk. Military-strategic concerns were certainly pervasive in this calculus, especially on the quantum-of-forces issue given the logistical advantages Pakistan enjoyed in Kashmir. However, it is undeniable that the reputational imperative highlighted in this work was independently salient to Nehru's decision making on the plebiscite issue.

Indeed, this is a case where we are clearly witness to the reputational tension between the desire to look resolute, on the one hand, and more accommodative, on the other, and how the two motivations can simultaneously influence policymaking. Therefore, at the same time that Nehru offered and remained committed to a plebiscite so as establish a benign international reputation for generosity and cooperation, we also see how fears that compromise in the face of an adversary's coercive acts would convey weakness drove New Delhi to be firm on the matter of the terms under which a plebiscite would be given effect.

Only in 1954 did Nehru abandon the idea of a plebiscite, insisting instead on settling the issue in keeping with the existing status quo. This the Indian government did directly in response to Pakistan's signing a military pact with the United States, a development that Nehru feared exacerbated the military-strategic and reputational costs of any concessions in Kashmir. For Nehru, the dramatically changed context made the loss of Kashmir strategically unviable. Such developments also clearly necessitated in Nehru's mind the adoption of an increasingly intransigent stance for reputational purposes so as to convey Indian resolve to a hostile and increasingly potent adversary. To the extent that communicating this resolve had become vitally important, India was willing to pursue it at the risk of undermining its reputation for generosity and cooperation, and an image as a nation of peace that it had been attempting to embellish with its otherwise conciliatory stance. This led to the categorical withdrawal of the plebiscite offer, a commitment that the Nehru government had been repeatedly reaffirming over the previous years. From this point on, India began functioning on the basis that Kashmir's accession to India was complete and nonnegotiable. That continues to be New Delhi's stance even today.

# 5

# The Dispute with China
## *The Formative Years*

India's territorial dispute with China has been as intractable as that with Pakistan over Kashmir. In contrast to the latter, however—a territory that held high salience for India in the immediate aftermath of partition—India's policies in the dispute with China during the Nehru period are puzzling because by 1960, the conflict essentially revolved around a piece of territory that was of ostensibly little importance to New Delhi. Toward the end of the 1950s, the period during which the conflict between the two countries assumed crisis proportions eventuating in war in 1962, it is now clear that China was willing to accept Indian sovereignty over territory that the latter held in the eastern sector in exchange for Indian recognition of Chinese claims over disputed territory in the western sector as part of a package agreement. In principle, such a solution should have been acceptable to a weaker India given that it involved retaining territory in the east that was of high salience to the country, in return for abandoning claims to territory in the west that Indian leaders from early on considered to be of little value. Moreover, New Delhi viewed its legal claims to the areas China sought in such an agreement as doubtful. In addition, a compromise solution fit in with Nehru's stated commitment in previous years to pursue a policy of friendship and accommodation with Communist China, a posture that led to concessions—derisively labeled by critics as "idealist"—over Tibet in 1954. Yet China's package offer proved unacceptable to Nehru. Rather, even more perplexing, and despite India's apparent military weakness compared to China, New Delhi decided in late 1961 to adopt the militarily provocative Forward Policy, escalating the crisis toward the disastrous war of 1962.

This chapter and the next illustrate how despite the lack of salience of the territory in the western sector, Indian intransigence on the entire territorial issue was driven primarily by reputational considerations, and specifically the mounting fear over time that concessions made from a disadvantageous bargaining position would signal weakness to Beijing and provoke greater challenges to India's territorial integrity and security.

Following an overview of the background to the dispute and a brief discussion of the alternative understandings of the Nehru government's policies, this chapter focuses on the earlier periods of the Sino-Indian relationship, from 1949 to 1956. The discussion will show how despite the dormancy of the dispute during this time, the underpinnings of India's later intransigence were present all along. While pursuing quintessentially accommodative policies with Beijing on the whole, there was a conscious decision made from very early on to adopt a posture of firmness on the territorial issue, partly for strategic reasons but more clearly for fear of the reputational costs of making concessions to an already stronger China. Beijing's overwhelming military dominance in the frontier regions, particularly following the invasion of Tibet in 1950–1951, and mounting evidence over time—in Nehru's view—of China's coercive and unilateralist tendencies exacerbated such fears in New Delhi. This context sets the stage for the discussion in the next chapter of India's refusal of Zhou Enlai's 1960 offer and thereafter the seemingly reckless pursuit of the Forward Policy in the lead-up to the Chinese initiation of war in 1962.

## The Territory in Question

Following independence from Britain in 1947, the Indian government had the immediate task of defining its claims with regard to the territorial boundary with China, the latter then embroiled in a civil war between the Nationalist and Communist forces. The task was a necessary one because the mountainous frontier region where India and China meet had never been delimited and demarcated consensually during the period of British colonialism in India. Two sectors of this border, as shown in map 5.1, were of particular concern to both states given the expanse of territory involved. The eastern sector near Burma, comprising some 35,000 square miles of territory, is largely coterminous with the region India called the North East Frontier Agency (NEFA), now known as the Indian state of Arunachal Pradesh. The western sector, on the other extremity of the Sino-India border region, in-

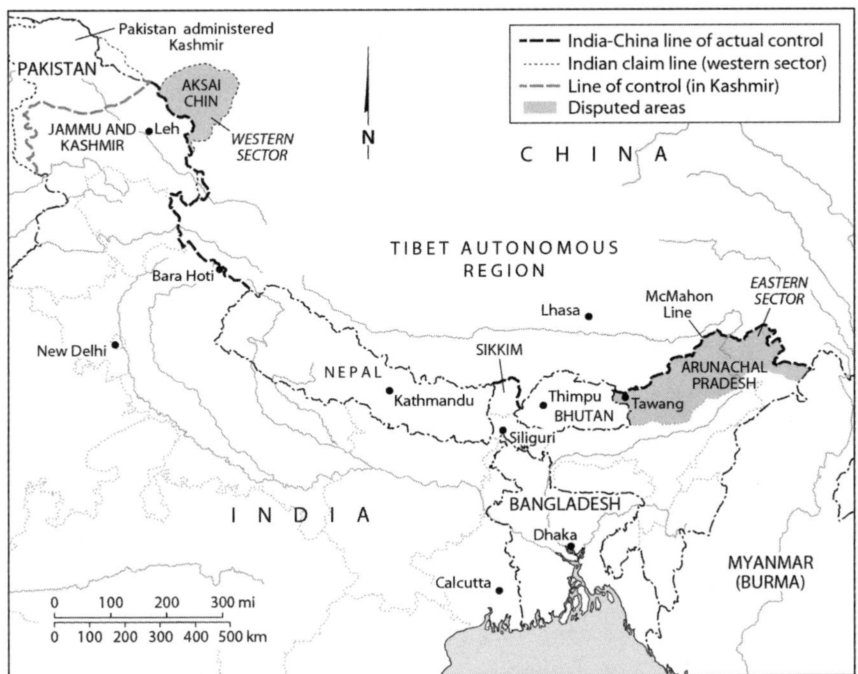


MAP 5.1 *Sino-Indian frontier dispute.*

cludes some 13,000 square miles of territory, of which the status of the Aksai Chin plateau bordering the Ladakh region of Kashmir would prove to be the most combustible issue.

In the eastern sector, shown in map 5.2, India claimed soon after independence that the border between the two countries had been delimited by the McMahon Line proposed by the British at the Shimla Conference between British, Chinese, and Tibetan representatives in 1913–1914, an agreement that the Chinese representative to the talks had initialed but his government never ratified.[1] This line drew the border between the two countries along the crest of the Assam Himalayas, leaving the area south of it with India. A region largely populated by tribal groups, the territory in the eastern sector holds little ethnonationalist significance for the Indian leadership. It is, however, strategically salient as something of a buffer area. A strong Chinese state that could project itself into Tibet and beyond, if in control of the Assam Himalayan region, and with easy and ready access to the plains of Assam, would pose a stark threat to the Indian northeast, a region where India was already vulnerable as it was connected to the rest of the country only by the narrow Siliguri corridor.[2] Furthermore, problems of internal political instability in the

MAP 5.2  *The eastern sector.*

region, where several groups had been fighting for their own state since independence, made control of NEFA indispensable to preserving the integrity of the Indian northeast.[3] Sardar Patel, India's home minister at the time, had alluded to this latter fact in a missive to Nehru in late 1950, noting that the area was populated by people who ethnically and culturally had "no established loyalty or devotion to India."[4]

In the western sector, shown in map 5.3, particularly with regard to Aksai Chin, the colonial power had left the boundary fairly ambiguous. British claims had fluctuated over time, largely shaped by bureaucratic infighting among colonial officials over the intensity with which they felt the desire to keep the region as a buffer zone between India and potential Russian expansionism. The extent of such concerns depended on fluctuations in Chinese power and reach in the region.[5] Three different lines had been proposed by India's colonial government at different times. The most expansive, northern-

MAP 5.3 *The western sector.*

most of these was the Ardagh-Johnson Line, which showed Aksai Chin as part of India. A second line, the Macartney-MacDonald Line, placed Aksai Chin within the confines of China's Xinjiang province. The final, least expansive line ran south of both borders and along the Karakorum range.[6] Having failed to resolve the border issue with China or settle on a firm line, the colonial power left independent India with a map that showed the boundaries in the western sector as undefined.

The territory itself, an uninhabited high-altitude desert extending west from the Tibetan plateau, was of little value in terms of symbolic significance, economic endowments, or strategic importance to postindependence India.[7]

Consequently, especially in comparison to the territory in the eastern sector, the salience of the land in the western sector was arguably negligible to the Indian leadership.[8] Not surprisingly, therefore, while India's claims in the region eventually settled somewhat along the most expansive of the British claim lines, the Ardagh–Johnson Line, there was never any real certainty in New Delhi about the value and validity of such claims. Moreover, these claims occupied very little attention and a clearly subordinate position to the McMahon Line in Indian thinking internally and in discussions with the Chinese immediately after independence. They acquired an unexpected prominence only in the later part of the 1950s and then motivated an intransigence that remains a puzzling aspect of the Nehru government's treatment of the Sino-Indian dispute.

### The Puzzle of Nehruvian Policy: The Alternative Arguments

That Nehru was unable to find or contribute to a compromise solution to the Sino-Indian dispute is in many ways a puzzle. It is particularly so given his own stated commitment to peace in general, and in particular to friendship and accommodation with China in the interests of solidarity among the Asian and newly decolonized countries. Indeed, in consonance with his "idealist" persona, as many have labeled it, the scholarly story that emerged in India and abroad in the immediate aftermath of the 1962 war was one that pointed to Chinese betrayal of a friendly India in pursuit of its illegal expansionist goals in the region.[9]

These narratives offered a view of Nehru that attributed to him a certain naiveté in his handling of China that made him largely incognizant of the threat China posed. In practically appeasing China with regard to Tibet in 1950–1951 and then again in 1954 and then leaving India undefended for the Chinese assault of 1962, Nehru by this account had exposed his essential idealism and sacrificed strategic thought at the altar of romanticism. To the extent that Nehru did have any misgivings about China, the failure to reorient policy to address them also further betrayed incompetence in the Indian leaders of the period.[10] This impression of a Nehru favorably disposed toward China to a fault was corroborated by evidence that prominent officials within the Indian administration such as Sardar Patel, G. S. Bajpai, and K. P. S Menon had expressed at various points misgivings about Nehru's approach to China. Nehru himself would add credence to such a view after the 1962 war, confessing that India, in relying on the good faith of other states (read China), had been "living in a world of unreality."[11]

Yet to the extent that Nehru was indeed partial to accommodation and peace with China and willing to make major concessions on issues such as

Tibet toward that end, the big question that remains is why the Indian government then adopted a policy of intransigence on the territorial issue. An answer to this emerged from later revisionist scholarship that contested claims of Nehru's idealism and at the extreme made the case that it was *his* government that had precipitated conflict by seeking to unilaterally impose a boundary on China. It was in fact China, as Maxwell, for instance, claims, that had been the victim of the unilateral assertion by India of questionable territorial claims, an intransigence that eventually left Beijing with little option but to use force.[12]

This refusal to compromise, most accounts suggest, was driven primarily by military-strategic and nationalist motivations. Some scholars have suggested that rather than driven by unmitigated idealism, Nehru's foreign policy had some real elements of realpolitik and strategic thought. It aimed at securing India's interests within the constraints posed by the country's limitations, and policy on the territorial dispute was therefore driven by essentially such considerations.[13]

An alternative account contends that central to Nehru's attitude on the territorial matter was a strong sense of nationalism. This nationalism manifested itself in, and was fueled by, Indian leaders' ideas and beliefs about the country's "historical" borders—as Hoffman has demonstrated—and their sense of postcolonial victimhood—as Miller has argued.[14] Miller indeed captures this logic succinctly in arguing that Indians (as well the Chinese) "harbor bitter resentment for the territorial damage inflicted on them by imperialist states and are determined not to give way on traditional territorial boundaries that are intimately tied to their nationalist beliefs and, hence, their identity."[15] By this account, then, Nehru's government adopted British-drawn boundaries wholesale because they genuinely believed that such lines had merely formalized what were precolonial India's preexisting traditional and customary borders with China. Nationalist feelings arguably also permeated an aggravated domestic body politic in the period of crisis beginning in the late 1950s, creating a set of irresistible domestic political pressures for Nehru.[16]

The security-seeking and nationalist arguments, in short, make the case that the level of firmness we see from New Delhi in this dispute is altogether unsurprising. As explanations for Indian conduct during this period, however, both of these alternative logics are incomplete, for three major reasons. First, it is apparent from internal documents that Nehru and his officials from early on viewed disputed territory in the western sector as being of little salience in military-strategic or nationalist terms. What is more, there was also clear acknowledgment in the government that India's claims to territory in the region lacked any strong legal or traditional justification. It was territory in the east that they viewed as crucial to the security of the entire Indian northeast and where India's claims were on firmer legal ground.

Given these facts, it would have been reasonable to expect, from both a salience and security perspective, that the Indian government would have been open to making concessions in the western sector in exchange for Chinese concessions in the far more valuable eastern sector. From a conventional military-strategic perspective, after all, while it made sense for Nehru to be firm in the eastern sector, there were very few benefits from picking fights in the west. Yet it was precisely such a solution that Nehru summarily rejected in talks with Zhou Enlai in New Delhi in April 1960. It was pursuant to Nehru's rejection of what Indian documents confirm to be Zhou's offer of a package deal—where Beijing would give up claims to the much larger territory in the eastern sector, in return for India's conceding to Chinese claims in the west—that both sides entered the slippery slope to war.

A second problem concerns the fact that not only did the Indian government reject Zhou's offer, but even more inexplicable for these arguments, New Delhi decided to then embark on the fateful and provocative Forward Policy little more than a year later, in 1961. As the Henderson Brooks-Bhagat report, a still classified official Indian postmortem of the 1962 war—parts of which have only recently been released by Maxwell—amply reiterates what was well known to both political and military leaders even then, the Indian army was woefully unprepared for any military confrontation with China at the time. Yet despite such debilities, New Delhi pursued a risky military initiative that seems unfathomable from a conventional security-seeking standpoint. That it did so in and over self-confessedly unimportant territory in the western sector makes the choice more puzzling. The more reasonable option would have been that of agreeing to the compromise solution Zhou had proposed rather than risking the possibility that the stronger Chinese would respond, as they did, to the provocations of the Forward Policy with war.

Third, as this chapter and the next highlight, domestic public opinion was not nearly as important in New Delhi's decision making as is usually made out to be. If it were indeed such pressures that were central to India's policy on China, logic suggests that we should have seen an Indian government that was willing to be far more conciliatory on territorial issues in earlier years, when an animated domestic public was much less of a factor. That it was able to make unilateral concessions on Tibet in 1954 certainly suggests that New Delhi had plenty of political room to maneuver in at that time. Yet the historical record suggests that the underpinnings for Nehru's proclivity to stand firm on territorial issues had in fact become apparent well before the time that domestic politics became a truly salient concern in New Delhi. Public opinion therefore, while not unimportant, especially later in the case, offers a far from comprehensive explanation for Indian policy.

The analysis that follows demonstrates how reputational concerns in particular were prominent in Nehru's thinking from very early on in Sino-Indian relations, well before the territorial conflict officially burst into the open in 1957–1958, and became stronger after that. At the same time that Nehru was pushing for friendly relations with Communist China, he clearly had fears and concerns about the latter's strength and expansionist tendencies, leading his government to assume a posture that laid the foundations for Indian intransigence in later years as reputational concerns congealed and exacerbated on the back of China's perceived perfidies. Again, as in Kashmir, security-related motives were certainly a driving force in Nehru's decision making, but even more so than in that case, they manifest themselves here not through the military-strategic but rather the reputational mechanism. Indeed, the big puzzles concerning Indian policymaking in the conflict with China during this period are inexplicable without factoring in the imperative of reputation.

## Indian Border Policy, 1949–1956

Immediately after independence, Indian maps with regard to the border with China were naturally those inherited from the British colonial predecessors. This meant that in keeping with British Indian maps, the McMahon Line was shown as the Sino-Indian boundary in the eastern sector, but in the western and middle sectors, Indian claims were left undefined.[17] With China embroiled in its civil war, the issue of the frontier with that country received little urgent attention from the Indian leadership, especially because they were immediately dragged into addressing the aftermath of partition and the rapidly escalating disputes with Pakistan, especially over Kashmir.

Indications in 1948 of an impending Communist victory in China first drew the attention of Indian officials to a potential frontier issue, but it was the progress of the Chinese invasion of Tibet in 1950–1951, intended to "liberate" Tibet and "stand guard at the Chinese frontiers,"[18] that truly activated thinking and policy formulation in India about the border with China.[19] From this time until the border dispute broke open in 1957–1958, India's policy on the issue was shaped by three basic constants: a focus on the eastern sector or the McMahon Line frontier, a policy of avoiding any discussion—or explicit raising—of territorial issues with Beijing, and an attitude of firmness with regard to Indian claims.

As Communist forces looked increasingly likely to emerge victorious in China, Nehru had started alluding to the need to pay greater attention to that frontier. By late 1949, he had begun contending that it was essential for India to develop communications infrastructure in the northeast, particularly road networks, cautioning that not to do so expeditiously was "risky business."[20] While he consistently underplayed the possibility of any immediate Chinese military threat on the Tibetan frontier,[21] he concurrently acknowledged that the movement of Chinese troops right up to the Indian frontier was troubling for not only India but also for the crucial Himalayan states of Nepal, Bhutan, and Sikkim.[22] Indeed, in relation to Nepal, Nehru bluntly asserted internally that while his government did "appreciate the independence of Nepal, we cannot risk our own security from anything going wrong in Nepal which permits either that barrier to be crossed or otherwise weakens our frontier."[23]

With the Chinese invasion of Tibet on October 7, 1950, Indian leaders' attention swiftly focused on the country's northeastern borders. Sardar Patel was, among others, most vocal in his identification of the development as a serious threat to the country's security. In an important note to Nehru, Patel branded China's actions in Tibet as "little short of perfidy," convinced that a strong and united China would function in imperialist ways and in all likelihood disown the McMahon Line.[24] Bajpai similarly expressed his fear that Beijing might now seek to heal the scars of past humiliations "on the basis of frontier rectifications that may not be to our liking."[25] Indeed, K. M. Panikkar, India's ambassador to China, had cautioned about such an eventuality as early as June 1948 when he had noted that China's occupation of Tibet risked meaning "the immediate revival of claims against Nepal, Bhutan, and Sikkim and also the denunciation of the McMahon line."[26]

Nehru was more immediately sanguine and circumspect than Patel and Bajpai about at least the short-term prospects of conflict—leading Bajpai to privately note that he had to "work hard to control his [Nehru's] enthusiasm"[27] about China; nevertheless, he was far from unperturbed. He conceded, in a note addressing Patel's fears, that the status of the border between the two countries had become an issue of concern and that there was now a possibility that Chinese troops would enter and take possession of territory that India claimed.[28] Bajpai's own take on China, it is worth noting, was very similar to how Nehru articulated the issue in later years. In his view, in India "China sees the only potential rival to political and economic equality in Asia and, therefore, jealousy rather than love is likely to be the real sentiment of China towards us. While we must cultivate her friendship, we must not be led away by false sentiments or illusions."[29]

In policy terms, the invasion of Tibet triggered moves by the Indian government to begin clarifying India's territorial claims. After all, previous Chinese governments had challenged the frontier as well; as one of his last acts, the Nationalist ambassador to India had reminded the Indian government that the Chinese did not recognize the McMahon Line. There was, therefore, every reason to believe that Communist China would soon follow suit.[30] New Delhi's immediate focus was the McMahon Line. One of Nehru's first acts consequently was to assert to his ambassador in Beijing, K. M. Panikkar, that there was no room for controversy over the territorial issue: "all frontiers with Tibet, that is, the McMahon Line, must stand as they are."[31] That this was to be his government's policy had in fact been noted by Nehru as early as December 1949, with the Communists having recently declared their intention to "liberate" Tibet. In a letter to the premiers of Indian states, Nehru had made it clear that much as he would like Tibet to remain autonomous, doing very much to give effect to such an outcome was "beyond our strength." Having said that, however, he also made it "dead clear" that his government would not "permit the slightest intervention, aggression or invasion of any Indian territory wherever it might be."[32] In parliament, Nehru clarified that the while the frontier in the west from Ladakh to Nepal owed its definition to use and custom, in the eastern sector the McMahon Line was indisputably India's boundary. India, declared Nehru, would not tolerate a breach of the latter, "map or no map."[33] The Indian prime minister believed that India's stance was "in fact on strong ground" legally, making any reconsideration of the McMahon Line unnecessary.[34]

By November 1950, the Nehru government had also formed the North and North-Eastern Border Defense Committee under the deputy defense minister, Brigadier M. S. Himmatsinghji. The committee, composed of delegates from several government ministries, the intelligence services, and the armed forces, was tasked with assessing the security situation in the regions bordering China. The committee submitted its two-part report in April and September 1951. Its recommendations were to guide efforts at strengthening Indian administrative control over and development of the communications infrastructure in the North East Frontier Agency (NEFA) along the McMahon Line, as well as the reorganization of the government's intelligence apparatus under the Intelligence Bureau. An infrastructural program to build roads and checkpoints along the frontier was also initiated by the government on the prompting of the report. Finally, the committee recommended that India firm up its territorial claims in sectors of the map shown to be undefined, and then take measures to ensure security of these territories from Chinese intrusion and occupation.[35]

Consequently, Nehru continued to emphasize in internal discussions the need to strengthen communication networks and checkposts, adding to intelligence capabilities, and developing the border regions economically so as to integrate them more closely to the rest of India without disaffecting the local population.[36] By this time, New Delhi had also presumably, again in accordance with the Himmatsinghji committee's recommendations, begun the task of defining and clarifying border claims, to be reflected in maps issued by the Indian government.[37] Indeed, as part of asserting such claims, in February 1951 India assumed military control over the Tawang tract in the NEFA region, territory that Nehru acknowledged was located on the Indian side of the McMahon Line but had always been under Tibetan control to that point.[38]

By early 1952, Nehru and his officials had begun to give consideration to the issue of how to approach the looming frontier dispute at the diplomatic level with Beijing. The primary dilemma confronting New Delhi at this juncture, it is apparent now, was less about the validity of Indian claims, particularly with regard to the McMahon Line, but more about how proactive and open India ought to be in addressing the territorial issue. Nehru's initial instinct was to instruct his ambassador in Beijing to explicitly raise the matter with Premier Zhou.[39] This was in keeping with the view of officials in New Delhi, Bajpai and Menon in particular, who preferred extending the scope of impending discussions over Tibet to cover the question of the border. These officials had envisaged being explicit on India's claims, and demanding Beijing's recognition of the border in return for concessions in Tibet.[40]

The Indian government's diplomatic approach to the issue, however, quickly settled into one predicated on delay and avoidance. From here on, New Delhi functioned on the assumption that the border had been settled by the McMahon Line, with no need for India to initiate or encourage any discussions with China. Nehru had anticipated such a policy in a 1950 note to Burmese leader U Nu outlining India's approach. His government, Nehru stated, intended to ignore Chinese maps, clarify their own claims with regard to the McMahon Line, and avoid raising any issue with China that would attract attention to "something which is rather complicated," exacerbating existing fears and suspicions on both sides.[41]

Such a stance was facilitated by what appeared to be Beijing's disinterest in the issue. In conversations with the Indian ambassador to his country, Zhou had claimed that Chinese maps were old and likely inaccurate,[42] and that barring the issue of the stabilization of the Tibetan frontier, there were no territorial issues between India and China.[43] Nehru was surprised, and even disconcerted, by Zhou's lack of interest in the matter. He wrote in reply to Ambassador Panikkar that it was "not advantageous" to India for issues related to Tibet to be discussed "piecemeal" and not as part of a general settlement. This was especially so because his government was "not particularly anxious to facilitate movement and retention of large numbers of Chinese troops in Tibet."[44]

A month later, Nehru reiterated that "any permanent or semi-permanent arrangements can be discussed only as part of general settlement of our interests in Tibet." These interests, he clarified, were "not confined to trade relations but involve political interests such as affirmation of the Frontier." Nevertheless, Nehru also seemed to appreciate the value of an avoidance-based policy predicated on an assumption that the border was settled as far as India was concerned. In the same communication, therefore, he also explicitly advised Panikkar that "it would be preferable not to mention this [Nehru's view about a general settlement] in your proposed note [to Zhou]. We had really intended this for your information only."[45]

The Indian prime minister recognized, as Panikkar had been suggesting, that there was some "advantage in our not ourselves raising this issue," even as he did not "quite like the Chinese premier's silence about it when discussing even minor matters." He therefore suggested that as long as Panikkar had made India's interests with regard to the frontier clear to the Chinese, as instructed earlier, "we can presume that Zhou Enlai's silence means some kind of acquiescence. It is not for us to suggest any reconsideration."[46] Once Panikkar—who had by now returned to New Delhi after completing his term in China—had confirmed that he had indeed made Zhou aware of India's position, Nehru concluded that his government would not raise the issue any further with the Chinese for the present, while sticking to their position that the boundary was well-defined and not subject to discussion.[47]

That Nehru was not unaware of the potential drawbacks of an avoidance approach is apparent from his missive to Panikkar a few days later in which he confessed to feeling that India's "attempt at being clever might overreach itself," and it was therefore perhaps better to be open and frank with Beijing.[48] Soon after, however, he reconsidered and accepted Panikkar's suggestion that no mention be made of the frontiers in discussions with China.[49] In parliament, Nehru clarified that although Chinese maps showed large territorial claims, at no point had Beijing raised the issue of borders. Furthermore, if China were to do so at some point, there was "nothing to discuss about the frontier. The frontier is there: the McMahon Line is there."[50]

This policy stance eventually made itself apparent as the two countries began talks over renegotiating India's interests in Tibet on the last day of

1953. Even before talks began, Nehru had made it known to his officials that India had no intention of raising the frontier question, "because we take it for granted." If the Chinese representatives were to raise the issue, members of the Indian delegation were instructed to express their surprise and let it be known that they had no authority to discuss an already settled matter. Indeed, if China sought to reopen the issue of the frontier, Nehru agreed with Panikkar's suggestion that Indian officials could walk out and break off the ongoing negotiations.[51] At the same time, in anticipation of potential trouble, Nehru was in no mood to "leave things to chance." He therefore reiterated the importance of strengthening coordination of defense and foreign policies with Bhutan and Nepal, as well as improving India's presence in the frontier areas, something he complained had already been inordinately delayed.[52]

The agreement over Tibet was successfully concluded in mid-1954. As part of it, India had made some substantial concessions on its interests in Tibet, inherited from the colonial government. For instance, while it retained its trade agencies, the Indian government surrendered its right to station military escorts there, as well as its control over the postal and telegraph services and twelve rest houses in the region. More important, the agreement also constituted India's recognition of Chinese sovereignty—not suzerainty, as was the case before—over Tibet.[53]

While Nehru publicly declared that with this agreement, India had won "a friendly frontier and an implicit acceptance" of the same, Indian policy betrayed more circumspection. In an important memorandum dated July 1, 1954, Nehru instructed his officials that all existing maps of the borders needed to be carefully examined and withdrawn if necessary. In their stead, new maps were to be printed clearly showing the north and northeastern frontier lines in accordance with Indian claims, with the new maps to state explicitly that there was no undemarcated territory. These new maps and future Indian pronouncements were also to give up referring to the McMahon Line, given its unfortunate British imperialist connotations. Finally, Nehru confirmed that the borders as indicated on these maps were final. Barring perhaps some minor alterations, they were not open to discussion with China.[54]

In general, then, New Delhi's policy continued to be one where there were no plans of taking the issue up immediately. However, if Chinese maps were to continue showing large parts of India as belonging to China, Nehru also did not intend to "put up with this for long."[55] Consequently, in speaking of Burmese anxieties about Chinese territorial claims in talks with Zhou in October 1954, Nehru only indirectly hinted at India's own fears by asking, "Supposing we publish a map showing Tibet as a part of India, how would China feel about it?"[56]

The updated Indian maps now showed the country's border with China in the east as running along the McMahon Line. In the west, a sector that had received much lesser attention from New Delhi, Aksai Chin was shown as part of India. This was in keeping with a decision made in 1953 to firm up India's claims in a region that until then had been marked as undefined in maps inherited from Britain.[57] However, in this western sector, New Delhi's claims did not adhere completely to the forward-most British line—the Ardagh-Johnson Line. Rather, as Raghavan has detailed, these maps showed a compromise line between the expansive Ardagh-Johnson line and the Macartney-MacDonald line, but still left Aksai Chin within Indian territory.[58]

This suggests two important things. First, the scant attention paid to territory in the western sector during this period reflects the low salience for India of the land potentially in dispute there. Indeed, Nehru and the Indian government were at this point preoccupied in internal discussions and those with Zhou with the obviously more important McMahon Line frontier. In contrast to the eastern sector, where India sought to rapidly extend administrative and military presence, little was done to cement India's claims in the west despite knowledge of some Chinese activity in the area as early as 1951.[59] As Noorani succinctly puts it, in the early years, "frontier consciousness centered exclusively on the McMahon Line."[60] Second, the decision to show a compromise line in the west also suggests a basic doubt in the Indian establishment about the extent of India's legal claims to territory in that sector. Both points would be confirmed in later years, as the next chapter details, but it is important to note that such doubts with regard to the western sector seemed to be present from early on, making the eastern sector the clear center of focus for the Indian government.

## Explaining India's Policy of Avoidance

Nehru's failure to raise the issue of the frontiers in these early years, especially when read in the context of his exchange with Patel in the wake of the Chinese invasion of Tibet, could arguably be seen as a demonstration of his naive idealism and obliviousness to a Chinese threat. After all, China's own internal weakness and vulnerability to external threats ostensibly made Indian interests in Tibet a major bargaining chip, one that India ought to have exploited to elicit reciprocal territorial concessions from Beijing, especially during the 1954 negotiations. Instead, New Delhi ended up surrendering all its special rights in Tibet and confirmed Chinese sovereignty over the territory, with very little to show for it in return on the border issue.

Yet Nehru was far from woolly-headed on this matter. He had actively grappled with the dilemma of whether to raise territorial issues immediately as part of any deal on Tibet or deliberately avoid the matter for the present. Indeed, a deeper perusal of the record suggests that Nehru's avoidance of the issue was, in its essence, premised on a posture of firmness and conceived of as an effort to buy time.[61] With the long term in view and having concluded that China posed little immediate threat, Nehru logically developed a preference for avoiding overt hostility with that country in the near term, with a view to building up bargaining strength for the eventuality that Beijing would broach territorial issues in the future.

Central to this approach was Nehru's—not unreasonable—conviction that the Chinese, faced as they were with the mammoth and costly task of domestic reconstruction, were highly unlikely to function in expansionist ways for some time. Geographical constraints presented by the mighty Himalayas only reinforced the sense that regardless of developments in Tibet, China would be "foolish" to pose any immediate large-scale threat on the Indian frontier.[62] Importantly, this seems to be an impression that was shared by other officials in the Indian government at the time. Bajpai, for instance, contended that a large-scale invasion of India by Chinese forces was unlikely, and what New Delhi ought to be more concerned about was the "possibility of small forces dribbling in through the numerous passes."[63] Such an assessment persisted in New Delhi well into the 1950s.[64] Nehru articulated this thinking in talks with John Foster Dulles in mid-1953 in pointing out that Beijing was too embroiled in domestic issues to indulge in "rash adventures." China, for instance, Nehru contended, could have easily invaded Burma and even had the excuse of the presence of Nationalist troops there, but it had not done so for the same reasons.[65] Mao's own confession that any war would destroy China's newly begun Five Year Plan and postpone the industrialization of China further corroborated for Nehru his belief that Beijing would not be so foolish as to act adventurously for some time.[66] In New Delhi, this context was viewed as allowing India and other countries the leeway to "await developments" rather than undertake any precipitous steps.[67]

Indeed, while China's myriad weaknesses made the likelihood of any immediate military threat from that country seemingly unfathomable, this certainly did not mean that New Delhi itself had the luxury of assuming potentially provocative policy positions. While the leadership in Beijing may not have had incentives at that point to initiate conflict themselves, there was no telling how they would have responded to India's explicit presentation of its territorial demands. For all of China's troubles, India continued to be the inarguably weaker party in the dyad, disadvantages that were especially apparent in the relative military-logistical positions of the two sides in the border areas. These weaknesses and constraints made adopting an overtly confrontational stance with China unnecessary and unwise for Nehru, especially when China was seen to pose little in terms of an imminent threat to India. Inviting open conflict at this point, moreover, made little sense to the Indian leader in that it risked encouraging Chinese hostility and aggression at a time when India was far from equipped to resist such acts.[68] Very early on, in responding to Patel and others, the Indian prime minister emphasized this very issue. "When you talk of defense," Nehru stated, "remember your resources; remember your capacity; and remember that defense consists of the economic position of a country, of the industrial potential of the country, plus the defense forces . . . you have to work within those limitations."[69] In this context of weakness, then, Nehru was determined to avoid conflict with China unless immediate interests on the border or in the Himalayan states were explicitly threatened.[70] Not surprisingly, then, Nehru reached the conclusion that "the present is not a suitable time to raise this [territorial] question."[71]

Consequently, even as Nehru had few illusions about the potential for Chinese expansionism, he had reached the determination that cordial, if not friendly, relations between the two sides could last for at least a few decades. In the meantime, there was hope that reducing Communist China's international isolation might help mitigate some of that country's aggressive tendencies.[72] Furthermore, as the Indian leader was reported to have noted in as late as 1955, India could "use the 25 years of peace just as well as the Chinese can, and if we just postpone our conflict, which I think may eventually occur, it would give us that much time to build up our own country."[73]

To the Indian prime minister, China was already a great power, particularly in military terms, and in ten to fifteen years, it was destined to be even stronger. India, already having to contend with Pakistan, needed a similar amount of time of peace in order to grow strong enough economically and militarily to be able to resist any Chinese threats to Indian security more effectively.[74]

Delay allowed India to wait things out rather than trigger immediate conflict and, in the meantime, strengthen its political, administrative, and military position in the area south of the McMahon Line. Such efforts had so far been implemented in an extremely lackadaisical manner, frustrating Nehru, who repeatedly urged his officials to treat the issue as a matter of great urgency. As Raghavan notes, "In these circumstances it is not surprising that he [Nehru] sought to avoid pushing the boundary question to the fore. India was far from consolidating its influence in the border regions and ill-prepared to counter any efforts by China to take possession of these parts. If the issue became an openly contested one, India might be unable to defend its claims."[75]

Panikkar had explicated exactly this rationale in a note to Bajpai early on, contending that if India insistently raised the issue immediately, China would have the choice of either accepting the McMahon Line or offering to renegotiate the frontiers. Since the former was unlikely, it was more advantageous for India to avoid the matter and function as if there was nothing to be discussed.[76] This logic continued to be relevant leading into the 1954 talks. While Nehru had already acknowledged that there was little India had the ability to do, or indeed wanted to do, to deny China what it desired in Tibet,[77] the ploy of using the issue as a bargaining chip on the matter of borders was far from guaranteed success. In fact, an opening of the territorial breach clearly risked unnecessarily actuating Chinese interest at a time when Zhou had not shown any desire to consider the issue, and, more important, India was not in any state of readiness to defend its claims were Beijing to begin contesting them.

It was far from illogical, therefore, for Nehru to avoid the matter entirely in the 1954 talks while helping resolve the status of Tibet. Ideally, and perhaps idealistically, he had reason to hope that Zhou had been sincere all along in his claims that there were no major territorial issues between the two sides and that in time, the border would automatically stabilize along India's claim lines without the need for negotiations. Satisfying China on Tibet arguably aided that possibility by encouraging more moderation in its leadership. Even if such hopes proved to be unfounded later, it still made little sense for India to immediately set a conflict in motion as opposed to delaying the eventual confrontation to a time when the country was better prepared.

Nehru explained this stance later, in a 1959 statement to parliament. He stated then that his government had felt that by holding their position, "The lapse of time and events will confirm it [the boundary] and by the time, perhaps, when the challenge to it came, we would be in a much stronger position to face it."[78] Foreign Secretary Subimal Dutt similarly recapitulated India's approach to the border. According to Dutt, the Indian government had worked under the assumption that the boundary was well known and that there was no reason for India to acknowledge or raise a dispute. "We were not ignorant of past disputes," Dutt contended, "but on balance we thought that the matter should rest with the Chinese to raise."[79] In the meantime, India intended to maintain normal relations with Beijing, buy time to build its own strength,[80] and "wait for easier days" in dealing with a potential Chinese territorial threat.[81] The 1954 agreement over Tibet served just such a purpose, premised on the principle that India should take advantage of any proposal, unless it was clearly undesirable, that afforded it time to build up strength.[82]

## The Reputational Imperative and Indian Firmness

Crucially, Indian policy during this period was not solely characterized by a desire to delay territorial issues with China to a more opportune time. Equally prominent were indications, especially after the 1954 agreement, that New Delhi had little inclination toward even acknowledging that a dispute might exist, let alone making any significant territorial concessions to Beijing. This was most explicitly true with regard to the eastern sector with which New Delhi was most preoccupied.

Such firmness pointed to Indian fears, which became heightened with time even in the western sector, that making any territorial concessions to a strong China would carry significant long-term costs. Importantly, while strategic concerns were no doubt salient in the NEFA, the documentary evidence points to a more explicit reputational imperative driving the Indian leadership's calculus. Even at this early stage, it was clear that New Delhi feared the possibility of concessions betraying weakness, and thereby encouraging further Chinese challenges and threats to India's sovereignty and security in the future.

Underlying the Indian government's reputational fears in relation to China was an acknowledgment of the large gap in military strength between the two countries, much to India's disadvantage. The Communist regime in China had emerged from the revolution in significantly better military shape than the Indians had in the aftermath of colonization and partition. Even at the end of their postrevolution military demobilization, the Chinese still possessed an army of 3 million soldiers. This was no surprise given the military imperatives of the revolution itself, but it also had something to do with Mao's deeply held beliefs about the utility of force in international politics. The Indian army, in contrast, which had been around 2 million strong at its peak during World War II, had shrunk in size to around 350,000 men once demobilization had been completed at the end the war and, following that, as a consequence of the division of resources between India and Pakistan. The context of stark military inferiority that the Nehru government was confronted with in dealing with Communist China was therefore indisputable.[83] India's preoccupation with Kashmir soon after independence served only to worsen this situation on the Sino-Indian border.

Supplementing Nehru's military-related concerns on the China front was the belief that the latter, in addition to possessing already substantial—and rapidly expanding—economic and particularly military strength, also had a tendency for expansionism. As early as January 1950, therefore, Nehru had informed the Burmese prime minister that given China's rapid growth and despite India's preference for friendship, "there are inner conflicts and frictions and suspicion of each other" that necessitated firmness from India in response to any "improper" demands from China.[84] The Chinese invasion of Tibet had only confirmed Nehru's concerns about Beijing's proclivities, leading him to conclude, in terms strikingly similar to those used after the 1962 war, that whether or not China had deliberately deceived India, it was probably true that "we may have deceived ourselves."[85]

New Delhi now recognized that the emergence of a great power on the country's frontiers was a troubling development,[86] one that naturally necessitated the waning of India's enthusiasm for China, to be replaced with caution.[87] It was clear that China was in its strength and activity already a great power and was likely to grow stronger. As India itself grew, there was a real possibility for conflict.[88] China's growth, moreover, appeared to be swifter, leading Nehru to conclude that India had to be "very, very wide awake" and be careful not to fall behind.[89]

Developments in Tibet made Nehru more "apprehensive of the long frontier," especially since China, like other great powers, was demonstrating a tendency to aggressively expand outward.[90] A strong China, the Indian prime minister contended, had itself demonstrated expansionist tendencies in earlier times, not always and necessarily in territorial terms, but certainly in seeking decisive influence beyond its borders.[91] Given that history (as Nehru saw it), the ascendance of an aggressive political philosophy with the Communist victory increased India's discomfiture. The fear was that since "China did not believe in treating other countries on equal terms," as soon as it had stabilized internally, it would seek to expand externally, both territorially and in terms of influence. India, the only potential obstacle to China in Asia, was likely to be a prime target.[92]

Consequently, Nehru noted in a missive to his ambassador in China the growing potential for rivalry between the two countries and acknowledged that the possibility of avoiding conflict had become an open and uncertain question.[93] Simultaneously, Nehru also clarified that India's interests with regard to the frontier overshadowed any held inside Tibet. For him, there was little contradiction in being friendly—by force of circumstance more than anything else—with regard to Tibet and equally firm and unyielding when it came to "vital interests" in the border areas and the Himalayan states.[94]

Importantly, the reputational logic behind Indian reluctance to even countenance the prospect of compromise on territorial issues was also made apparent in internal discussions in New Delhi. Even as the Communists had declared their intention to "liberate" Tibet, Bajpai observed that the Chinese, "like any other Communists, reacted well to firmness but would exploit any sign of weakness." As Raghavan correctly notes, this would be the underlying logic of Indian policy on the border issue in the period that followed.[95] Over the next few years, with China's growing strength, especially relative to India in mind, Nehru contended that India's policies on the frontier issue had to be shaped not only by the present but aimed at the future.[96] Consequently, it was clear to Nehru what New Delhi's attitude toward China ought to be, especially on territorial issues. He articulated these ideas in his December 1952 instructions to N. Raghavan, Panikkar's successor as ambassador to Beijing:

> Our attitude towards the Chinese government should always be a *combination of friendliness and firmness. If we show weakness, advantage will be taken of this immediately.* . . . This applies to any development that might take place or in reference to our frontier problems between Tibet and Nepal, Bhutan, Sikkim, Ladakh and rest of India. In regard to this entire frontier we have to maintain an attitude of firmness. . . . Bhutan is independent in a way but is protected by us and its foreign affairs are our responsibility. . . . This is only for your information and guidance. Nothing need to be done about it at present.[97]

The potential for Chinese expansionism, Nehru contended, would only be exacerbated if India failed to deal with Beijing firmly. With regard to the frontier, this meant that India had to "maintain an attitude of firmness. Indeed there is nothing to discuss there."[98] The new government in Beijing had to be made to appreciate that India would hold firmly to its opinions and interests and that its policy of friendship was "subject always to not giving in on any matter that we consider important or vital to our interest."[99] How important such concerns were to Nehru is indicated in his reported advice to an Indian cultural delegation to China at this time: "Never forget that the basic challenge in South-East Asia is between India and China. That challenge runs along the spine of Asia. Therefore, in your talks with the Chinese keep it in mind. Never let the Chinese patronize you."[100] In keeping with such concerns, as tensions over the impasse in Korea and then the death of Stalin in early 1953 heightened Indian anxieties about China, Nehru scuttled a proposal floated by the Burmese leadership for a pact of nonaggression between India, China, and Burma. In explaining India's stance to U Nu, Nehru argued that while he was open to the idea in principle, "the Chinese government should not be made to think that we want this pact because of our weakness and therefore we want [a] favor from them. They do not respect those who show weakness. We have to be both friendly and firm."[101]

The satisfactory conclusion of the 1954 agreement on Tibet, and the declaration of the Panchsheel principles—the five principles of peaceful coexistence[102]—did little to dampen Nehru's fears. Despite public displays of great bonhomie, Nehru privately tempered the mood by opining, "In the final analysis, no country has any deep faith in the policies of another country, more especially in regard to a country which tends to expand."[103] While relinquishing certain inherited Indian rights in Tibet was, as R.K. Nehru characterized it, "a concession only to realism,"[104] the most the Indian prime minister expected from the agreement was curbing "to some extent undesirable urges in the other country."[105] Because a "communist government especially functions often in a peculiar way," it was wise not to rely wholeheartedly on any assurances the Chinese government had made.[106] The agreement over Tibet was therefore not a "permanent guarantee" of Beijing's friendship. Chinese expansionism owed itself not only to communism but had been "evident during various periods of Asian history for a thousand years or so."[107] Nehru now saw India—and the rest of Asia—as potentially confronting a new such era.[108] In this context of China's growing strength and its potential use, the reputational imperative had assumed increasing salience in the Indian government's thinking. This became patently apparent as Sino-Indian relations descended toward war in the next few years.

## Conclusion

This chapter has served three purposes. First, it has identified the key puzzle in India's approach to the dispute with China in the Nehru period: its pursuit of a surprisingly intransigent stance over territory that was ostensibly of not much salience to the country. Moreover, India did so in full awareness that its military forces were in no condition to successfully prosecute a war with China if the latter happened to initiate one. Such conduct, dealt with in detail in the following chapter, cannot be accounted for by alternative explanations that ground themselves in either security-seeking motivations or the nationalist salience of the territory.

Second, the historical discussion has also made the case that despite the dispute's largely dormant status during this period, the foundations of Indian firmness were in fact in evidence much before the border issue erupted into crisis in the late 1950s. Rather, and contrary to the conventional wisdom that presents Nehru's early attitude toward China as one driven by a naive idealism, it is clear that even as it pursued what appeared to be quintessentially accommodative policies with Beijing, most notably on the issue of Tibet, the Indian government had simultaneously determined that on territorial issues, they would stand firm. Even the decision to avoid broaching the topic altogether in the course of the 1954 talks with the Chinese is understandable from this perspective as motivated primarily by the calculus that it was wiser to try to delay eventual conflict with the Chinese to a time when India might be better prepared for it.

Finally, a detailed look at the documentary evidence from this early period also provides clear hints as to the reputational bases for why Nehru felt the need to assume a largely unmoving attitude on this matter. It is apparent that even at this early juncture, the Indian prime minister was conscious of the yawning gap in the two sides' bargaining strength in the border areas. This, combined with the fact that Nehru seemed to have already formed an impression of the Chinese as potentially expansionist, partly because of his reading of their history and partly as a consequence of their actions in Tibet, led to fears in New Delhi that being overly accommodative to Beijing in a context of military disadvantage risked being viewed by the other side as evidence of weakness. Friendliness on other fronts, it was consequently felt, needed to be balanced with resolve on matters such as that of the border. It was these concerns that acquired increasing prominence in Nehru's thinking in the years to follow and help account for the puzzle of Indian intransigence in the approach to war in 1962.

**6**

# Opening the Territorial Breach

## The Building Crisis

Beginning in 1956, the Indian policy of delay and avoidance became progressively unsustainable. Increasing Chinese activity along the frontier, and the continued publication of Chinese maps laying claim to vast tracts of the disputed territory, had compounded the "sense of disquiet" in New Delhi.[1] By mid-1956, Nehru was warning his officials that Zhou's earlier explanations for Chinese maps (that they were old and erroneous) notwithstanding, Beijing's acceptance of Indian claims could not be taken for granted. After all, despite India's functioning on the basis that there was no dispute, the Chinese had in fact "never admitted this clearly, though they did not deny it either."[2] Intelligence reports from Tibetan sources that the Chinese were actively exploring their claims with regard to Nepal, Bhutan, and Sikkim;[3] infrastructural developments by China on the Tibet frontier;[4] and perhaps most important, repeated incursions of People's Liberation Army (PLA) troops into Burmese territory in August 1956 only disconcerted Nehru further.[5]

With these developments in mind, New Delhi decided to adopt a more explicit position on territorial issues. At an immediate level, a decision was made to send a friendly but firm communication to China.[6] Nehru also concluded at this point that the time had come to broach the subject informally with Beijing—informally because he was cognizant of the fact that raising the issue publicly, particularly in parliament, would engender rigidity domestically and reduce room for some flexibility, perhaps in the western sector, in the future.[7] Consequently, in talks with Zhou on December 31, 1956, and January 1, 1957, Nehru at long last explicitly raised India's concerns with regard to the McMahon Line. Zhou, according to Nehru, responded by stating that although China had never recognized the line, "it is an accomplished fact, we should accept it," pending Tibetan approval.[8] The Chinese premier also, Nehru claimed, agreed in this meeting with the latter's contention that barring two or three minor issues, which could be settled soon, the border between the two countries was known and undisputed.[9]

But Nehru's relief at Zhou's assurances was momentary and fleeting. In late 1957, Chinese authorities announced the completion of the construction of a road through the Aksai Chin plateau in the western sector, indicating to the Indian government that the Chinese had established a permanent presence there.[10] India sent military patrols to the area in summer 1958, which confirmed that the Chinese road did in fact pass through territory that India also claimed. The Indian government's initial response was to register an informal protest.[11] Nehru's first note, on December 14, 1958, asserted that there was "no question of these large parts of India being anything but India."[12]

Zhou's response immediately worried Nehru and his officials. In his note, the Chinese premier let it be known that the Sino-Indian border had never been delimited and that the issue had not been raised earlier "because conditions were not yet ripe for its settlement." China was willing, however, to take "more or less a realistic attitude" toward the McMahon Line but needed time to address the situation. In the meantime, he suggested that both sides adhere to the status quo.[13] The statement implied to officials in New Delhi some doubts in China about the McMahon Line and that in the western sector, the Chinese saw no problems with their presence in Aksai Chin. The exchange consequently marked the beginning of a series of communications between the two leaders that progressively heightened alarm in New Delhi about Chinese intentions.

These apparently extensive Chinese territorial claims, in addition to the escalating anti-India rhetoric emanating from China in response to the brewing rebellion in Tibet, deepened perceptions of Chinese hostility in India.[14] Zhou's September 8, 1959, note formally declared that Chinese maps reflected the true customary boundary between the two countries, shocking the Indian leadership.[15] As the Nehru government saw it, not only were the Chinese claims troubling in themselves, but they were also left sufficiently vague so as to make possible their extension at a later date.[16] Gone also was Zhou's earlier explicit assurance of accepting the McMahon Line alignment, with only a vaguer formulation now of Beijing seeking to resolve the issue by reference to "the historical background and existing actualities."[17] This was also the period when the Chinese ambassador had noted in a communication to the Indian government that just as it made little sense for China to "antagonize the US in the east and again to antagonize India in the west," India could surely not afford to have two fronts. In India, this note was taken as an implicit threat of impending trouble if India did not settle the dispute on Chinese terms.[18]

Around these developments, two military clashes soured the atmosphere even further. The first skirmish took place in late August 1959 in the Longju area in the eastern sector over posts that India had set up, the Chinese argued, beyond the McMahon Line. Beijing was correct in so contending; nevertheless, the use of force to rectify the disagreement had grated on Nehru, who labeled it as "the culmination of progressive Chinese unfriendliness towards India."[19] A more severe firefight took place a couple of months later on October 21, 1959, in a Chinese ambush on an Indian police patrol in the Kongka Pass area of Ladakh in the western sector. This clash, which left five Indians dead and several more injured and captured, marked a serious spike in tensions. It exacerbated Indian fears, aggravated domestic opinion, and increased the urgency of dealing with a deteriorating situation. New Delhi's immediate response was to adopt a firm diplomatic stance, demanding Chinese withdrawal from occupied areas in Ladakh and the North East Frontier Agency (NEFA) as a precondition to any talks. Furthermore, India made it clear that no negotiations could be held on the basis, as the Chinese suggested, that the entire boundary was undelimited.[20]

Consequently, Zhou's November 7 suggestion that the status quo be maintained along the frontier, with each side's forces withdrawing 20 kilometers from the line of actual control[21], was viewed as unacceptable in New Delhi. "We cannot," Nehru wrote to Zhou, "agree to any arrangement, even as an interim measure, which would keep your forcible possession intact."[22] Such was the level of mistrust that the Indian leaders viewed the Chinese offer as a trick. Beijing's proposal would have equated China's claims in the west to the Indian position in the east, which was intolerable to Nehru. Furthermore, given Chinese strength, the kind of withdrawal that Beijing envisaged New Delhi undertaking in the east would have created a serious exploitable strategic advantage for China in the area.[23]

Nehru's counteroffer sought instead the withdrawal of the Chinese from all disputed territories and proposed—only in the western sector—the withdrawal of both sides to behind the other's claim lines.[24] Were these preconditions met, Nehru conveyed, his government was willing to immediately negotiate minor rectifications on the entire border and even submit such issues to mediation or arbitration based on historical evidence.[25] As Zhou noted, this proposal in effect required China to withdraw from more than 33,000 square kilometers of territory that it in fact held in the west, whereas Indian forces had no presence in the area to revert from.[26]

Having rejected multiple calls from Zhou for negotiations, Nehru finally agreed to "talks"—not "negotiations," he would clarify publicly—to be held in late April 1960 in New Delhi.[27] In these talks, Indian records corroborate, Zhou proposed an agreement suggesting that China was willing to recognize India's claims in the eastern sector in return for Indian reciprocity in the western sector. Indeed, as early as October 1959, the Indian foreign secretary had anticipated that by speaking of the "realities of the situation," Zhou likely implied exactly such a solution.[28] Prior to the talks, a Chinese note of April 3 had been interpreted in precisely this manner in the prime minister's office as suggesting "compromise on the basis of give and take."[29]

During the talks themselves it became "obvious" to the Indian leadership that this was indeed the case. As Dutt put it in a note to heads of Indian missions abroad:

> The Chinese aim is to make us accept their claim in Ladakh as a price for their recognition of our position in NEFA. Throughout the discussions they have invariably connected Ladakh with NEFA and stressed that the same principles of settling the boundary must govern both areas. It was obvious that if we accepted the line claimed by China in Ladakh they would accept the McMahon Line. There might be need for minor frontier rectifications, but that would not create much practical difficulty.[30]

The Chinese, according to the Indian foreign secretary, wanted to treat the dispute as one of delimitation, with each side to hold what it possessed and not make any further territorial claims. Once negotiations were agreed to, Beijing further hoped that

> neither side should make a territorial claim as a precondition. China is not making any such claim to the NEFA and undertakes not to cross the line up to which Indian control has extended. Similarly, India should recognize that Chinese control extends up to the line shown in the Chinese maps and should not try to cross that line. . . . The Indian claim to Ladakh must be treated in exactly the same bar as the Chinese claim to the NEFA.[31]

What the Chinese were proposing in effect, another Indian official has claimed, was this: that "you occupy NEFA, we will keep on making our claim on our maps etc. We will occupy Aksai Chin, then sometime later we will settle it."[32] Zhou himself developed some of these ideas in his six-point proposal at a press conference at the end of the New Delhi talks.[33]

India rejected Zhou's proposed solution. And while the leaders of the two countries had determined to have officials of the two sides jointly investigate the historical evidence, that effort seemingly went nowhere. Indeed, by 1961,

Nehru had publicly declared India's case to be foolproof and reiterated that the issue could be settled only by Chinese withdrawal, not by "horse trading."[34] Indian government communications to Beijing continued to declare that while New Delhi was willing to reenter negotiations, this required as a prerequisite the restoration of the status quo that existed prior to China's occupation of nearly 20,000 square kilometers of Indian territory in the western sector since 1957.[35] At the most, as a communication from May 14, 1962, conveyed, India was agreeable to the Aksai Chin road being used by Chinese civilian traffic pending negotiations and settlement of the border issue.[36]

As tensions escalated in mid-1962, in no small part due to India's Forward Policy (discussed shortly), and China moved toward the option of using force, there was a brief period where it appeared that the Indian government might have been willing to loosen its position. In the first few months of 1962, New Delhi seemed willing to agree to more relaxed terms that demanded only that China display a willingness to pull back from occupied territory in the western sector through perhaps a token withdrawal before India could agree to negotiations.[37] In July 1962, substantive discussions were held in Geneva between Defense Minister Krishna Menon and Chinese Foreign Minister Marshal Chen Yi. Immediately after, there were hints that New Delhi might being willing to negotiate without preconditions. India's July 26 note to the Chinese seemed to suggest as much. That did not last for long, however. In their next note, Indian officials reverted to their earlier stance. An aggravated domestic public likely had much to do with this reversal, as did concerns over increasing military tensions on the borders, but no small part can be attributed to Beijing's response to the initial note, which was dismissive of the Indian offer and demanded that India first "unequivocally and publicly withdrew all fictitious and false claims on Chinese territory."[38] From this point on, all hope for a negotiated solution had effectively dissipated, and developments swiftly moved toward the outbreak of war in October 1962.

## The Aksai Chin Puzzle

The Nehru government's rejection of Zhou's offer in the New Delhi talks proved to be a critical inflection point in the deterioration of Sino-Indian relations. The Chinese proposal had presented the possibility of resolving the territorial dispute on ostensibly reasonable terms, through a process of—as the Chinese put it—give-and-take. Its rejection by New Delhi, and the subsequent resort to more forceful means, played no small role in the eventual decision by Mao and Zhou to unleash the might of the People's Liberation Army (PLA) to unilaterally settle the issue.

That Nehru rejected such a proposal is perplexing for several reasons. For one, it went against the persona Nehru himself had cultivated: of an idealist who aspired to have fraternal relations between India and China and had sought—to a fault—to be accommodative of the Chinese. The clearest expression of such an attitude lay in Nehru's approach to the Tibetan issue, on which New Delhi had made substantial concessions in the landmark 1954 agreement.

Beyond Nehru's alleged idealism, a doubtful contention in itself given the Indian prime minister's early skepticism about China, the decision to reject Zhou's offer is made more perplexing by the fact that in terms of both salience and India's legal position in Aksai Chin, New Delhi had clearly concluded by the time of the 1960 talks that its claims were far from ironclad. This was true as much in 1959–1960 as it was in the early 1950s when New Delhi had paid little attention to the western sector and devoted its entire focus to the NEFA area. Indeed, Nehru admitted as much later in a speech to parliament in February 1961.[39]

Shortly after the discovery of the Chinese road in Aksai Chin, India's foreign secretary and Nehru's confidant on the issue, Subimal Dutt, wrote several notes to Nehru and other officials regarding India's claims in the region. In these notes, Dutt presented his conclusion that the country's case in Aksai Chin did not "seem to be based on very sure grounds." Therefore, one option for New Delhi, he suggested, was "for us to reconsider our position in regard to Aksai Chin, and if our claim is not based on substantial evidence, to give it up."[40] Even apart from legal claims, moreover, the foreign secretary made clear the thinking in the Indian government about the value of the territory. For Dutt, the remoteness of Aksai Chin meant not only that the territory was of doubtful importance—the Indian army chief even declared the territory as being of "no strategic importance to India" in January 1959[41]—but also that there was little in practical terms that India could do to obstruct Chinese activities in the area. Indian officials were clearly aware from early on that conflict in the western sector was likely to be both costly and futile.[42]

As Dutt further clarified in another note to Nehru, he saw the problem with India's position as lying primarily in the fact that New Delhi's claim line in the western sector was based on a British-drawn line that, contrary to the McMahon Line, had been meant even by the British "to serve only as a basis of possible discussion with the Russians and the Chinese." What was more, since the British themselves had never formally proposed this line as a border to China, it could not be relied on to serve Indian claims. All of this had been confirmed by research conducted by the Indian Historical Division, on which Dutt had based his assessment.[43] Such a conclusion is in consonance with

Maxwell's assertion that the Ardagh-Johnson Line, on which India's claims were broadly based, was never taken seriously by even the British. Rather, the British had intended to use such expansive claims to have China—when its leaders were finally ready to negotiate a boundary—agree to the compromise Macartney-McDonald Line that left Aksai Chin with China.[44]

That Dutt's assessment was shared by actors outside the prime minister's office is confirmed by B. N. Mullik's account. According to Mullik, even as more intelligence about Chinese activity in Aksai Chin began to filter in in early 1958, both the Ministry of External Affairs (MEA) and the army had communicated to the political leadership their attitude that "this part of the territory was useless to India. . . . The boundary had not been demarcated and had been shifted more than once by the British. . . . It would be pointless to pick up quarrels over issues in which India had no means of enforcing her claims."[45] The MEA had furthermore concluded that "in any protest we lodged we could not be on firm grounds."[46] R. K. Nehru similarly revealed later that even as early as "1953, our experts had advised us that our claim to Aksai Chin was not too strong."[47]

Not surprisingly, then, this uncertainty regarding India's claims in Aksai Chin was reflected in some of the Indian government's early pronouncements after the crisis had broken into the open. This was true of communications to Beijing, where in response to a Chinese note of November 3, 1958, for instance, the Indian government stated only that "whether the particular area is in Indian or Chinese territory is a matter of dispute."[48] Publicly, too, particularly in parliament, Nehru made it apparent over the next year that the dispute in the western sector was considered by his government as fundamentally different from that over the McMahon Line. Nehru claimed in a September 10, 1959, speech in parliament that India had always "looked upon Ladakh area as a different area, as I may say so, some vulgar area so far as the frontier is concerned because the exact line of the frontier is not at all clear as in the case of the McMahon Line."[49] Aksai Chin, moreover, he repeatedly pointed out, was practically uninhabited and had such difficult terrain that the Indian government had found it difficult and impractical to exercise any presence there.[50] In this "barren, uninhabited region without a vestige of grass and 17,000 ft. high," moreover, it was acknowledged that the Chinese had greater strategic interest and evidentiary claims, which for Nehru made the territory "peculiarly suited obviously for some kind of consultations and decision as to the facts, because the facts are very complicated."[51]

Indeed, in reacting to Zhou's combative letter of September 6, 1959, Nehru had clarified in parliament that while there was very little scope for movement on the McMahon Line,[52] Aksai Chin was more "a matter for argument." He could not say "what part of it may not belong to us, and what parts may," there never having been any delimitation of the region.[53] Even with the escalation of tensions in late 1959 and following talks with Zhou in 1960, at the same time that he declared India's case in the west to be strong, Nehru also conceded that determining claims over historical jurisdiction in the region was an "extraordinarily difficult thing" in the face of rival maps and evidence.[54]

All of this suggests that for much of this period, the Indian government might have had some basis for flexibility over claims in the western sector. Corroborating this is testimony by R. K. Nehru, India's ambassador to Beijing until 1958, that Nehru was well aware that China could not be expected to give up everything, especially in Aksai Chin, territory that was recognized to be of great value to Beijing.[55] More important, R. K. Nehru has claimed, "Until 1960, we ourselves were not sure that the territory belonged to us and we were thinking in terms of giving up our claims as part of a satisfactory settlement."[56]

With this being the case, how do we account for India's puzzling failure to agree to a solution along the lines Zhou offered in 1960? The agreement would have, after all, only denied India territory that it seemed to have little interest in in the first place and ostensibly helped avoid the possibility of conflict and war with a stronger China.

## Reputation and Indian Intransigence on Aksai Chin

The reputational imperative is instrumental to explaining this Indian intransigence. By 1956, the Indian government's preexisting concerns regarding Chinese intentions had only exacerbated with the continued publication of offending maps and the increasing instances of PLA incursions across the border.[57] Therefore, despite the 1954 agreement on Tibet, Nehru had continued to note with trepidation the problems posed for India by an already strong China that would grow more potent and dominant in Asia in the coming years.[58] Geographical barriers, it was felt, would contain China in the near term, but it was what Beijing might choose to do in a decade's time that really concerned the Indian prime minister, making the task of further integrating the restive population of the Indian northeast of increasing urgency.[59] Already, Apa Pant, the political officer serving as India's envoy in Sikkim, had been warning about China's road building and other infrastructural efforts that provided it better access to "the ill-defined border areas, and to take possession of these as on their side of the frontier . . . at an opportune moment."[60]

The 1956–1957 talks with Zhou left Nehru reassured to only a very limited extent. He continued to be suspicious of what he viewed as China's history of "vast efforts of constructive expansion"[61] and feared that Beijing could at any point officially lay claim to the vast tracts of Indian territory that had been represented as part of China in maps since before the Communists had assumed power.[62] Signs that the Sino-Burmese boundary talks were floundering thanks to what he viewed as China's failure to adhere to previous commitments to the Burmese reinforced Nehru's sense of disquiet.[63]

In this context of deep suspicion, the discovery of the Aksai Chin road, the communications exchanged with Beijing, and the failure of talks over a small tract of land called Bara Hoti all exacerbated reputational concerns in New Delhi. The latter disagreement (over Bara Hoti), involving a tiny area in the middle sector, had persisted since 1954. India had been planning discussions over it since 1955, partly to develop an "inkling into the Chinese mind in regard to frontier questions in general."[64] Such talks did not materialize until 1958, but when they did, the seeming intransigence of the Chinese over even this minor piece of territory had left Dutt highly disconcerted.[65] This growing wariness of a stronger China, and ever more so the seeming willingness of Beijing to exploit its advantages for expansionist purposes, seemed to confirm Nehru's early fears that concessions, even on land as unimportant as that in the western sector, would betray weakness and provoke further Chinese transgressions in the future.

Such fears were reinforced by the fact that Nehru viewed Zhou's recent assertions of his country's territorial claims as a bad-faith reneging on prior understandings. For all his suspicions and despite the fact that he himself at the time had rejected the idea of officially raising the border issue, Nehru still believed that the two leaders had informally struck what one scholar has termed a "moral agreement" premised on "gentlemanly reciprocity" in the 1954 talks.[66] That understanding—that in exchange for Indian concessions in Tibet, Beijing would recognize India's territorial claims, and especially the sanctity of the McMahon Line—were assumed to have been made more explicit in later meetings in 1956–1957. Evidently at no point in those talks had Zhou made any mention of the territory in the western sector, territory that the Chinese leadership must have been well aware was part of India's official map claims. As a result, as Nehru wrote to Zhou on September 26, 1959, he had hoped that with the 1954 agreement, "the main problems which history has bequeathed to us" had been settled once and for all.[67]

Later on in the 1960 talks with Zhou, Nehru, not surprisingly, repeatedly alluded to this theme of Chinese duplicity. In their first meeting, on April 20,

1960, in fact, he complained to Zhou about it. Nehru's remarks on that occasion bear quoting in detail:

> On the last occasion when you were here I mentioned to you that there are no major problems before us but only a few minor ones and which could be discussed and settled by mutual consultations. That was our belief. Therefore we were greatly surprised to find that steps had been taken on the Chinese side which, according to us, clearly infringed our frontiers. What distressed us most was that if the Chinese government did not agree with us, they should have told us so. But, for nine years nothing was said, despite our stating our views to them in clear terms. . . . Then came the agreement of 1954 and Bandung and all that which helped the growth of our relations and served to remove the idea that there was any basic conflict between us. But then in the last year or two the frontier questions loomed up. When the Chinese maps came to our notice, we brought it to the notice of the Chinese government many times. The answer we received was that these maps were old and had to be revised and that the Chinese government did not attach very great importance to them. . . . Therefore it came as a great surprise and distress to us that some six months or eight months ago China should lay claims to these areas. We just could not understand it and this produced a feeling of great shock, as happens when firm beliefs are upset suddenly.[68]

Evidently the discovery of the Aksai Chin road, Chinese occupation of thousands of square miles of India-claimed territory in the western sector, and Zhou's declaration of extensive Chinese territorial claims were all viewed by the Indian leadership as manifestations of Chinese perfidy and expansionist intentions. As Indian officials complained, "No question of the frontier of the Tibet region with Ladakh was ever raised during all these years."[69] In the Indian view, then, quite apart from China's growing strength, it was the country's perceived proclivity to renege on prior commitments and unscrupulously exploit its power advantages at opportune moments—a tendency that had manifested itself first in Tibet in 1950—that was especially concerning. In Nehru's mind, moreover, it was apparent that all his earlier friendly overtures to Beijing had unfortunately been misconstrued by the Chinese leadership as signifying weakness and therefore exploited.

Indeed, Indian officials processed such behavior by China as part of a general trend of its growing international assertiveness. In addition to the Sino-Burmese territorial dispute, where talks were deadlocked, with the Burmese holding Beijing responsible,[70] reports of Chinese interference in Yugoslavia, which President Josep Tito characterized as demonstrating "expansionist tendencies,"[71] led Nehru to conclude that the attitude of the Chinese had perceptibly "stiffened." This turn of events required that India "be particularly careful in the future in what we say and do in regard to China specially"; if China could do this with Yugoslavia, there was "no particular reason to imagine that they cannot or will not do so in the case of India."[72] Closer to home, in Sikkim[73] and Tibet,[74] there were increasing reports of Chinese pressure and allegations in China of Indian complicity in Tibet suggested to Nehru that the issue was serious.[75]

Given these fears, the prospect of negotiations on the basis of a coercively and unilaterally created status quo, and the principle that the entire frontier was not delimited, as the Chinese were arguing, was unacceptable to Indian officials. And indeed, with Zhou's notes being seen as having left the actual extent of Chinese claims vague, portending the possibility of further challenges in the future, the dangers of appearing weak to a stronger power that was viewed as prone to exploiting such advantages quickly became a constant theme in Nehru's public and private utterances.[76] For Nehru, "for the first time a world power or would-be world power" sat on India's frontiers,[77] a development that had "all manner of forebodings" for India's future security.[78] This China, moreover, owing to a combination of its strength and an "abnormal state of mind,"[79] seemed to Nehru to care little for peace and exhibited tendencies of what he contended was China's "national trait": expansionism.[80] Indeed, by April 15, 1959, Nehru had informed Vijayalakshmi Pandit that the Chinese had become increasingly arrogant and were throwing their weight around.[81] In essence, then, what India now faced was "a great and powerful nation which is aggressive. It might be aggressive minus Communism or plus Communism," but it was there nonetheless.[82] Consequently, in a note to state chief ministers, Nehru openly acknowledged the "indefinite" nature of the frontier but also emphasized that China was a "powerful country bent on spreading out to what they consider their old frontiers, and possibly beyond."[83]

Meekly submitting to a strong and assertive China was out of the question for the Indian leadership given the perceived reputational costs. As Nehru saw it, sustainable long-term friendship could not exist between the weak and the strong, and especially "between a country that is trying to bully and the other who accepts to be bullied." It was unclear, he noted, whether Chinese behavior was a mere expression of local aggressiveness, a quest to "show us our place," or something deeper.[84] A settlement of the territorial issue was therefore very unlikely, except on Indian terms, because Beijing had to be made to realize that "the time for any country to display arrogance in dealing with India" was long past.[85]

India had no choice but to stand firm and work toward a position of parity with China because the voice of a nation counted only when it was backed up by strength.[86] As Nehru declared in the aftermath of the Kongka Pass incident, India now confronted a "situation which can only be faced by strength," a strength that "can be built up in many ways—armies, etc.—but basically again it has to be built up by the industrial background that you have."[87] In this context of India's material weakness, if friendship was the ultimate goal, it would not come "by adopting a weak attitude to a strong country."[88] A weak India, Nehru asserted, would garner little respect in the rest of the world, and least of all from the Chinese, if it did not demonstrate resolve.[89]

In keeping with this thinking, Nehru publicly declared that India would not be willing to give up even one inch of territory if it were to be done under compulsion or force. It was "the pride and arrogance . . . of a strong and aggressive power" that was showing in Chinese behavior, and to India, it was not "a yard of territory that counts but the coercion. Because, it makes no difference to China or India whether a few yards of territory in the mountains are on this side or on that side. But it makes a great deal of difference if that is done in an insulting, aggressive, offensive, violent manner, by us or by them. All that counts."[90] Toward the end of September 1959, Nehru also refused U Nu's offer to serve as a go-between to India and China for fear of conveying Indian anxiety and fear to Beijing, and thereby encouraging further Chinese pressure and demands.[91] And if through conciliatory gestures to their other neighbors Chinese leaders had sought to signal good faith to India, the effect was in fact completely the opposite. Indian officials viewed such efforts as two-faced attempts to pressure India through isolation and embarrassment by painting New Delhi as unreasonable and Beijing as generous. According to Dutt, the Chinese were "trying to tell all Asian countries that they would like a settlement and so on but at the same time extending their occupation and using force in protection of what they consider is their territory."[92]

Having determined that it had no choice but to adopt such a position of firmness, the government of India in late 1959 sought to bolster its self-confessedly questionable historical claims in the western sector[93] by dispatching Sarvepalli Gopal of the Indian Historical Division to London for that purpose. As Maxwell has pointed out, Nehru could have used the opportunity to instruct Gopal to find what Indian officials were aware was readily available historical justification for a compromise boundary in the western sector.[94] Instead, Dutt instructed his subordinates to provide Gopal with a list of "points on which further evidence should be secured in London."[95] On his return, and even before he had presented his research, Gopal unsurprisingly found Nehru in a mood of "defiance and resistance against the idea of handing over territory to the Chinese" and seeking to be convinced of India's case.[96] At the end of the meeting, Nehru is said to have concluded, "I think that our case is a strong one and I see no reason why we should weaken in it at any point."[97] Equipped with Gopal's evidence in February 1960, Indian officials expectedly went into the April talks with Zhou fully prepared to reject any arrangement involving a territorial quid pro quo.[98] Dutt continued to decry Chinese attempts to use such a formula to justify claims over land occupied only recently and concluded that Indian firmness in the talks had likely impressed the Chinese leadership.[99]

On Aksai Chin specifically, it was clear well before the 1960 talks that India intended to stay firm, especially if China did not reverse its unilateral advances. This was borne out clearly in Dutt's thinking, who, despite having conceded the weakness of Indian claims and interests in Ladakh, nevertheless recommended to Nehru a posture of firmness. The logic behind this stance was ostensibly that it was inadvisable from New Delhi's perspective for the Chinese to be allowed to get away with the "impression that they can unilaterally assert their authority without any regard to past discussion."[100] Such an "attitude of indifference," the foreign secretary feared, was likely to "serve as an encouragement to the Chinese authorities to take unilateral action in the other contested areas also."[101] Indeed, even with regard to the dispute over Bara Hoti, Dutt contended that while in principle the territory could be easily conceded because it was small and immaterial to India, the trouble lay in the Chinese repudiation of the entire frontier, including on the issue of border passes, the status of which the Indian government believed had been settled by the 1954 agreement. On these latter issues, it was argued, India could not "afford to make concessions," since compromise on Bara Hoti on such terms would have indicated weakness and encouraged greater Chinese demands all across the border areas.[102] As Dutt later revealed, Nehru's own fear was that "even if India gave in to the Chinese claim in Ladakh, other demands would not be long in coming."[103] Morarji Desai, finance minister at the time, had similarly informed British interlocutors that the cabinet believed that conceding territory in Ladakh would be "the thin end of a wedge."[104]

It was little surprise, then, that India's policy during this period was predicated on maintaining firmness over New Delhi's basic demands. Underlying the rejection of Zhou's 1960 offer—and Indian insistence that negotiations could not take place on the basis that the entire border was undelimited and without the Chinese first withdrawing from occupied territory—was the fear that accepting Beijing's terms would encourage a stronger China to pose further territorial and perhaps other challenges in the future. New Delhi therefore viewed Chinese proposals, including the package offer, as tricks that could not be taken at face value or expected to exhaust Chinese claims.[105]

In keeping with the logic of the reputational imperative, Nehru and his officials considered the implications of such concessions for how the Chinese would view India as deeply worrying given that they were clearly speaking from a position of disadvantage in bargaining strength. Such concerns were, moreover, exacerbated by perceptions in the Indian government that they had been the victims of a constant barrage of Chinese unilateralism and coercion, which the latter steadfastly refused to acknowledge or rectify.[106] Expressed in theoretical terms, Beijing's seemingly coercive approach had served only the function of provoking the Indian government into putting even greater stock in their reputation and increasingly assume a posture aimed at establishing their resolve. The secretary general of the MEA, N. R. Pillai, articulated this thinking: if India "gave way now on this matter, it would only encourage the Chinese to feel that they [India] were weak and to press even more ambitious claims later on."[107]

The essence of India's stance, then, according to R. K. Nehru, was one of keeping talks going while not surrendering on the border issue and building up strength at the same time. That a give-and-take solution was probably unacceptable to India even before the 1960 talks is apparent from a note that the Indian ambassador in Beijing wrote in the previous month reiterating that while India would be prepared to consider minor alterations on the frontier, there could be no talks based on an assumption that the entire frontier was undelimited.[108] While there was recognition that China could not be expected to give up all claims in the western sector, compromise for India was conceivable only under conditions where the Chinese accepted Indian sovereignty in the eastern sector and withdrew from Aksai Chin. After that, negotiations could be confined to the latter region—conditions, in other words, where any concessions India made did not amount to capitulation, and hence a signal of weakness.[109]

In the pursuit of such a face-saving resolution of the issue, however, and reflecting the fact that Nehru was never completely closed to the idea of compromise, New Delhi was not averse to some imaginative thinking. As Raghavan has recently discovered, India's president at the time, S. Radhakrishnan, had suggested to the British high commissioner, Malcolm MacDonald, a few days before Zhou's arrival in April 1960 that Nehru was open to a formula that would have allowed the Chinese to retain the "substance" and concede the "shadow" in Ladakh. In other words, China could retain de facto control of the territory in return for conceding de jure Indian sovereignty over it, thereby offering India a reputational escape from the situation.[110]

Aksai Chin, in any case, had now become the fulcrum of India's diplomatic activity. In accordance with this position, once the April talks had failed, the Indian members to the 1960 delegation-level talks held between June and

December of that year were instructed to take up discussion of Ladakh first, and only carry documents related to that sector, especially given that the Chinese had already shown little willingness to produce all of their maps.[111]

## The Forward Policy

Having rejected Zhou's 1960 offer, the Indian government soon began to supplement firmness at the diplomatic level with the adoption of more active military measures in Ladakh. By mid-1960, the political leadership had begun to push for more aggressive patrolling of disputed areas in the western sector not yet occupied by Chinese troops, with the understanding that at the same time, Indian forces were to try and avoid clashes with the Chinese. Indeed, by May 1960, New Delhi had even begun to seriously contemplate going beyond patrolling to establishing military posts in unoccupied territory, an effort that was temporarily forestalled by a reluctant army leadership that only recently had been assigned responsibility for that section of the frontier following events at Kongka Pass.[112]

Such plans acquired increasing urgency with growing intelligence over the next year that pointed to a steady buildup of Chinese military posts in Ladakh. In response, in a meeting on November 2, 1961, the Forward Policy was conceptualized. The plan primarily sought to forestall any further ingress by China into Ladakh in particular, a region where not only had the presence of adversary troops expanded in recent months and years but so had Beijing's claims, as maps that the Chinese delegates presented at the official talks in 1960 suggested. The new policy required Indian troops to patrol as far forward as possible toward India's claim line in Ladakh—by December 1961, the instructions were expanded to include NEFA—and establish military posts with the aim of preventing "the Chinese from advancing any further and also dominating from any posts which they may have already established."[113] Physical confrontations and military clashes were to be avoided, however, barring instances where this was necessary for self-defense.[114]

By March and April 1962, Indian troops had established some forty of these posts in unoccupied sections of the western sector, according to one account.[115] In the eastern sector too, twenty-four posts had been created along the McMahon Line by mid-1962.[116] Once such posts were established, Indian policy for them was to hold firm when faced by intimidation or threats from superior Chinese forces. The latter had resumed their own forward patrolling in the western sector on April 30, as a Chinese note of protest informed New Delhi. In keeping with this Indian stance, in May 1962 the political leadership instructed a post in the Chip Chap valley to hold firm against Chinese advances, despite the army western command's request for permission to withdraw. Shortly after, in July, an Indian platoon at Galwan was similarly instructed, and even ordered to open fire in response to a Chinese siege. By this point, commanders in Ladakh had been given the authority to open fire first on Chinese troops who approached too close to Indian posts.[117]

If New Delhi's rejection of Zhou's 1960 offer is puzzling given the relative lack of importance India attached to territory in the western sector, the decision to pursue the militarily provocative Forward Policy is perhaps even more surprising. Quite apart from the fact that this fateful policy arguably precipitated Beijing's eventual decision in 1962 to initiate what turned out to be a disastrous war from an Indian perspective, embarking on such a risky military initiative was ostensibly unfathomable from an Indian security standpoint given the country's significant military disadvantages.

That there were yawning gaps in the military capabilities of the two sides, much to the disadvantage of India, is beyond doubt. Burdened with having to manage the threat from Pakistan, fight internal insurgencies, and fulfill UN peacekeeping commitments, not to speak of the lack of urgency the Nehru government had seemed to attach to upgrading military capabilities in the early years, the Indian army had been underequipped, undertrained, and badly stretched for too long. To expect this force to compete against a PLA that was riding high on performing giant killing feats in the Korean War a few years earlier, and more directly had rapidly expanded its presence on the borders with India in the years since taking over Tibet, was ambitious to say the least. Encapsulating this mismatch, Whiting has estimated that in the approach to 1962, Chinese troops enjoyed a five-to-one advantage in terms of manpower over Indian forces in the border areas, as well as qualitative superiority in firepower, boasting of heavy mortars and automatic rifles, while Indian troops had only a few 3-inch mortars, machine guns, and World War I vintage rifles.[118] A detailed American Special National Intelligence Estimate assessment of the Sino-Indian military balance prepared for President Kennedy shortly after the outbreak of war in 1962 reached similar conclusions. In addition to their clear advantages in terms of troop numbers, the Chinese were understood to have an air force boasting of some 2,000 jet fighters and 460 bombers, as opposed to India's 315 and 320, respectively. Extrapolating from the Korean experience, American intelligence officials also viewed PLA troops as adept at surmounting the sorts of logistical challenges facing them in the zone of conflict.[119]

Furthermore, documentary evidence makes clear that Indian leaders during this period—both political and military—were by no means unaware of the severe disadvantages confronting the Indian military in any foreseeable contest with the superior Chinese forces. In 1959, while continuing to discount the possibility of a major war being initiated by the Chinese, the army's general staff was also functioning on the assumption that were a larger attack to happen, there was not much that Indian forces could do about it without accepting some loss of territory. As Raghavan notes, "Requirements of a larger invasion were apparently neither considered nor projected by the military. This was consonant with the military's belief that it was up to the politicians to ensure that such an attack did not occur."[120]

Such concerns about India's military preparedness to fight the Chinese continued over the next two years and up to the time the decision to pursue the Forward Policy was made. A paper by the chiefs of staff from January 1961 concluded that while they could make troop-level recommendations to fight a potential limited war on the borders, if the conflict expanded to "a full scale conflagration amounting to an invasion of our territory, then it would be beyond the capacity of our forces to prosecute war." This was "because of limitation on size [of forces], the paucity of available equipment and the lack of adequate logistical support."[121] In accordance with such an assessment, military officials had even apparently conveyed unease about the Forward Policy at the November 2, 1961, meeting.[122] Nehru himself confessed during this time that India's forward posts were likely to be "in constant danger of attack with larger numbers" that the Chinese possessed.[123] General K. S. Thimayya, army chief until May 1961, summarized this view a few months before the war itself in stating that he could not "even as a soldier envisage India taking on China in an open conflict on its own. China's present strength in manpower, equipment and aircraft exceeds our resources a hundred-fold with the full support of the U.S.S.R. . . . It must be left to the politicians and diplomats to ensure our security."[124]

The most substantive dissection of the extent of the Indian military's weaknesses in relation to China prior to the 1962 war was delivered by the Henderson Brooks-Bhagat report, an official postmortem of the debacle commissioned by the government of India after the war. This report, parts of which have only recently become available publicly, amply reiterates what was well known in Indian policy circles at the time: the military was woefully unprepared for any confrontation with China. The report summarized what was known then about the relative military strengths of the two sides:

> The Chinese had a well equipped division with supporting arms deployed against Ladakh. Further, the Chinese had developed roads to all the important areas they held and thus could concentrate large forces at any given place. As against this, we were thinly spread-out, with no supporting arms worth the name and with poor communications between the various sectors. *Thus, in case of hostilities, we would be defeated in detail.*[125]

Such a military context made the kind of assertiveness that the Forward Policy entailed an incredibly risky, and therefore surprising (if not foolhardy), undertaking. Indeed, given these conditions, it was more reasonable for the Indian leadership to agree to the compromise solution that Zhou offered. Certainly, at the least, it made little sense to risk provoking the stronger Chinese into a war that India was clearly unprepared to contest over a piece of territory that was acknowledged to be of little importance.

## Explaining the Forward Policy

Explaining India's seemingly irrational adoption of a more active military stance along the frontier requires extending the logic of reputation building to the Forward Policy decision. Even before this point, India's leaders had become intent on demonstrating their resolve by refusing to make ostensibly reasonable concessions on the territorial issue. Nevertheless, New Delhi's initial posture right before and after the 1960 talks, in keeping with what would be considered reasonable for a weaker power, gave little consideration to undertaking militarily assertive or provocative actions in addressing the brewing conflict with China. With regard to the western sector specifically, Nehru's September 13, 1959, directive to his officials had made clear that things were to be left as they were. Indian troops were to avoid skirmishes with the Chinese "not only in a big way, but even in a small way" until it was forced on them. The expectation was that China would not seek to transgress in the region any farther and that the matter could be addressed later as part of a broader diplomatic consideration of border issues.[126]

Progressively after the failure of the 1960 talks, however, as it became evident to Nehru that diplomatic firmness alone was doing little to deter the Chinese from advancing toward their newly extended claim line in Ladakh, existing policy began to be viewed as unsustainable in New Delhi. In response, the Forward Policy was envisaged not necessarily as a means to militarily rectify territorial losses in the western sector. No doubt the establishment of such presence, if it were successfully accomplished, carried with it the benefit of strengthening India's bargaining position in the area. This in turn promised to provide New Delhi with a situational context from which it could more reasonably call for withdrawal by the Chinese troops in the western sector as part of a process of joint (rather that unilateral) withdrawal.[127] "Possession," as Nehru noted in the November 2 meeting, "was nine-tenths of the law."[128] Notwithstanding such considerations, however, the basic fact remained, as the Indian political leadership clearly acknowledged in the lead-up to the decision to adopt the Forward Policy, that their military confronted distinct numerical and logistical disadvantages in the border areas. Given this, it clearly made little sense for India to pursue a strategy aimed at outcompeting the Chinese on territorial possession.

Instead, Nehru and his officials viewed the Forward Policy primarily as a means of stemming China's unilateral military expansion in the western sector by demonstrating resolve and firmness by way of what amounted to symbolic or token resistance.[129] The strategy, in other words, represented a more limited set of military goals assumed in the hope that even a symbolic presence in the area of contention would be sufficient to restrain the Chinese. As the army chief of general staff, Lieutenant General B. M. Kaul, said later, regardless of the actual balance of capabilities, India had no choice but to adopt the Forward Policy, failing which China "would have kept advancing up to her claim line and India, being the weaker country, could have done nothing about it. It would then have been a fait accompli."[130] In Kaul's recollection of the thinking in New Delhi, it was better for Indian forces to establish as many forward posts as possible in Ladakh, "even though in penny packets, rather than wait for a substantial build-up," in the conviction that "the Chinese will not attack any of our positions even if they [the Indian ones] are relatively weaker than theirs."[131]

Such thinking had been anticipated much earlier in the aftermath of the Kongka Pass incident when MEA officials had expressed their opinion that the Chinese were likely to fill in uninhabited areas in the western sector when possible but would not "shoot their way through."[132] A few months prior to the Forward Policy decision itself, the logic found its more extreme expression in the reaction of M. J. Desai, the new foreign secretary, to the discovery of a freshly established Chinese post in the Chip Chap valley. Desai is reported to have contended then that "one of the most effective methods of stemming Chinese policy of gradually creeping westwards across our borders in Ladakh would be to give them an occasional knock during these chance encounters." Engaging in such "short offensive action aimed at inflicting casualties and for taking prisoners," he seemed to be believe, would be sufficient to deter the Chinese by effectively demonstrating Indian resolve.[133]

Desai's enthusiasm was curbed for the time being by the greater circumspection of military leaders. However, the general contours of this view—that the Chinese would not undertake an all-out offensive and therefore symbolic acts would be sufficient to deter China—received further confirmation in an Intelligence Bureau report of September 26, 1961, that had suggested exactly that. The report claimed that "where even a dozen men of ours are present, the Chinese have kept away."[134] In the absence of such a presence, however, the Chinese were expected to fill out their 1960 claim lines. The decision to pursue the Forward Policy was made on the basis of this fundamental belief that a more active presence in the unoccupied portions of the disputed territory would be sufficient to deter Beijing by demonstrating Indian resolve to resist Chinese ingress. Contrary to Desai's thinking, however, Nehru's initial instructions envisaged all this being done "without [Indian troops] getting involved in a clash with the Chinese unless this becomes necessary in self-defense."[135]

Presumably in accordance with this thinking, confrontations in May and June 1962 in the Chip Chap valley and Galwan areas of Ladakh elicited instructions from the Indian political leadership for troops to stand firm in the face of Chinese pressure and to use force if necessary in doing so. In the former case, one hundred Chinese troops had advanced toward the Indian post in the Chip Chap valley on May 6, 1962, with the apparent intention of launching an assault, leading the Western Army commander, Lieutenant General Daulat Singh, to put in a request to the army chief for permission to immediately withdraw the post. The request was denied, however, by both the army chief and prime minister for explicitly reputational reasons. Both believed that a failure to put up resistance threatened to betray lack of resolve on India's part and encourage further challenges by the Chinese to other posts India had recently established. Nehru consequently demanded that the post stay firm in the expectation that doing so would deter enemy troops, an expectation that proved correct: Chinese forces eventually withdrew from the standoff.

In the second such encounter a month later, on July 4, Chinese troops completely surrounded a recently created Indian post in upper Galwan and established a virtual siege within a hundred yards of the post. In this case again, Indian officials warned the Chinese of their intention to stay firm and instructed troops to resist with fire and force if enemy troops moved any closer. The next day, Chinese troops pulled back somewhat from their positions. Although they continued to surround the Indian post, tensions were dampened enough for New Delhi to be able to claim that it had won a war of wills.[136]

While the increasing tensions such encounters represented certainly worried Nehru, the fact that Chinese troops eventually withdrew in these instances served to reinforce the belief in New Delhi that the Forward Policy was indeed bearing fruit in expected ways and that token resistance was proving to be sufficient to deter Chinese advances. For Nehru, these encounters had demonstrated the worst the Chinese would do, leading him to reinforce his instructions to military officials that Indian posts maintain their positions under all conditions, partly in order to "study the 'behavior pattern' of the Chinese."[137] In essence, the political leadership believed that "if India challenged China . . . it would call China's bluff."[138] Indeed, such reputational considerations ostensibly even influenced the timing of India's military action against Goa around the same time, in December 1961. In implicit reference to the Sino-Indian dispute, Nehru had noted in that context that failure to act in Goa could have adversely affected "the position of India generally in regard to other problems that we face, including other borders."[139]

By mid-1962, the Forward Policy was also playing out in a more active manner on the eastern front along the McMahon Line. Toward September and October, tensions in that region became concentrated over an Indian post called Dhola directly below the Thagla ridge. While the Chinese claimed, correctly according to the 1914 treaty map, that this area lay on their side of the McMahon Line, New Delhi believed that the correct boundary lay along the watershed and hence on its side. The original map, in this view, was incorrect because the mapmakers' intention had all along been for the line to run along the ridgeline. As part of the Forward Policy, therefore, the Indian army's Fourth Division had been ordered to secure that area. In response, on September 8, PLA troops occupied the Thagla ridge and menaced the Dhola post, further precipitating the crisis.[140]

Given what had come before, New Delhi's reaction was unsurprising. In a meeting chaired by Defense Minister Krishna Menon, it was determined that the Indian army would undertake Operation Leghorn with a mission of expelling Chinese troops from Thagla, by force if necessary. In demanding action from his skeptical subordinates, the army chief, L. P. Sen, made it clear that the political leadership was not willing "to accept any intrusion of the Chinese into our territory and if they come they must be thrown out by force." New Delhi, as Raghavan points out, saw the PLA action "as foreshadowing a Chinese strategy of responding to the forward policy in Ladakh by opening a new front in the east. To deter further incursions in NEFA, India had to demonstrate resolve in the Thagla area. If not, the PRC would be emboldened to conduct piecemeal intrusions all along the McMahon Line."[141] Indeed, so intent was the Indian leadership on establishing their resolve in the eastern sector that the foreign secretary (Desai) instructed the army chief in a September 22 meeting that the PLA presence in the Dhola area had to be reversed even if it came at the expense of territorial losses in the western sector.[142] Nehru himself is reported to have declared to his officials on October 3 that his forces had to "take—or appear to take a strong stand" on the issue and force a Chinese withdrawal from Thagla or "*at least try to do so to the best of our ability.*"[143] On October 10 PLA forces launched an offensive to overrun the Indian post. While army officials reacted with shock, Nehru was unperturbed. He proceeded on a prearranged trip to Ceylon the next day, having instructed his troops that Operation Leghorn would continue.[144]

To the extent that this Indian expectation of being able to deter China by occasional demonstrations of resolve proved to be disastrously flawed, and the Forward Policy entailed a grievous error of judgment on the part of decision makers in New Delhi, it is clear from this discussion that it had little to do with a misreading of the military situation on the ground or, more precisely, an overestimation of India's military capabilities. The excesses of the Forward Policy were predicated on the belief that China would be restrained in its reactions, and certainly would not undertake a massive invasion of India. It is also important to note that this was not Nehru's conviction alone; the assessment was shared and reinforced by the Indian military leadership as well. As Kaul had noted, as late as June 1962, he too was "convinced that the Chinese will not attack any of our positions even if they are relatively weaker than theirs."[145]

Such confidence was based on the notion that China's internal and external troubles were sufficiently severe to restrain the Chinese from reacting forcefully. The temporary domestic travails that China was undergoing in the early 1960s owing to rebellion in Tibet and the emerging failure of the Great Leap Forward were apparently sufficient for the Indian prime minister and his subordinates to conclude that China could not afford a major offensive any time soon.[146] For Nehru, the Chinese "were in no position to divert their attention to anything except putting their own internal matters right," meaning that if India "dealt with them strongly, we should have the better of them."[147]

Indeed, the fact that India's own external relations were experiencing something of an upswing, especially with the Soviet Union, only added to the Indian prime minister's confidence that Beijing was in no position to trigger a war. Various developments beginning in the early 1960, not least growing evidence of an emerging Sino-Soviet split, had led Nehru and his officials to believe that Premier Nikita Khrushchev of the USSR disapproved of Chinese conduct on the border issue and was surely tilting toward India. Moscow had even agreed to supply India with MiG-21 aircraft and other military equipment in 1962.[148] Convinced that the Soviets would serve to restrain any Chinese temptations to war, Nehru found it unimaginable "that a war between India and China will remain confined to these two countries." "It will be a world war and nothing but a world war" if Beijing was foolhardy enough to start one, the Indian prime minister believed.[149] With these other, more systemic factors in play, Nehru was able to justify not putting too much stake in "all the brave words that are said in these communications to us by the Chinese government."[150] Not surprisingly then, as the Henderson Brooks–Bhagat report concludes, it was these "preconceived notions of the lack of reactions by Chinese" rather than sound military judgment that underlay the Indian decision to adopt the Forward Policy, a posture for which the army was clearly unprepared in pure capability terms.[151]

To Nehru's and India's misfortune, Mao correctly recognized this source of India's misplaced confidence.[152] In response, with the diplomatic avenue deadlocked and military eyeballing and skirmishes extending from Ladakh to the NEFA, Chinese troops launched massive military offensives in both the western and eastern sectors on October 20, 1962. The hostilities were briefly halted on October 24, only to resume again three weeks later.[153] In the interim, Zhou had called for talks, which were to be preceded in part by India's withdrawal from territory acquired as part of the Forward Policy. Nehru rejected this. "India," he categorically stated, "cannot and will not accept a position under which Chinese forces continue to commit aggression into Indian territory, occupy substantial Indian territories and use these as a bargaining counter to force a settlement on their own terms."[154] With no hope for negotiations, Beijing resumed its military offensive. By the end of the war on November 21, Chinese troops had shattered Indian defenses and advanced up to their claim lines in both sectors, only to unilaterally announce a ceasefire and intention to withdraw in the eastern sector to behind the McMahon Line. In the swift loss that had, as Guha puts it, "represented a massive defeat in the Indian imagination," 1,383 Indian troops were killed and approximately 3,968 were taken prisoner, with yet another 1,696 determined to be missing.[155] India had been "shocked out of" what Nehru himself now confessed as "an artificial atmosphere of our own creation" that had until then left the country and its leaders increasingly "out of touch with the realities of the modern world."[156]

## Domestic Politics as Alternative Explanation

It has been argued that beginning in late 1959, with news of the Chinese road in Aksai Chin becoming public, the skirmish at Longju, Zhou's September 8 note outlining China's extensive claims, and following that the Kongka Pass incident, an aggravated public opinion and parliamentary opposition narrowed any scope for flexibility that the Indian government might have had earlier.[157] Nehru's decision in the midst of these developments, on August 28,

1959, to release white papers detailing correspondence with Beijing ostensibly served to effectively restrain the government further in its China policy by inflaming public opinion, parliamentary opposition, the Indian press, and indeed even Nehru's own party members.[158] Raghavan writes that Nehru was forced now to "assess constantly what the political marketplace would bear, and to adopt only those policies which could conceivably be sold to the public."[159]

Testimonies of several prominent Indian officials of the time corroborate this logic in suggesting that were it not for his sensitivity to the pressures exerted by public opinion, Nehru would have likely found it easier to be more conciliatory to China, including accepting Zhou's 1960 offer. Krishna Menon, for one, suggested later that Nehru was "concerned about what people would say. . . . Panditji was very sensitive to public opinion in that way."[160] Nehru himself was reported to have stated at a private meeting before the 1960 talks that "if I give them that I shall no longer be Prime Minister of India—I will not do it."[161]

While such public opinion pressures on the Nehru government were undeniable, the discussion offered in this book demonstrates that rather than serving as the fountainhead of Indian policy, domestic politics played a more limited reinforcing role. To the extent that public opinion did matter, it did not force Nehru in directions opposed to his government's preferred policy. In fact, much before this public opinion became active, it is apparent that Nehru and his officials had determined that compromise on even an admittedly unimportant piece of territory risked betraying weakness to a strong and aggressive China, with dangerous portents for the future. Indeed, as several scholars of the conflict have suggested, for all his suspicions of China, Nehru might well have been willing to cut a deal with Zhou in earlier years. That possibility, however, had been squandered by Beijing's decision to preemptively occupy territory in the western sector and build a road there, committing thereby what Nehru perceived as perfidious aggression.[162]

The basic underpinnings of Indian policy had therefore been set by Nehru's office prior to and independent of any public pressure. To that extent, Maxwell is likely correct in his assertion that while public opinion might have made it difficult for Nehru to change course, such pressures "did not make him do anything he was not himself inclined to do; nor did they prevent him from doing anything he really wished to do."[163] Noorani similarly states that for all the pressures of public opinion, Nehru had not held "a different view of the past. He had himself mobilized public opinion. Had he so willed . . . a policy based on the historical truth and sensible diplomacy conducted in private could have cleared a route that would assuredly have led to accord."[164] Indeed, it has been argued that were Nehru genuinely convinced that a significantly different approach to the dispute was wise and appropriate, he could have, though with some difficulty, carried both parliament and public opinion with him.[165] The last point is perhaps a significant overstatement of what Nehru would have been able to do once parliamentary and public opinion had become animated over the border issue. Nevertheless, there is little evidence that Nehru held a view of the situation significantly different from and more conciliatory than the public after August–September 1959.

It is no surprise, then, that having initially declared that it was "wrong to be swept away by public opinion,"[166] Nehru did little to resist parliamentary and public opinion on the China issue. This might also explain Nehru's surprising decision to release the white papers in August 1959, when he himself had acknowledged that public diplomacy on such issues, by rousing nationalist feelings, made a flexible approach impossible.[167] In 1956, in fact, the Indian prime minister had advised the Burmese leader to agree to informal and secret talks with Zhou because with formality and publicity, "there is a tendency to adopt rigid attitudes. Once this rigidity comes in, then it becomes very difficult to deal with the matter."[168]

One can therefore postulate that perhaps with no interest in budging from his own basic position Nehru saw benefit in stoking the parliamentary and public outcry that releasing the white papers was sure to result in as a useful bargaining tool with the Chinese. If Beijing did accede to all of Nehru's demands regarding prerequisites to negotiations, he could have then sold whatever concessions he was willing to make in the western sector on the back of having elicited a significant Chinese withdrawal. As one contemporary account speculated, "Why did Nehru publish the White Papers? They were bound to unleash nationalist passion in India, probably to a degree which could deprive him of any leeway for negotiating. Pique? Nationalist passion in himself? Or calculation, for instance to exert pressure on China as well as to anticipate criticisms of his border policy in India?"[169] Indeed, on the very day of the release of the white papers, an Indian note informed the Chinese government that New Delhi had until then "observed discreet reticence about these incidents" despite concern in public and parliament, implying that New Delhi now saw little benefit in doing so in a context of China's continued "unilateral application of force."[170] Nehru himself later stated that by publishing the white papers, what he was "aiming at is either winning over the other party or weakening the other party in its own opinion and in the world's opinion and in my own."[171]

TABLE 6.1

*India in the Sino-Indian dispute: A summary*

| Period | Bargaining Strength | Adversary Coercion | Policy | Reputational Explanation |
|---|---|---|---|---|
| 1949–1957 | **Weak** China was much stronger in military terms, especially in the border areas | **Minimal** No direct coercion; but Beijing's conduct in Tibet was indicative of such tendencies | **Delay/Firmness** Avoided raising issue; position premised on standing firm on map claims; some indirect hints of compromise in the west | Delay in hope that India would be better able to resist China later; firmness driven by fear that concessions from weakness would invite more challenges |
| 1957–1961 | **Weak/Declining** India continued to be weak as China strengthened its position | **High** Discovery of Chinese presence in Aksai Chin; assertion of Chinese claims diplomatically; military skirmishes | **Intransigence** Progressively more intransigent on entirety of claims; rejection of package deal; rejection of negotiations without Chinese withdrawal in the west | Intransigence to establish resolve in the face of a stronger power that was also coercive; negotiations or concessions without at least Chinese withdrawal risked signaling weakness |
| 1961–1962 | **Weak/Declining** Military balance was in China's favor by a large margin; PLA power projection in disputed areas was dominant | **High** Prior aggression yet to be reversed; evidence of continuing Chinese expansion in the west | **Intransigence/ Force** Adoption of the Forward Policy aimed at establishing military posts in areas unoccupied by Chinese in Aksai Chin | Use of force (despite military weakness) as a symbolic means of demonstrating resolve primarily to deter Chinese expansion, but ideally to compel withdrawal |

## Conclusion

Indian policy in the lead-up to the war of 1962 with China is puzzling in two significant ways. First, given the nature of the stakes and Nehru's supposedly idealistic view of the prospects of Sino-Indian ties, it is difficult to explain why New Delhi brushed aside the Chinese premier's 1960 offer of a deal that would have left India with territory of most value to it in exchange for letting China hold land that Indian officials thought of as being useless to them. A second quandary pertains to why the Nehru government displayed this intransigence and, what's more, soon after pursued an even riskier and militarily provocative Forward Policy in full awareness of the fact that the country clearly lacked the military wherewithal with which to back up such a stance in the event that the Chinese responded with greater force.

This chapter has demonstrated how the reputational imperative was a crucial, and thus far unexplored, factor influencing Indian decision making during this period. New Delhi's rejection of Zhou's package offer at the 1960 talks, by this account, had very little to do with any salience—strategic or symbolic-nationalist—that he attached to territory in the western sector. Similarly, domestic political pressures, while important, are less persuasive as a determinant of Indian conduct than is commonly believed to be the case. Rather, Nehru and his officials assumed an intractable posture on self-confessedly unimportant territory primarily because they feared that making any concessions to a stronger China, especially in a context of Beijing's perceived unilateralism, would communicate the sort of weakness that Chinese leaders were historically prone to exploit. Such reputational concerns were in fact apparent, as the previous chapter has detailed, from very early on, but they acquired even greater urgency toward the late 1950s. The Forward Policy was similarly driven less by some sense that Indian troops would be able to successfully reverse earlier PLA advances, but instead by the thinking that taking such action, however symbolic, was the least India could do in order to establish its resolve. The hope in New Delhi was that this, along with China's internal and external frailties, would be sufficient in forcing the adversary to put a brake on making further military advances and perhaps even make the sort of pullbacks that Nehru required as a prerequisite for negotiations. This assessment proved to be disastrously incorrect and led instead to China's decision to prosecute a punishing war in late 1962.

The war having humiliatingly confirmed India's profound weakness against China, it is not surprising that the reputational fears that had animated New Delhi all along only intensified after it and that negotiations and compromise became even less palatable to Nehru. Regardless of Beijing's declaration of a unilateral cease-fire and withdrawal in the eastern sector, the Indian prime minister persisted in his demand that Chinese troops and officials withdraw at the least to the status quo prior to September 8, 1962 (maintaining India's territorial gains made as part of the Forward Policy) before any talks could be held. For India to relent on this, Nehru contended, "would mean not only letting him [the aggressor, China] have what he wanted but exposing our country to further inroads and demands in the future." In the face of parliamentary criticism that even this was giving up too much, the Indian prime minister argued that getting China to agree to his demands would have constituted a major victory for India—and therefore a basis on which to enter into negotiations—as it would have indicated China's acceptance of its initial aggression. Anything beyond that had little chance of Beijing's agreement and would, moreover, show India in poor light in the international community.[172] According to Gopal, even after the Chinese withdrawal, Nehru was absolutely unwilling "to consider negotiations which were not backed by strength."[173]

The dramatic developments of the last few years had in effect only re-inforced in Indian minds the belief that Communist China was indeed expansionist. For Nehru, "whenever in her history China has been big and powerful, it has tried to expand and overawe surrounding countries and bring them within its circle," and it was India's refusal to accept Chinese hegemony, rather than the territorial issue alone, that had evoked Chinese wrath.[174] In parliament, Nehru declared that "China as constituted today is an aggressive and expansionist country, possibly with vast designs for the future."[175] India's intransigence was therefore necessitated not only by issues of territory but also by the need to signal that India would not succumb to China's attempts at coercion and hegemony and further undermine its own tattered status and prospects for the future. The reputational costs of compromise for India had now been magnified, rendering the dispute only more intractable for the years to come.

**7**

# Mao's China in the Sino-Indian Conflict

The thrust of the argument of this book so far has been that factoring in a reputational imperative is crucial if we are to understand some of the central, and often puzzling, aspects of Indian decision making in its territorial disputes during the Nehru era. Reputational considerations were vital in instances of both surprising conciliation despite high salience of territory and intransigence where territory of low importance was involved. As the theoretical argument of this book makes clear, however, there is no reason to expect such concerns to be exclusive to India alone. Indeed, as this chapter seeks to illustrate, the reputational imperative may also give a better account of some of the surprising elements of Chinese decision making in territorial disputes with India and other smaller neighboring states in the late 1950s and early 1960s. Before proceeding, however, I note that what follows is by no means a definitive account of Chinese decision making. Beijing's thinking during this period is, if anything, arguably shrouded in even more mystery than that of New Delhi. Only recently have scholars been able to begin the admirable task of piecing together the different strands of this story from newly available primary documents, the result of which has been at least two notable and comprehensive works on China's territorial disputes.[1] Consequently, this chapter aspires to little more than serving as a preliminary exercise at establishing the plausibility of the fact that some of the more unexpected aspects of Chinese decision making with regard to the territorial disputes with India and others during this period were influenced to a salient degree by the reputational imperative.

In contrast to Nehru's intransigence, the Chinese leadership displayed a surprisingly marked tendency for conciliation and a preference for a give-and-take approach over competing territorial claims in the period under consideration, even choosing, as Hyer puts it, to cede in some cases "territory believed by both parties to belong to China historically."[2] In the Sino-Indian case, the clearest expression of this approach came in the 1960 talks during which Zhou made the package offer to Nehru. Such concessions were unexpected for two reasons. First, there was some salience associated with the territory in the east that the Chinese leaders were willing to give up as part of a deal. There is no doubt an argument to be made that the barren and sparsely inhabited frontier regions were of low intrinsic value to the Chinese leadership and that even then, it was land in the western sector that was of far greater strategic salience to China, given that it served as the best overland link from an unstable Tibet to the rest of the country.[3] Yet it is also true that the Chinese leaders viewed their claims in the eastern sector as perfectly legitimate and that the contested territory was in fact not completely shorn of nationalist importance to them. Their own extensive claims were premised on the need to redress the century of national humiliation when a weakened Qing dynasty had been forced to cede extensive territory and influence to foreign powers.[4] It is not surprising, then, that even in 1936, Mao had been speaking of "the immediate task of China to regain all our lost territories."[5]

The McMahon Line specifically was regarded as one of many such illegal impositions on the country and the Indian leadership's insistence on its maintenance as the assumption by the latter of the mantle of British colonialism. Early Communist propaganda in China in fact viewed Nehru as a "running dog of the Anglo-American imperialists," necessitating that India too be liberated from the grip of Western imperialism.[6] As Zhou consequently wrote to Nehru much later in 1959, British expansionism in Tibet and Xinjiang constituted "the fundamental reason for the long term disputes over and non-settlement of the Sino-Indian boundary question." What surprised his government was New Delhi's demand to give "formal recognition to the situation created by the application of the British policy of aggression."[7] The Chinese premier expanded on this theme of the McMahon Line being a colonial imposition in the 1960 talks with Nehru:

> From the beginning, mention of this [Simla convention and the notes] has been a shock to the Chinese people, and it hurt their feeling because these are the legacies of imperialism.... [The British] brought pressure on China and Tibet to come to India and negotiate with McMahon. Moreover, the British representative, without letting the Chinese representatives know about it, secretly exchanged notes in Delhi before

the Simla convention was signed and the McMahon line was fixed as a result of this exchange of notes.[8]

Second, even on security-seeking grounds, an argument can be made that it made little sense for China to be so conciliatory toward India. If Beijing's core concern was stabilizing the Tibetan frontiers, then the territory in the eastern sector should have been, as one scholar has contended, as important as that in the west.[9] Both sectors bordered the Tibetan landmass, and while there certainly was strategic importance attached to the road connections through Aksai Chin, the borders in the eastern sector were by no means insignificant in that they provided the primary points of ingress and egress in and out of India for Tibetan rebels.

Moreover, the Chinese leaders were, counterintuitive to standard bargaining expectations, open to making these substantive concessions on their stated claims despite the undoubted military advantages they enjoyed against India in the disputed regions. Indeed, China's superiority in terms of both manpower and firepower, proven incontrovertibly a few years later in war, logically allowed Beijing to pursue more assertive means in order to both deter India from its alleged mischief making in Tibet, as well as to impose a solution on the country on the territorial issue, all while needing to make little to no compromise on its territorial claims. Such an approach, moreover, fit in with Mao's and Communist China's penchant for realpolitik, as well as their belief in the efficacy of military means, convictions that had already stood the test of war in previous years against stronger adversaries.[10] Yet the Chinese leadership surprisingly chose the path of compromise instead.

As puzzling as Beijing's choice to adopt a conciliatory approach until 1962 is its decision to then abruptly abandon it and initiate an expansive and punishing war on India late in that year. If a threat context, both domestic and international, had indeed required conciliation in earlier years,[11] very little had arguably changed by 1962, with the looming failure of the Great Leap Forward policy and a severe downturn in ties with the Soviet Union supplementing the Chinese regime's troubles.[12] Indeed, if reversing Indian advances made as part of the Forward Policy was the motivation, a more limited offensive in the western sector would have sufficed. Furthermore, having launched the offensive and swiftly decimated Indian defenses and occupied all of the disputed territory, the Chinese decision to unilaterally withdraw from much of the occupied area is puzzling. Logistical and international political concerns notwithstanding, the Chinese leadership certainly had the option of holding territory as a bargaining chip to force Nehru into compromise. Not doing so, Beijing must have realized, was certain to relegate the prospect of resolving the dispute to the distant future. A wounded and humiliated India was, as was soon proven, unlikely now to make the kinds of concessions it was unwilling to make even before defeat in war.

How then do we account for these policy decisions? After providing an overview of China's early strategy of delay on the territorial issue, this chapter illustrates how the reputational logic can add to our understanding of Beijing's major decisions during this period: of being conciliatory initially, to initiating war a few years later, only to then decide to not capitalize on the gains of war by carrying out a unilateral withdrawal from most of the occupied territory.

## The Early Years of Delay, 1949–1957

Like Nehru, the Chinese demonstrated a marked disinclination early on to raising or addressing the nascent territorial dispute.[13] This was apparent in Zhou's response to the Indian ambassador's allusion to the issue in a meeting in September 1951: he suggested that barring the stabilization of the Tibetan frontier, "there was no territorial dispute or controversy between India and China."[14] In 1952, when K. M. Panikkar broached the issue once more, Zhou again demonstrated little interest in a discussion.[15] Chinese maps representing large swathes of territory that India claimed as part of China were also explained away as old and inaccurate.[16] His government, Zhou explained, had simply not had the opportunity to survey the frontier and revise old nationalist maps.[17] Of course, Beijing was likely well aware of India's stance on the issue. Nehru had, after all, been declaring in parliament that his country's boundaries with China—the McMahon Line in particular—were beyond dispute.

True to form, the Chinese, like the Indians, avoided raising the issue during the landmark talks over Tibet, and even after as India began producing maps that showed the entire boundary as firm and therefore in keeping with its stated claims.[18] Such prevarication on Communist China's part is not surprising. Having only recently emerged from a draining civil war, the Communist regime faced the mammoth task of cementing political authority against internal and external threats.[19] In such a context, antagonizing India, whose cooperation Beijing required in dealing with the immediate challenge in Tibet, made little sense. India, after all, enjoyed great advantages in Tibet in the form of political ties and easier geographical access to the region.[20] Delay, in addition to helping China firm up its position internally, also allowed Beijing to rapidly improve its military position, and hence bargaining strength, in the Sino-Indian frontier region over the next several years. As Chinese troops pushed up to India's Tibetan frontier for the first time in decades, they also used this period of diplomatic inactivity on the territorial issue to build up physical presence in what until then had been the no-man's-land of Aksai Chin, including building an all-weather road connecting Xinjiang and Tibet through the region.[21]

That the Indians themselves sought to avoid the territorial issue facilitated this stance, as did the fact that New Delhi also quickly moved in the early years to assuage fears in China about Indian intentions in Tibet. China's invasion of Tibet had briefly instigated a sharp exchange between the two governments, as Beijing accused India of intervening in China's internal affairs under foreign influence.[22] Yet those tensions quickly subsided as New Delhi showed little enthusiasm for backing Tibetan appeals for independence at the UN.[23] India's relinquishing of all special rights and status in Tibet as part of the 1954 treaty culminated the process of India's reassurance of China. Nehru indeed justified these concessions publicly in India as based on an acceptance of facts on the ground, as well as his government's desire not to be associated with the extraterritorial rights that had resulted from British imperialism.[24] At the same time, Nehru also played the role of Communist China's constant champion in the international arena, from backing its demands for the Chinese seat at the UN to supporting its claims to Taiwan.[25]

China's refusal to raise the territorial issue also hinted at early signs of a willingness to compromise, especially in the eastern sector. The Chinese premier explained to Nehru in late 1959 that the issue had never been raised "because conditions were not yet ripe for its settlement and the Chinese side, on its part, had had no time to study the question."[26] If one were to interpret the statement at its most benign, China's disinterest was merely a function of having accepted the McMahon Line as the de facto boundary, leaving little to dispute or discuss until a more opportune time.[27] Such an interpretation is not unreasonable given Zhou's attitude on the issue in the 1956–1957 talks with Nehru, the first instance where he explicitly addressed the issue of the McMahon Line. In those meetings, he had noted that China's disinterest in the issue in previous years was partly a result of a disinclination to alter the McMahon Line delineation.[28] While his government did disagree with the legality of that line, Zhou assured Nehru that his government did not desire to change an "accomplished fact."[29] The plausibility of such a reading is only enhanced by China's tolerance during this period of Indian actions and statements asserting sovereignty all the way to the McMahon Line and Beijing's attitude toward the eastern sector in later talks.

Interestingly, however, especially given India's later attitude, this delaying strategy also meant that during his discussions with Nehru, Zhou left uncontested the Indian prime minister's assertion that with the status of the McMahon Line confirmed, the frontier between the two countries would be well known and undisputed barring a few minor issues.[30] The Chinese premier had, of course, failed to raise the issue of the western sector, which he was no doubt aware formed part of India's extensive map claims. Zhou's failure to refer at any point to claims in that region, ones that were objectively far more important to China in strategic terms, until the Indians threw open the issue in 1958 suggests that compromise was going to be much less palatable to Beijing on that front. Fatefully for the conflict, it also left Nehru with the impression that China had agreed to recognize Indian territorial claims in return for concessions in Tibet.[31] That Zhou did not broach the topic of Aksai Chin, all the while that the People's Liberation Army (PLA) was actually expanding their physical presence in disputed areas, consequently became central to Nehru's sense of Chinese betrayal.

## Beijing's Move Toward Compromise

Once the territorial breach was opened with the Indian government's initiating diplomatic correspondence and protests in 1957–1958, Zhou continued to hint at the possibility of conciliation at the same time that he was now more explicitly asserting his government's territorial claims. In a January 1959 missive, he suggested that Beijing found it "necessary to take a more or less realistic attitude" on the matter. He cautioned nevertheless that China "cannot but act with prudence and needs time to deal with the occasion." In the meantime, the Chinese premier suggested that the two sides adhere to the existing status quo as a provisional measure.[32] Nevertheless, for much of 1959, there was little in the nature of urgency on the part of the Chinese leadership in addressing Indian complaints. Indeed, until September there was a period of a few months with little direct communication from Zhou to Nehru.

This swiftly changed later in the year. On September 8, the Chinese premier for the first time clarified the nature of his government's claims about what they viewed as the "traditional" boundary in the frontier areas. He nevertheless did restate at the same time that China sought a friendly resolution of the dispute based on "the historical background and existing actualities."[33] By November, Zhou was urgently calling for direct talks with Nehru and suggested that in the meantime, both sides withdraw their armed forces 20 kilometers behind "the so-called McMahon line in the east, and from the line up to which each side exercises actual control in the west."[34] Nehru's counterproposal, of confining the withdrawal formula to only the western sector, proved unacceptable to the Chinese leadership, but Zhou nevertheless persisted in pushing for talks, even suggesting that they be held in neutral Rangoon in December.[35]

Beijing's repeated entreaties resulted in Nehru's eventually acceding to talks, to be held in April 1960. The talks failed spectacularly, but they famously involved the most explicit expression of the package offer: China's willingness to resolve the dispute on the basis of give-and-take.[36] By late 1959, it is apparent that the Chinese regime had seemingly decided on such a negotiated approach to the conflict, with Mao even confiding to Soviet officials in October that "the McMahon Line with India will be maintained" and that China "never, under any circumstances, will move beyond the Himalayas."[37] Beijing had concluded, as one member of the Politburo Standing Committee summarized, that "China should make some concessions, India should make some concessions, [and] in this way reach an agreement through mutual compromise."[38]

Spurned by Nehru, over the next year the Chinese nevertheless continued to convey, including through the Burmese leader U Nu, their wish to resolve the dispute peacefully. In 1962, the Chinese reportedly even informed leftist Indian journalists that in addition to accepting the McMahon Line delineation in the east, Beijing was also willing to offer New Delhi joint use of their road in Aksai Chin and the formation of a joint body to consider the delimitation of the frontier in that sector.[39] In July 1962, a few months before the war, Foreign Minister Marshal Chen Yi is said to have hinted in his talks with Krishna Menon that his country was willing to make further concessions in the western sector.[40]

## Explaining Compromise

That the desire to address and resolve the brewing territorial conflict with India acquired new urgency in Beijing at the time that it did is not surprising. Recent scholarship on China's territorial disputes has offered convincing accounts for how both internal political developments and a worsening international environment made delay as a strategy no longer sustainable.[41] On the domestic front, by 1957–1958, armed resistance in Tibet had been growing and Beijing had lost control of much of Tibet itself, barring Lhasa. By March 1959, the situation had deteriorated to a full-fledged rebellion with massive demonstrations rocking Lhasa, resulting in a crackdown by the PLA.[42] In Beijing, the troubles in Tibet were immediately linked to India, with Kalimpong in India understood to be the "commanding center" where the rebellion had been conceived, apparently with New Delhi's connivance.[43] Indeed, by mid-1958 even Nehru was aware that relations "with China are not as good as they have been in the past, chiefly because they think that we are conniving at the act of Tibetan emigration."[44]

In keeping with this perception of Indian complicity in Tibet, Zhou made a public statement on May 6, 1959, suggesting that "the center of the Sino-Indian conflict" lay in the fact that the Indian government "had inherited England's old policy of saying Tibet is an independent country." On the same day, an article from the Xinhua news agency personally revised by Mao had accused Nehru of being a bourgeois successor to British imperialism and of conspiring to restore Tibet's feudal system.[45] Zhou also declared in a May 1959 meeting with ambassadors from socialist countries that he believed that Nehru sought Tibet to "serve as a 'buffer' under the Indian sphere of influence, and become their protectorate."[46]

New Delhi's eventual decision to grant asylum to the Dalai Lama, impose a trade embargo on Tibet, and diplomatically escalate the territorial issue around the time of the outbreak of revolt in Lhasa confirmed these linkages for Beijing.[47] Zhou noted as much in one of his communications to New Delhi, pointing out that Indian troops had become increasingly assertive in the disputed border areas following the outbreak of troubles in Tibet.[48]

The record of the 1960 talks with Nehru confirms Zhou's preoccupation with Tibet at that time. In their first meeting, the Chinese premier had chosen to draw Nehru away from speaking about the frontier dispute in general to focusing on Tibet. As he noted, "Of course both aspects are related: (i) international developments in Tibet, and; (ii) border question arising out of Tibet."[49] The next day, in talks with Ambassador R. K. Nehru, Zhou made the connection even clearer in stating that the outbreak of tensions "was a logical outcome of the revolt in Tibet and the coming of the Dalai Lama into India."[50] Much later, in explaining the 1962 war, Mao similarly noted that the problem was never "of the McMahon Line, but the Tibet question."[51]

With domestic conditions deteriorating further on the back of a developing food crisis attendant on the disastrous Great Leap Forward policy, the situation confronting China in the international realm was no less disconcerting. As relations with the Soviet Union began to see a sharp downturn and hostile American presence and involvement in the region escalated, including in Southeast Asia, it is no surprise that the leadership in Beijing viewed tensions with New Delhi as a troubling development.[52] Indeed, in an indication of the linkages between their domestic and foreign difficulties, the Chinese had recently become aware of American efforts—through a CIA program—at actively fomenting the rebels and undermining China's position in Tibet. India, Mao suspected incorrectly, was conspiring in facilitating the CIA's covert operations.[53]

Given this context of intense vulnerability from both the inside and outside, it is reasonable to conclude that Chinese leaders viewed compromise with India as a means of somewhat mitigating the intensity of the threatening circumstances that they confronted. As Whiting argued in one of the early pieces of scholarship on the Chinese approach to the Sino-Indian conflict, the country's "overall policy derived from a sense of weakness and vulnerability."[54] Reaching an agreement on the territorial issue potentially raised the hope of greater cooperation from India in stamping out domestic threats, particularly the rebellion in Tibet, and thereby stabilizing that long border.[55] In terms of the external threat, as Hyer notes, Beijing adopted a conciliatory approach in order to combat the "strategic imperatives of China's [threatening] international environment."[56]

The evidence is thus overwhelming that security-seeking drivers are key to explaining Chinese leaders' decision to compromise in their territorial disputes with India and others. However, such arguments also beg some further questions about why China chose that path and what specifically led its leaders to expect that their concessions would elicit cooperation and friendship from India. After all, while the lower, though not negligible, salience of the territory in concern no doubt made conciliation easier, a military solution was always an eminently viable option for Beijing. The PLA's superiority over their Indian counterparts was substantial enough, as was proven a few years later, such that it logically allowed the pursuit of more assertive means in order to put a stop to India's alleged mischief making in Tibet and impose a solution on the territorial issue. Indeed, confident local military commanders were encouraging political leaders to consider punitive military action against the Indians during this time.[57]

Further recommending an approach based on the use of force was the fact that it would have served the purpose of deterring India and other adversaries by establishing Chinese resolve while also requiring no territorial concessions from Beijing. Widespread compromise, by contrast, did not necessarily guarantee a more benign security environment. It equally risked confirming to others that China was indeed weak and vulnerable and therefore ripe for further exploitation. In short, there is nothing logically self-evident about how Beijing chose to deal with the new security context. Finally, the fact that Chinese leaders had, even in earlier years, indicated a willingness to accept the McMahon Line delineation suggests that the incentive to compromise was not purely a consequence of the concatenation of threats that China faced in the late 1950s, even if the timing of the offer was certainly their result.

The reputational imperative, I suggest, helps shed light on why Chinese leaders pursued the compromise option and expected that doing so would prompt friendlier policies from India. In contrast to how New Delhi viewed China during this period, the long-term threat that Beijing perceived from India was relatively muted. This was less because of some perceived lack of hostility on the part of India—there were several reasons, including Tibet and ideology, for the Chinese leadership to mistrust the "bourgeois-nationalist" Nehru regime[58]—and more due to the distinct military advantages that the Chinese enjoyed over India. These were advantages, moreover, that Mao and his associates expected to increase as the regime resolved its internal political and economic troubles.[59] Reinforcing this material aspect of China's military prowess were Mao's deeply held beliefs in the efficacy of force, confirmed in Korea, in dealing with any security challenges—beliefs that served to augment the regime's confidence that they could prevail in any military conflict through sound strategy and morale.[60] More crucial, these military advantages were particularly stark in the frontier regions, lending Beijing dominant bargaining leverage all across the border.

Given such undisputable advantages in the bargaining context, it was not unreasonable for leaders in Beijing to expect that any concessions that they made to India would carry few reputational costs. In fact, and to the contrary, Chinese leaders expected that making large concessions from a position of strength would show them in a favorable light to India and other neighbors by demonstrating generosity and reasonableness. It was this display of generosity that was key to Beijing's hopes of eliciting reciprocal cooperation from New Delhi in quelling the rebellion in Tibet and stabilizing the southwestern border without having to use China's ostensible military advantages to coerce concessions from India.[61]

This logic also fits with Zhou's insistence in the 1960 talks that India accept the illegality of the McMahon Line and the undelimited nature of the Sino-Indian frontier as a prelude to any compromise. As one Chinese official put it during those talks, "To still hold on to the illegal McMahon Line and want us to recognize it, creates difficulties. We are anxious to reach a settlement based on historical conditions and existing realities by mutual consultations and on a reasonable basis."[62] New Delhi's acknowledgment was crucial to establishing the legitimacy of China's contesting territory along the McMahon Line in the first place, and thereby Beijing's generosity. Without it, Chinese concessions arguably risked looking less like generosity and more as a retraction of claims that had been baseless and expansionist in the first place, as New Delhi had been asserting all along.

Admittedly, there is little direct evidence to suggest that Beijing was indeed thinking along these lines. However, indirect evidence, including the Chinese leadership's emphasis on the reputational imperative later on in the lead-up to war, indicates some merit to this line of argument. Indeed, Indian government officials seemed to recognize and even take exception to the Chinese contention that they were being generous and reasonable. Such irritation was evident in one communication from the Indian embassy in China to New Delhi following the 1960 talks, complaining that officials in Beijing "generally tried to explain that the Chinese side made proposals for a reasonable settlement of the boundary question . . . by stressing the constructive efforts of Zhou Enlai, the reader is left in little doubt as to why no agreement was possible."[63]

Perhaps more revealing, this was also the time that Beijing had been pursuing much the same policy with other bordering nations with which it had territorial disagreements. By making generous concessions—reflecting in some cases almost the entirety of the claims of the other side—to significantly weaker neighbors such as Burma, Nepal (both in 1960), and Pakistan (in 1963), Chinese leaders had clearly sought to develop a benign reputation in order to elicit the cooperation of those countries in dealing with the internal and external travails that had driven Zhou to approach Nehru as well.[64] After all, even more than in the case of India, China could have reasonably and relatively costlessly pursued more unilateral means of stabilizing the frontiers with its smaller neighbors, making unnecessary any territorial compromise.

That Beijing still sought territorial agreements with these countries that meticulously ensured that they "did not bear the clear marks of overweening Chinese power" illustrates clearly the reputational imperative at work.[65] Zhou had been explicitly committing to such an approach since the 1955 meeting in Bandung during which he had suggested that his government would "use only peaceful means" in dealing with border disputes; in the meantime, he was "willing to maintain the present situation" without prejudice to either side's claims.[66] By 1960, as talks with the Burmese government (and others) were initiated, Beijing was prepared to be magnanimous because of its professed disapproval of "great nation chauvinism"[67] and the desire to promote "solidarity among Asian and African countries."[68] Indeed, by this point Zhou had developed a set of four principles that were to guide his government's approach to negotiations. Two of them called for China to give up historical claims based on the country's imperial past and avoiding any acts that would betray "big nation chauvinism."[69] Interestingly, as Lall has pointed out, even on procedural issues, the Chinese sought to signal generosity from a position of overwhelming strength. In dealing with Nepal, for instance, Beijing allowed Kathmandu to host two of the three boundary committee meetings instead of assuming the mantle of senior partner and insisting that talks be held in China.[70] Zhou himself neatly encapsulated the reputational imperative at work in Chinese decision making a few years later in remarks following the Sino-Pakistan territorial agreement; he noted that "since China is bigger than these neighboring countries . . . China always made more concessions to the opposite party in the process of mutual accommodation in order to seek a settlement of the question."[71]

It is no stretch to conclude that the concessions Zhou was willing to make to India were motivated by a calculus similar to that which drove compromise with the other neighbors: being accommodative from a position of strength would signal generosity and thereby encourage cooperation from the other side. Indeed, the timing of the agreements with Burma and Nepal suggests that India was central to Beijing's calculus in even those cases. By swiftly initiating and concluding agreements with those two countries before talks with New Delhi in April 1960, Zhou arguably sought to signal to Nehru that such generosity was available to India too. As the Chinese premier explicitly noted during a stopover in Rangoon en route to India in March 1960, he had hoped that the Sino-Burmese agreement "would be advantageous for discussing the problem with India." A *People's Daily* article from February had similarly asked, in implicit reference to India, why "events that have happened between China and Burma [could not] also occur between China and other Asian countries?"[72]

In the 1960 talks, the Chinese premier made this link more explicit. In response to Nehru's complaints about Chinese maps, he noted that Beijing had "already reached an agreement with Burma and the entire boundary question will soon be settled. The same should be applicable to the Sino Indian boundary question and we feel that there are no difficulties that cannot be overcome."[73] The point was articulated in much greater detail on the sidelines of the Nehru-Zhou talks two days later by Chen Yi in a meeting with Sardar Swaran Singh, a minister in Nehru's cabinet, in the following terms:

> I must make it clear that we do not recognize the McMahon Line. We did not want to take great parts of Burmese territory south of this line. The Burmese Government also understood clearly that the McMahon line was not mentioned and there would be local adjustments of boundaries based on survey etc. Non-recognition of the McMahon Line did not mean China extending her claims over any territory. The Burmese Government understood the Chinese non-recognition of McMahon Line and were not apprehensive. The Sino-Burmese boundary is to be drawn on the basis of actual jurisdiction, geographical features, local adjustments etc. . . . China and India are great countries and, therefore, their standard should be higher, at least the same as that in the settlement of the boundary questions between China and Burma.[74]

As discussions continued into the next day, Chen Yi emphasized the generosity underlying his government's dealings with the Burmese government, in hopes no doubt of convincing the Indian leader of China's reasonableness. Specifically, he pointed to the section of the border between China and Burma that had been delineated by a line, distinct from the McMahon Line, agreed to in 1941 by the British and KMT governments. Chen noted:

> I hope the Indian friends would consider this example and also the attitude of the Chinese government to the Sino-Burmese boundary line drawn in 1941. If the Chinese government did not follow a policy of settling questions with brotherly South-East Asian nations in a friendly manner, it was possible for us not to recognise the 1941 line. This boundary line was drawn by British colonialism at a time when China was in dire straits fighting for its existence against Japan. Our attitude was not to draw this line again and we said that as the treaty was formally signed by the Chiang-Kaishek Government, we would accept it. Though the Chinese government was unhappy about the 1941 line in the interests of the Sino-Burmese friendship and for implementing international obligations we accepted it. . . . Gen. Ne Win, the then Burmese Premier, told Premier Zhou about the Chinese rights to a silver mine south of the 1941 line. Premier Zhou immediately replied to him that "We give up that." He did not even ask for my opinion though I was present.[75]

Not surprisingly, then, with Nehru's rejection of their proposed terms, the Chinese contended that "anyone in the world with common sense" would wonder "since the Burmese and Nepalese Governments can settle their boundary questions with China in a friendly way through negotiations . . . why is it that the Indian Government cannot negotiate and settle its boundary question with [China]?"[76] Indeed, soon after the failure of the 1960 talks, the Chinese premier took some consolation in the fact that at least in terms of the reputational stakes, the talks had "isolated" Nehru "and proved that while we are willing to resolve the boundary issues, he is unwilling to solve the boundary problem; we have gained the initiative."[77]

In offering to address the territorial issues with India in a spirit of give-and-take, the Chinese leaders believed they had been reasonable and generous, as they had been with other weaker neighbors. To accede to the entirety of India's demands, which sought to deny China of both physical possession of the disputed territory in the western sector as well as any historical-legal claims to it, was a different matter altogether. That not only involved giving up territory in the west that was of great strategic salience to the country—salience that had, if anything, increased manifold with the rebellion in Tibet—but also risked carrying significant reputational costs. To succumb to such demands and give up territory that China actually held, and Nehru had previously acknowledged meant little to India, was, in Beijing's view, going far beyond reasonableness to abject surrender. As Zhou noted in the

1960 discussions with Nehru, in a formulation similar to the latter's complaint regarding Chinese claims, "In the early days after the foundation of the Republic of China we sent troops and supplies to Tibet from Sinkiang through Aksai Chin area. It was only last year that the matter was brought up by India and it was a new territorial claim made by India." Moreover, Zhou further pointed out that Nehru had "acknowledged in Parliament that this portion of the boundary was somewhat vague. In Indian maps different lines and different colors have been used."[78] The nature of India's terms, therefore, by denying China of both territory and *locus standi* over the land in dispute while retaining the moral high ground for New Delhi, made concessions in the west reputationally unacceptable to Beijing. Having been imposed on by imperialists in the past, when "our Indian friends want to bully us," Zhou complained to the Indian vice president, "Then we do not know what to do." Indeed, in yet another parallel to Beijing's approach to other neighbors, the Chinese premier further claimed on this occasion that his government had been generous even with regard to the logistics of the meeting. As he put it:

> When Prime Minister Nehru invited Premier Zhou to Delhi they [the Chinese government] had at first considered reiterating their invitation to come to China or alternatively of fixing the meeting, as proposed earlier in Rangoon. But after consideration the Chinese Government had felt that in the interest of friendship Premier Zhou should come to Delhi for these discussions. This again was a proof of Chinese sincerity.[79]

For Zhou, refusing to acknowledge China's claims to what its leaders viewed as their own territory in the west made India's demands "unfair" and far from "equitable."[80] New Delhi's position on the western sector was viewed as an "absurdity" and hardly serious and fair unless the Indian government was prepared to apply the same principle equitably to the eastern sector as well. China was, after all, not "a defeated country,"[81] and while its government was willing to negotiate and settle all boundary issues with its neighbors, it could not "allow itself to be plunged back to the position of the injured old China."[82] The Chinese belief that, as one scholar has put it, "Nehru sought to cut the Aksai Chin road as part of an effort to force the PLA out of Tibet"[83] and the Indian resort to the Forward Policy in 1961 only reinforced Chinese stakes in the western sector. To accede to the entirety of Nehru's demands was therefore completely out of the question for Beijing. A give-and-take solution was much more palatable. Beijing's hope, as Chen Yi articulated it, was that "India and China should shake off the legacy of imperialism and settle all boundary questions on a basis which is reasonable and satisfactory to both."[84]

## Initiation and Aftermath of the 1962 Offensive

As important as the reputational imperative had been to the choice and nature of concessions that China was willing to offer India and others in the approach to 1962, it soon became similarly significant to Beijing's surprising decision to abandon the conciliatory approach and launch a blistering military offensive against India along the frontier in October and November 1962. In initiating war, the Chinese leadership certainly sought to put an end to the Forward Policy and reverse any Indian gains from what Zhou referred to as Indian "nibbling" in the western sector.[85] The use of force therefore ostensibly served Beijing as a useful means of arresting and reversing the decline that it had seen in its position in the western sector, before Indian positions became less easily surmountable. Notwithstanding such considerations, however, if the Chinese leaders' intention was only to reverse Indian gains made as part of the Forward Policy, they could have reasonably confined their military offensive to the western sector. That they did not do so suggests that significant reputational goals underlay the initiation of war as well. In demonstrating the full extent of their strength, Chinese leaders had as one of their primary goals the establishment of a reputation for resolve against attempts by others at pressuring the country into concessions. In this way, it hoped to deter India (and possibly others) from troubling China again for a significant period of time and, as Mao believed, "create 10 years of border stability."[86]

From late 1961, in fact, the Chinese had been warning India of exactly this possibility. With Indian troops steadily "pressing forward on China's borders," Beijing cautioned New Delhi in November that "it would be very erroneous and dangerous should the Indian government take China's attitude of restraint and tolerance as an expression of weakness."[87] After all, the Chinese Ministry of External Affairs argued, New Delhi ought to have recognized that if its logic that India had full rights to create posts in the western sector were accepted, "the Chinese Government would have every reason to send troops to cross the so called 'McMahon Line' and enter the vast area between the crest of the Himalayas and their Southern foot."[88] The Indian government's "deliberate attempts to realize [its goals] by force," Beijing consequently threatened, "is most dangerous and may lead to grave consequences."[89]

With little change in India's actions on the ground, Zhou had instructed his military commanders by May 1962 to begin preparations for war. Chinese troops patrolling the western sector were instructed to dominate nearby Indian posts without resorting to force and instead attempt to compel Indian troops to withdraw through a show of firmness.[90] At the same time, however,

Chinese officials cautioned India against persisting "in its act of playing with fire in an attempt to assert its territorial claims by armed force." New Delhi, it was made clear, would be making a "fatal mistake if it should think that China is flabby and can be bullied in view of her self-restraint and forbearance."[91] Even as tensions mounted toward war and as the Chinese built up military pressure in the Thagla ridge area in the eastern sector in September 1962, a communication from Beijing called on India to stop pursuing a policy of "sham negotiations and real fighting" and made one last offer to "welcome negotiations if seriously intended." It suggested a firm date of October 15 for when talks could be held without preconditions. If Nehru refused, the note promised, China "will resist, whenever attacked."[92] Another note sent the same day warned New Delhi that "shooting and shelling are no child's play; and he who plays with fire will eventually be consumed by fire."[93]

The Nehru government continued to ignore these warnings. Indeed, Indian leaders were now increasingly making public statements promising to evict Chinese forces from occupied territory.[94] In an October 11 press conference, Nehru himself declared, "Our instructions are to free our territory." When that was to happen was left completely up to the Indian army.[95] In this context, the decision was made in Beijing to initiate a massive offensive. By now, Chinese leaders were convinced that New Delhi viewed accommodation and restraint as weakness, which precipitated further Indian brazenness. Mao had decided that "a very strong jolt [was] necessary to cause Indian leaders to acquire a sober appreciation of Chinese power" because India had seemingly "not learned the lesson that the Americans had learned in Korea—to respect the power of New China."[96] In Zhou's assessment of the Sino-Indian dynamic at this point, similarly, "when you have no room for retreat and you do not counterattack, that is really showing weakness and they will believe that you are easily cowed." More direct reference to a reputation-building imperative came in Mao's statement to the party politburo on October 18, days before the offensive started. In it, he explained that if China were to "counterattack one time, then the border will become stable and the boundary problem can be peacefully resolved." The attack, however, Mao clarified, was designed only to "warn and punish, only to tell Nehru and the Indian government that they cannot use military means to resolve the border problem."[97]

That a reputational imperative was in play in Chinese decision making is also borne out in more indirect ways. This is particularly true of the nature of Beijing's global outreach surrounding the decision to go to war, especially in the African and Asian world. Much of this diplomatic activism, it must be acknowledged, amounts more strictly to image (rather than reputation) building and preservation, in that there is little evidence to suggest that it directly and primarily aimed to influence the target audiences to act in a certain manner. Nevertheless, to the extent that Chinese leaders also had reason to believe that their actions on the Sino-Indian matter would influence the attitudes and conduct of others toward them, especially of countries in their strategic neighborhood, it is reasonable to expect that they were also sensitive—especially given the sense of encirclement that they were feeling at the time—to the possibility of reputational blowback in the case of war. There was value, consequently, in trying to ensure that if blame were to be apportioned internationally after a war, much of it would fall on Nehru's truculence. Furthermore, and more indirectly, the exercise also offered the possibility that it would help prevent the eventuality of war altogether by pressuring New Delhi into assuming a more conciliatory stance for fear that a failure to do so risked emerging from the conflict with an international reputation for being unreasonably intransigent and even belligerent.

The "international audience," in other words, "had become a salient target for Chinese exploitation of the border crisis."[98] Beijing had presaged this dimension of its calculus as early as November 1960 when a PLA directive to units on the western border had ordered military restraint by noting that the "provocation and attacks" of India could not be viewed "merely from the military standpoint." "We must not," the directive urged,

> replace policies with emotion and erroneously regard the struggle strategy of avoiding armed clashes as an indication that we are weaker than the neighboring country . . . [by striking back] we might gain a greater military victory, but politically we would fall into the trap of the other side. . . . By doing our utmost to avoid armed clashes with them . . . in the political and foreign policy struggle, we will be in the position of initiative, reason, and advantage from beginning to end.[99]

As General Lei Yingfu later recalled, many military officials who had been advocating for war remained puzzled about why "having commanded three major military campaigns such as the war against the United States in Korea . . . was Mao so 'soft' on India." Chinese leaders instead were more focused on making "a strong impression on global public opinion that the PLA had controlled itself" and that the country had "friendly designs."[100] Consequently, in a July 14, 1962 meeting, Mao again warned that while India's activities as part of the Forward Policy had given China plenty of reason to go on the offensive, restraint had to be maintained so as to reveal Nehru's true intentions and establish India as the aggressor (and China as the victim) in the eyes of the international community.[101] In the same vein, an October 3 note to the Indian government pointed out that it would not be "difficult for the Asian countries and all peace-loving countries to see . . . that the Chinese Government is sincerely working for a peaceful settlement."[102] Prior to the offensive itself, Chinese officials used the first anniversaries of border agreements with Nepal and Burma to publicly emphasize how their government had been willing and able to swiftly negotiate mutually acceptable border agreements with neighbors other than India. Indeed, as the Chinese government took pains to emphasize, it had done so on the basis of incredibly generous terms for those smaller states.[103]

Once the war began, Beijing's unusual decision to halt the offensive briefly to renew an offer to Nehru that both sides withdraw to behind the line of control existing prior to India's Forward Policy and then proceed to negotiations seems similarly reputationally motivated. Revealingly, Zhou's letter to Nehru at this point was accompanied by a simultaneous transmission to several African and Asian countries highlighting the renewed offer to India and appealing to their good offices to help resolve the dispute peacefully. The note also explicitly, and incorrectly, laid sole blame for the war on a fictitious Indian offensive of October 20. Nehru's response on October 27, demanding Chinese withdrawal to restore the status quo prior to September 8 before he would consider discussing further measures, constituted a rejection of Zhou's offer.[104] In dismissing the counterproposal, the Chinese premier's November 7 missive, not coincidentally released publicly as well, protested that while China had "not tried to force any unilateral demand on the Indian side on account of the advances gained in the recent counter-attack in self-defense," Nehru's terms had again unfairly demanded from Beijing "humiliating conditions such as forced on a vanquished party." Zhou's note also made extended reference to Asian and African nations having appealed to both sides to settle the dispute "on the basis of mutual understanding and mutual accommodation," stating further that he was "convinced that their intentions are good and their viewpoint is correct."[105] Wrapping up this public relations exercise at reputation and image management, Zhou sent out another letter to African and Asian leaders on the eve of the launch of the second offensive. The note restated in detail China's case and emphasized its peaceful intentions and actions all along, while accusing India again of having "embarked on the road of military adventure" having seen an "opportunity ripe for launching massive armed attacks."[106] What followed was the second phase of military action, this time completely routing Indian troops all along the disputed frontier.

Given how reputational considerations had influenced the Chinese decision to first offer compromise and then go to war, as well as the nature and public packaging of the offensive itself, it is not difficult to understand the logic behind Beijing's final puzzling act: its abrupt decision on the thirty-second day of fighting to unilaterally declare a cease-fire and announce its decision to withdraw all troops to positions 20 kilometers behind the November 7, 1959, line of control. No doubt, the logistical difficulties that Chinese troops were bound to face with the onset of winter contributed to the decision. The same goes for the changing international context, where the end of the Cuban missile crisis opened up the possibility of great power support for India against China.[107] Once the war began, in fact, it had become clear that the Kennedy administration was inclined to assist the Indians in fighting the Chinese. By November 1962, the US Air Force and Britain's Royal Air Force had already airlifted some crucial military supplies to equip Indian soldiers on the battlefront.[108]

Nevertheless, it also remains true that in a very basic sense, by the time the unilateral cease-fire was announced, the Chinese offensive had already achieved what it had been designed to do in the first place: in Zhou's famous words, to "teach India a lesson."[109] With that goal served, it is not surprising that Beijing chose to cease fire and withdraw. From a reputational perspective, the decision was also in keeping with what had come before. By demonstrably choosing not to exploit their undisputed military might and actual territorial gains, Chinese leaders reasonably hoped to preserve and reinforce the impression of generosity they had been seeking to build since the late 1950s with their neighbors, including India, by pursuing the path of compromise in their boundary conflicts. Consequently, the cease-fire came into effect on November 22, and on December 1 Chinese troops began their withdrawal. Further demonstrations of purported generosity followed in the next weeks and months as all captured equipment and personnel were repatriated to India and Beijing desisted from anything in the nature of boisterous celebration of the victory at home.[110]

## Conclusion

At the end of the war, the Indian leadership had been left convinced that a duplicitous China had all along been motivated by expansionist goals and the desire to undermine India's position in their quest for Asian leadership. Yet as this chapter has argued, China had been surprisingly conciliatory and moderate in its actions during this period of the Sino-Indian territorial conflict. Chinese decision making on territorial issues seemed only minimally (if that) concerned about any such rivalry. It was instead driven more by the immediate needs of stabilizing the country's frontiers and relations with neighbors. Beijing was therefore willing to make surprisingly substantial concessions to India and its other neighbors. Indeed, even as the Chinese pursued a deliberate policy of delay on the territorial dispute in earlier years, it was apparent that they were always open to eventually making large concessions to India in the eastern sector—the section of the frontier that was most salient to Indian security concerns—in return for Indian concessions to Beijing's claims in the Aksai Chin area that was considered strategically vital to China. Only with their failure to get Nehru to agree to Zhou's package offer in 1960, the initiation of India's Forward Policy, and New Delhi's refusal to accede to or suggest what Beijing considered to be reasonable terms for negotiations was the decision made to go to war. Even then, the war was aimed at punishing India rather than delivering a fait accompli or exploiting military advances to coerce India into making concessions.

This chapter has also shown that the severe internal and external threats China confronted beginning in the late 1950s do go far toward accounting for the urgency with which Beijing began to address territorial issues. However, as table 7.1 summarizes, the reputational imperative helps us better explain both the surprisingly conciliatory nature of China's eventual stance on these territorial issues, as well as the decision to go to war in 1962. By this account, China's overwhelming bargaining advantages over India, owing primarily to the country's military predominance in the contested frontier areas, facilitated compromise by leading decision makers in Beijing to believe that the reputational consequences of doing so were likely to be not just benign but even positive. By making large concessions from a position of strength, China was hardly likely to be viewed as weak and exploitable. Rather, the hope was that by demonstrating the extent of Chinese generosity, compromise would serve to be reputationally advantageous, and thereby both mitigate fears of the country in the neighborhood and elicit more cooperation from India (and others) in helping China address its more urgent security challenges. Using force, though logically viable as an option, had the major disadvantage of risking the reinforcement of existing fears of Beijing as overbearing, and consequently vitiating China's security environment even further at a crucial time.

With attempts at peaceful resolution of the dispute based on mutual compromise derailed by Nehru's seeming intransigence, and more moderate attempts at deterring India through threats of the use of force having failed, Beijing resorted to war in 1962 primarily as a means of rectifying misapprehensions in India that China's weaknesses had made it vulnerable to exploitation. The application of overwhelming force was therefore aimed to a significant degree at reputation building, but in this instance to establish one of resolve in the face of India's Forward Policy. The unilateral cease-fire and withdrawal sought to mitigate any potential negative reputational repercus-

TABLE 7.1

*China in the Sino-Indian dispute: A summary*

| Period | Bargaining Strength | Adversary Coercion | Policy | Reputational Explanation |
|---|---|---|---|---|
| **1949–1957** | **Strong** China was significantly stronger in military terms, especially in the border areas | **Minimal** No major coercion from India, although it was suspected of mischief in Tibet; Nehru made major concessions on Tibet in 1954 | **Delay** Avoided raising issue; strong indications that China was predisposed to accept the McMahon Line delineation in the east | Delay allowed for dealing with more urgent internal threats and solidifying Chinese presence at borders, especially in the western sector (nonreputational) |
| **1957–1961** | **Strong** China continued to strengthen its presence in the border areas and western sector, despite domestic troubles (Tibet and famine) | **Minimal to Moderate** Little direct coercion on the border issue from India; New Delhi was perceived to be fueling rebellion in Tibet, however, and raising border issues to that end | **Compromise** Initial assertion of expansive claims, but matched with hints of willingness to concede in the eastern sector; package offer in 1960 confirmed this | Beijing believed it was speaking from strength, as in the case of other neighbors, and so any large concessions would be viewed not as weakness but as generosity, and encourage cooperation from India |
| **November 1961– October 1962** | **Strong** PLA power projection continued to be dominant and was not substantially challenged by the Forward Policy | **High** Rejection by India of several offers of negotiation was followed by the militarily provocative Forward Policy | **Threats and War** Initiation of war in October 1962, following several threats warning that India's actions were inviting it | China believed Nehru had misconstrued earlier generosity for weakness; war intended to punish India and establish Beijing's resolve |
| **November 1962–** | **Dominant** Chinese strength was indisputably confirmed in its overwhelming of Indian defenses in the war | **None** China initiated the war | **Compromise** Unilateral withdrawal (instead of exploiting military gains) suggested Beijing's reversion to 1960 position | War had established Chinese resolve to resist coercion; unilateral withdrawal refocused on communicating generosity |

sions from the use of force by seeking to reinforce China's earlier efforts at signaling its generosity to New Delhi and other international audiences.

The immediate Chinese aim of using force to deter India and stabilize the Sino-Indian frontier for the foreseeable future was achieved through the wildly successful war. However, if Beijing had hoped that the war and China's conduct in its aftermath would also convince Nehru of the need to resolve the territorial dispute at the bargaining table, such expectations were soon dashed. In India, the humiliation of war had only added to the preexisting litany of complaints and mistrust of China, leaving New Delhi if anything more intransigent than before.

**8**

# Conclusion

This book has sought to overcome some important lacunae in the scholarly work—both theoretical and historical—on India's handling of its major territorial disputes with Pakistan and China during the Nehru era. It has done so by proposing a novel reputational theory for state behavior in territorial disputes. This framework, the reputational imperative, makes two important contributions to our understanding of how states conduct themselves in international relations in general and in territorial disputes in particular. First, it demonstrates how decisions to compromise or be intransigent on territorial claims, and the extent of each, are significantly and independently influenced by what leaders perceive to be the implications of such choices for their country's international reputation. Second, it has offered a more complex portfolio of reputational goals that feature in state decision making, including reputations of not just resolve but also more benign ones for generosity and cooperation. Doing so has facilitated developing more specific and finely grained expectations about the conditions under which states are, or are not, likely to lay stress on particular kinds of reputation building, making compromise more or less likely.

How leaders assess the prospective reputational import of their decisions is, I argue, shaped by the bargaining context, a function of perceptions on each side about relative bargaining strength and the recent history of bargaining tactics used by an adversary. Where the bargaining context is favorable, this theory suggests, state leaders are likely to find it easier to make concessions on their claims in the belief that compromise from a position of strength is more likely to carry reputational benefits (of appearing generous) rather than costs (of appearing weak), whereas intransigence, by conveying a bullying disposition, might generate unnecessary reputational blowback. Similarly, the more unfavorable the bargaining context is, the more likely state leaders are to remain firm, for fear that compromise in the face of an adversary's strength or coercion will communicate weakness, whereas intransigence will convey the positive impression of resolve, and thereby serve to deter the other side.

The empirical record, as the previous chapters have demonstrated, bears out this theoretical argument for the most part. It helps makes sense of, for instance, the variations in Nehru's approach to the Kashmir dispute after independence and especially the failure of the plebiscite option. Importantly, the case study of the dispute suggests, neither did nationalism render Kashmir indivisible for India nor did some fundamental insincerity on the part of the Nehru government preclude the conduct of a plebiscite. Instead, for many of the early years, the Indian prime minister was open to making large compromises on Kashmir and continued to adhere to his government's initial commitment to a plebiscite. This he did in the belief that being conciliatory from a position of strength posed little risk of appearing weak and served instead as an indication of New Delhi's generosity, whereas being intransigent and reneging on the plebiscite commitment promised damaging any chances that India would cement a more benevolent reputation and image for generosity and cooperation internationally.

Rather, until late 1953, the plebiscite option languished, largely owing to Nehru's firm prerequisites for a vote being held in the state. Military-strategic considerations were certainly important in this story. However, a reputational calculus was independently important in Nehru's stubborn insistence on such terms, motivated by the fear that making the generous concessions that India was willing to make without ensuring the reversal and punishment of Pakistan's initial aggression hazarded demonstrating an Indian tendency to yield to coercion and encourage greater demands from the adversary. Only after 1954, when the US-Pakistan military pact severely compounded the long-term threat Pakistan posed to India, did New Delhi withdraw the plebiscite offer. Again, however, this decision owed itself to a great degree to Nehru's belief that a changing bargaining context had severely exacerbated the perceived reputational costs of making major concessions on Kashmir. India now confronted the risk of any substantive compromise being viewed in Pakistan as succumbing to the latter's growing bargaining strength, thereby necessitating that New Delhi demonstrate greater resolve.

The reputational imperative similarly makes explicable the otherwise puzzling intransigence of the Indian leadership over the self-confessedly unimportant territory of Aksai Chin in the Sino-Indian dispute, territory that had in fact occupied very little of the Indian leadership's attention prior to 1957. It was not, the account shows, some unreasonable pig-headedness on the part of Nehru or overwhelming domestic pressures alone that bred this surprising firmness. Rather, strong fears within Nehru's government that such large concessions would signal Indian weakness, and encourage more demands from a stronger and potentially aggressive and duplicitous China, were central to making compromise unpalatable in New Delhi. Indeed, so severe were these reputational concerns that they drove the Nehru government to adopt the disastrous Forward Policy, while being fully aware that Indian forces were in no shape to fight the Chinese, and in the hope and expectation that ever minor and symbolic demonstrations of resolve would be sufficient to restrain Beijing from further expansion in disputed areas of the western sector.

China's record of compromise in its territorial disputes with India and other smaller neighbors in the 1960s adds validity to this reputational argument. In this case, the intensification of internal and external security threats late in the 1950s did trigger the need in Chinese leaders for action on the territorial front. But compromise, rather than the use of force, was incentivized by the expectation in Beijing that large concessions made from a position of strength would be reputationally beneficial in signaling generosity to others and thereby eliciting their cooperation in helping China manage its more immediate security challenges. Mao, Zhao, and their colleagues therefore, counterintuitively, did little to exploit the People's Liberation Army's (PLA) undoubted military superiority to coerce their weaker neighbors into conducting themselves in a more accommodative manner or to impose a solution to territorial issues on them. While in India's case this meant offering a package deal, Beijing was even more generous with other much weaker neighbors, in most cases agreeing to virtually all of those countries' territorial claims. Indeed, China's eventual initiation of war with India in 1962 was similarly driven in important ways by the reputational imperative, aimed primarily at demonstrating resolve in the face of India's perceived unilateralism as part of the Forward Policy. Beijing's puzzling decision to first use force and then unilaterally withdraw from all of its claimed territory in the eastern sector can be accounted for by this desire to first demonstrate firmness through force and then reinforce to India and other neighbors China's essential generosity through the unilateral withdrawal.

## Does Reputation Matter?

The argument offered in this book has focused on how leaders think about reputation formation. The case studies also afford us some limited insights into the other question that has animated the theoretical study of the phenomenon in international relations: whether reputations form at all, and if they do, whether they do so in the manner that leaders expect. On this question, the evidence seems to be mixed. There is indication that states do make some dispositional attributions about other states. Nehru and his officials clearly believed the Chinese and the Pakistanis to be almost congenitally hostile and expansionist and constantly updated that impression with every act of perceived duplicity or unilateralism by the other side. Mao and his colleagues similarly carried some deeply set views about Nehru, which led them to some highly consequential misperceptions about India's role in Tibet, as well as the basis of the country's stance on territorial issues. To the extent that such attributions clearly influenced the eventual actions of both India and China, this suggests that decision makers are not incorrect in putting some stock in their reputations.

However, it is also clear from these cases that some of the recent scholarship by, for example, Mercer and Press is correct in suggesting that reputations do not form or change as easily or in the manner that leaders seem to believe they do. Both Nehru and the Chinese leaders had no success in changing the other's preexisting impressions about themselves. Despite New Delhi's generous concessions on Tibet in 1954, Beijing continued to mistrust Indian intentions, and Zhou's 1960 offer did little to assuage Nehru's negative views of China. Consequently, in the approach to war, both countries had trouble establishing the reputations that they sought: India for resolve and the Chinese for generosity. Pakistan's leaders similarly never attributed even a modicum of sincerity and generosity to Nehru's conciliatory position in the early years of the Kashmir conflict. India's assertions of resolve with Pakistan similarly did little to restrain the country in the long term and certainly did not influence its leaders into assuming a more conciliatory position in tune with New Delhi's demands in later years. To the extent that there is any circumstantial evidence of success in these cases, it perhaps comes from China's compromises with other neighbors, such as Nepal and Pakistan, where benevolence arguably translated into much friendlier relations with those countries in later years.

All of this suggests that reputation management is a much more complex enterprise than leaders perhaps believe and that the demands and thresholds for its formation and change are often incredibly high. A couple of preliminary propositions on the kinds of factors that might matter in this regard might be worth noting. For one, it seems reasonable to expect that single acts, however consequential they might be, will not generate reputational attributions unless they are part of a pattern that audiences can identify with some consistency over a certain period of time. In the absence of such regularity, it is likely that states will attribute the causes of any acts to situational rather than dispositional factors. In China's case, for instance, it could be argued that the fact that Beijing made individual concessions to its neighbors in the context of widespread compromise with all its neighbors over that period helped provide more traction to achieving its reputational goals. Nevertheless, it is perhaps also true that if Beijing had not followed with further acts of seeming generosity, Nepal and Pakistan would have likely explained away China's initial compromise on territorial issues by way of the country's situational constraints—its domestic and external weaknesses—during that time.

Second, the efficacy of acts aimed at building reputation might also depend on the context in which they are carried out. Here the literature on costly signaling might be useful, in that it tells us that efforts at communicating certain information about oneself is more likely to be viewed as credible depending on the costs one is willing to risk in the process.[1] Efforts at signaling generosity may therefore, for instance, be most effective when the costs of compromise are potentially high and the benefits of doing so are seemingly negligible. Chinese concessions, by this logic, would have had an even greater chance of being read as generous the more salient the territory was to them and if they were made at a time when Beijing had no incentives to compromise because it did not confront any severe internal or external threats. Similarly, establishing resolve will be more successful the larger the domestic political and other sunk cost risks that states assume in the process. India, in this view, perhaps failed to convince Beijing of its resolve in part because New Delhi simply could not get Chinese leaders to understand the domestic costs Nehru faced if he chose the path of compromise. Also, by limiting military expenditures aimed at strengthening the army in the border areas in previous years, the Indian prime minister had also arguably failed to assume the sort of sunk costs that might have convinced Beijing of the credibility of India's firmness.

The findings of this book that reputations do not form as state leaders expect them to does not therefore indicate that reputation as a concept itself is useless. Rather, it points to an urgent need to conceptualize reputation better in order to discover how state leaders think about it, as well as rectify misconceptions they might hold about how reputations form.

## Territorial Disputes and Enduring Rivalries

As I noted early in the book, much of the theoretical literature on wars and enduring rivalries in international politics has identified the existence of territorial disputes as being the most important factor behind why states go to war and why they end up in long-lasting rivalries. Indeed, the two dyadic relationships that this book has been concerned with—the India-Pakistan and Sino-Indian ones—represent two of the most dangerous and consequential rivalries in contemporary world politics. More often than not, this scholarship has found, states that are party to territorial disputes prefer to assume the undoubted costs of conflict and war rather than make the sorts of concessions that would lead to their peaceful resolution. Over time, as these countries experience repeated crises and wars that progressively reinforce the hostility between the contestants, their relationship settles into the sort of uneasy and dangerous equilibrium that characterizes international rivalries.[2]

The reputational considerations flagged in this work also have something of value to tell us about the origins and persistence of these territorial disputes and rivalries. In fact, in both cases dealt with in this book, it is clear that the intractability of the disputes owes itself to some degree to the intensification of reputational fears on at least one side over the course of the conflict. In Kashmir, the initial terms the Indian leadership set for the plebiscite had much to do with the reputational fears that had been animated in New Delhi in the wake of the tribal invasion from Pakistan. A few years later, Nehru's abandonment of the plebiscite in response to Karachi's entrance into a military pact with the United States was driven by similar concerns. Similarly in the Sino-Indian dispute, what objectively appeared as a reasonable solution became progressively problematic for reasons connected to reputation. The adoption of a firm stance by the Indian leadership on the prerequisites to any negotiations, and the resort to limited military measures through the Forward Policy, had a strong reputational logic attached to it, intended to avoid any impression in Beijing that New Delhi would succumb to Chinese strength and repeated instances of perceived unilateralism.

The Chinese resort to force in 1962 had its own reactive reputational logic aimed at signaling to India that intransigence, threats and use of military force would be repelled ruthlessly. While the unilateral withdrawal by Chinese troops soon after the offensive sought to present Beijing's intentions in a benign light, the practical consequence of the use of force nevertheless had been to heighten reputational fears in the Indian leadership, making talks, let alone compromise, more unviable for the next several decades.

Indeed, to the extent that coercion by an adversary animates fear in states that making any concessions will make them look weak, it is reasonable to hypothesize that repeated crises and wars (often perceived to have been caused by the adversary) concretize the reputational stakes on both sides of a rivalry, making compromise increasingly difficult. What may result over time could be something like a reputational dilemma wherein policies and actions that state leaders undertake to minimize the reputational costs (and maximize the benefits) of compromise for themselves often seem to have the sometimes inadvertent consequence of exacerbating the reputational fears of an adversary, making concessions on the latter's part even less likely.[3]

All of this is to say that in theoretical terms, there might be value in explicitly introducing the reputational mechanism as a potential contributor to rivalry formation and persistence. In practical terms, the implications of this observation might mean that in framing potential solutions to these complex conflicts, policymakers will need to be more overtly sensitive to what each side has at stake in terms of their reputations.

## Territorial Disputes: Beyond India and China

The findings of this book have implications for cases beyond Indian and Chinese decision making alone. Indeed, the importance that leaders attach to reputation has manifested itself in other cases in the region as well. This is perhaps best exemplified in the fact that even weak states with little military capability have periodically shown the tendency to adopt intractable positions on their territorial claims for reputation-building purposes, regardless of the immense risks associated with such a posture. This has been notably true of how weaker countries in the region have dealt with their territorial disputes with China. Preliminary evidence from those cases points to the fact that in the early 1960s, states like Burma and Nepal went into their negotiations with Beijing with demands that almost the entirety of their claims be met and refused to make even minor concessions in some instances.

Burma, for instance, demonstrated a willingness to tolerate deadlock with China for several years prior to negotiations in the early 1960s, while being itself faced with serious domestic challenges at the time.[4] Nepal similarly went into its talks with China with the attitude that "notwithstanding its size or might if any power attempts to occupy or control even an inch of territory of another Asian country, such attempts will definitely disrupt peace in the world."[5] In assuming this firm stand, Kathmandu had been encouraged by New Delhi, with Nehru insistent that "in their [Nepal's] anxiety to settle their problems with China they should not give the appearance of having been scared."[6] Indeed, King Mahendra's audacious statements during his September–October 1961 trip to Beijing, even with a territorial settlement overwhelmingly favorable to Nepal's claims already having been agreed to, are even more revealing. In public pronouncements during that visit, Mahendra surprisingly alluded to China's history of expansionism and "tendency to ignore just and rightful claims, and the rights and susceptibilities of her small neighbors."[7] He also expressed his hope that China would not "repeat past mistakes" and would "take lessons from history and not adopt the path of encroachment upon and interference in the political sovereignty and territorial integrity of her neighbors."[8] While some of this firmness can no doubt be explained by reference to the domestic political costs politicians face when compromising, that the Nepalese ruler was willing to adopt such a provocative tack perhaps indicates equally the import of the reputational imperative in his attitude to the territorial dispute with a much stronger China.

Just as clear, a desire for a reputation for generosity has arguably manifested in India's efforts in recent years to expeditiously resolve all outstanding issues, including relatively minor territorial ones, with Bangladesh on terms that seek to avoid an impression of Indian hegemonic imposition. After several failed efforts to do so since the 1970s, both sides signed a new protocol in September 2011 seeking to give effect to the 1974 land boundary agreement and bring the dispute over several small enclaves of territory on both sides of the border to a close. The agreement involved swapping Indian enclaves in Bangladesh with those of the latter in Indian territory. New Delhi also agreed not to be compensated for the nearly 16 square miles of net loss in territory that such a settlement involves. Ratification of the deal, pursuant to the Indian parliament unanimously approving a constitutional amendment bill, followed in June 2015 during Indian Prime Minister Narendra Modi's visit to Dhaka where he also announced a new $2 billion line of credit for Bangladesh.[9] While no doubt a minor concession, the Indian willingness to agree to, as one observer of the dispute has put it, an "uncompensated cession of undisputed territory" suggests an "imperative of good neighborliness" and generosity as motivating India's recent conduct toward Bangladesh, in return for which the Indian leadership no doubt expects greater sensitivity from Dhaka to New Delhi's own security and other concerns in the region.[10]

Such a reputation for generosity is also something India has increasingly sought to cultivate in the broader South Asian region in recent years. Indeed, the resuscitation of negotiations with Bangladesh happened in part as a consequence of New Delhi's conceptualization in the late 1990s of what came to be known as the Gujral Doctrine,[11] which, as its first principle, articulated the idea that India would no longer seek reciprocity in relations with its smaller neighbors and would instead assume a posture of generosity and magnanimity.[12]

All of this suggests that the reputational dynamics identified in this work ought to be generalizable beyond South Asia and the cases addressed in this book. They should not only help further the conversation on the theoretical role of reputational concerns in international relations in general, but also give us a better understanding of specific aspects of state behavior in cases of territorial and other conflicts over time and across the world. More work is required to specify when and how reputations matter for state leaders, what other considerations influence such a calculus, and test such expectations against a larger and more global set of cases than this book has sought to do. Such research will not only help scholars better explain state behavior in international relations but also complement the theoretical work on reputation formation by providing researchers with better-developed baseline theories of the reputational bases of decision making with which to contend.

## Reputation in Intrastate Conflict: Nehru and the Nagas

The argument made in this book should also extend to a topic that has been at the core of research on reputation in territorial disputes: intrastate separatist conflicts. Indeed, preliminary evidence from the Indian government's treatment of the case of Naga separatism in the Indian northeast in the 1950s points further to the importance of the reputational imperative.

In addressing that challenge, which began soon after independence as leaders of the Naga tribe began demanding a separate state for their people,[13] the Indian government was seemingly driven by much the same reputational logic that characterized its thinking on India's interstate territorial disputes. As the separatist movement gathered steam in the next few years, for Nehru it was unquestionable that the "real solution will require a political approach and an attempt to make the Nagas feel that we are friendly to them and that they can be at home in India." To this effect, he was clearly willing to make large concessions short of offering the group independence. However, his government could do so only, Nehru contended, from a position of undisputed strength. This meant in May 1956 that "the present is not time for the political approach, because it may be construed as a sign of weakness."[14] In an obvious parallel to how Nehru thought of China, he asserted that this reputational consideration was particularly crucial in dealing with the Nagas for whom "weakness is something approaching a sin. Friendliness of course should always be there, but no step which appears to be a surrender through weakness."[15]

The first priority for Nehru therefore was "resisting violence and breaking the bone of the resistance movement," because making any political concessions or commitments before having done so was "likely to be regarded as the precursor of approaching surrender . . . and tend to further stiffen their [the rebels'] backs."[16] What Nehru desired instead was for his government to make it perfectly clear that "we are not going to negotiate with anybody on the basis of threats and violence."[17] Once he felt that Indian forces were succeeding in breaking down military resistance Nehru decided to "give fresh thought to this matter"[18] and became "prepared to consider any reasonable approach to this problem which promises a settlement."[19] As Nehru noted at this point again, his only worry throughout had been that "hostile elements should be encouraged in their hostility in the future and imagine that by violence and killing they can gain their ends." However, since "they must have realized by this time that they cannot coerce the Government of India into doing anything because of their violence," time appeared to be "ripe for a fresh attempt to be made" at pacifying them.[20] Once a settlement was reached, Nehru thought, India could withdraw forces from the Naga areas to the more important Pakistan frontier "without any loss of prestige" because the act made from a position of strength "might well appear as a generous gesture showing confidence in the Nagas."[21] "Our approach has all along been," Nehru later recounted, "friendly, but a friendly approach means nothing at all unless it is also a firm approach. Otherwise, the friendliness is only supposed to be weakness and fear. Therefore, it has to be firm and at the same time a friendly approach."[22]

While not more than a snapshot of a brief period in India's handling of Naga separatism, what this discussion does suggest is that not only is there merit to looking for more generalizable accounts, such as this one, of India's (and other states' in general) conduct across interstate territorial disputes, but that the insights offered here have potential viability in thinking about state behavior in managing both internal and external threats. It also points to another area ripe for fruitful research: that which lies at the interstices between secessionist and interstate territorial disputes. As the discussion in this chapter specifically, and in the book as a whole, has shown, states often face both internal and external challenges to territorial integrity, challenges that are in many cases linked to each other. State responses to such a combination of challenges have varied widely. Beijing, for instance, chose in the 1950s and 1960s to compromise externally so as to avoid making even moderate concessions at home. In contrast, Indian and Burmese leaders generally displayed a preference for making concessions at home over giving up territory to an external challenger. Why this is so, and especially how considerations identified in this book play into choices of compromise and intransigence in one domain rather than the other, is an intriguing question worthy of further inquiry.

## Implications for the Present and the Future

Finally, what do this research and its findings mean for the period beyond the scope of this study, particularly for the contemporary state of the Kashmir and Sino-Indian conflicts? It cannot be denied that the passage of time has complicated their dynamics only further. Domestic constraints on political leaderships in particular are likely more potent today than they were in first decade or so of these disputes, for several reasons. First, repeated crises and wars have generated and exacerbated, particularly in the defeated parties, public memories, narratives, and discourses of the adversary's hostility and treachery.[23] In India, the scars and shame associated with the Chinese offensive in 1962 and in Pakistan the Indian "fraud" in Kashmir, and then the mutilation of the country itself in the war of 1971, have undoubtedly imbued disputed territories with even greater nationalist salience than they initially possessed. Second, governments today enjoy neither the political dominance nor the unquestioned legitimacy that a Nehru or a Mao held in the early years after independence, which makes them even more susceptible to domestic political constraints, rendering reputational concerns as a factor that only further complicates the prospects for peaceful resolution.[24]

Nevertheless, this book has also demonstrated that the implications of nationalism and domestic opinion have often been overblown and that the resolution of disputes over territory, even those of nationalist importance, may be possible if the solutions proposed are sensitive to the strategic and reputational interests of disputants. Ensuring this is crucial to making any potential settlements acceptable to both political leaders and domestic public opinion. Proposed solutions that keep such considerations central, this book suggests, offer the most likely path out of these intractable territorial conflicts.

### Kashmir

All of this will require no doubt a great deal of imagination, not to mention luck. In Kashmir, this might mean solutions that are unlikely to involve transfers of territory or mechanisms (such as a plebiscite) that may result in such transfers but nevertheless might feature some kind of relaxation of Indian sovereignty over the state in order to accommodate Pakistan. Such an outcome could be sold by New Delhi, both at home and abroad, as a demonstration of Indian generosity toward Pakistan and the Kashmiri people from a position of strength. In Pakistan, to the extent that Indian concessions mitigate the strategic threat—possibly through a drawback of Indian military presence in Kashmir—and at the same time impart Islamabad with some semblance of symbolic parity in the disputed state, compromise may become both acceptable to its leadership and explicable domestically.

Indeed, secret back-channel discussions between New Delhi and Islamabad in two instances, first in 1999 and then from 2004 to 2007, indicate the exploration of solutions along precisely such lines. That these talks happened with a Hindu-nationalist Bharatiya Janata Party (BJP) in power in India in 1999 and a military regime ruling Pakistan from 2004 to 2007, again suggests the limits of nationalism in thinking about the conflict. It also points to another potential avenue for extension from this research: the possibility that given the reputational tensions highlighted in this work, leaders who have already established reputations in one dimension will be most able to pursue policies that risk that reputation and seek one on a different front. In clearer terms, it may be that leaders already known for their hawkish credentials will find it easier to pursue policies that would in general risk communicating weakness in order to convey generosity, while those who are established doves can best afford to take actions that threaten to undermine that reputation and establish resolve instead.[25]

In any event, the first attempt at back-channel talks between India and Pakistan failed with the Indian discovery of the Pakistani military intrusion into Kargil in June 1999. However, as Wirsing has suggested, it did demonstrate that "given suitable circumstances the elected leaders of India and Pakistan are quite capable of engaging one other in dispassionate, imaginative, and constructive dialogue about Kashmir."[26] In the second instance, according to journalist Steve Coll's account,[27] both sides agreed to explore a solution that involved what the Indian prime minister, Manmohan Singh, would term making "borders irrelevant" by allowing the free movement of people and goods from both sides of the line of control, with Kashmir itself to be made highly autonomous.[28] With a gradual recession in violence, it was envisaged that both sides would slowly begin withdrawing their troops from Kashmir; still later, once these measures had proved sustainable, the line of control could become the international border. Furthermore, on issues of joint interest, a "joint mechanism" involving Kashmiris, Indians, and Pakistanis was mooted, which the Pakistani negotiators sought to be akin to a plan for shared governance. By early 2007, both parties had reportedly come perilously close to agreement, only to see a precipitous drop in President Pervez Musharraf's popularity at home—unrelated to Kashmir and which eventually led to his ouster in 2008—putting paid to the effort. The fear in Pakistani government circles that Musharraf's own unpopularity at home would have made an otherwise sellable solution domestically unviable made putting off the issue unavoidable.

The failure of these efforts, and many before and after them, does point to the tragic complexities and challenges—too numerous to detail here—that beset the conflict and the possibilities for solution.[29] Yet that talks such as these were possible in the first place also suggests that Kashmir is far from indivisible and the conflict not nearly as intractable as it may seem if only both sides could be empathetic to the other's strategic and reputational concerns.

### The Sino-Indian Conflict

In contrast to Kashmir, the Sino-Indian territorial dispute, despite having persisted for as long, is in many ways a much simpler affair. The 1960 model, a formula reflecting the existing status quo, still seems ostensibly to be the most reasonable and logical basis for resolving the territorial dispute. The 2005 guiding principles for settling the dispute agreed to by the two countries seem to suggest as much.[30] The relative stability along the line of actual control for nearly two decades, thanks in part to confidence-building measures instituted by both sides beginning in the 1990s, facilitates this process.[31] That India is much stronger now relative to China than it was in the 1950s and 1960s also makes a settlement along the status quo more feasible by, arguably, somewhat dampening reputational fears in New Delhi.

Nevertheless, and contrarily, there are also reasons to expect that reputational considerations will continue to be salient in the management of the territorial dispute. For India in particular, although its growing strength is certainly reassuring, as long as it continues to speak to Beijing from a position of relative weakness, and the emotional baggage of the 1962 war persists, it is likely that any acceptable solution to the frontier question will still require concessions by Beijing beyond the current status quo. This is perhaps even more true considering the context of an expanding rivalry between the two countries in recent years. Indeed, the intense attention that renewed Chinese military activity on the borders and in the seas, and growing engagement by Beijing in India's neighborhood and beyond, have attracted in New Delhi conveys the kind of long-term fears of China that persist in India.[32] Under these circumstances, to concede the status quo in a final settlement without any Chinese concessions in the western sector, even symbolic ones regarding the principles of negotiation, will ostensibly be viewed as problematic by Indian leaders in that it would amount to a blanket acceptance of China's earlier aggression and therefore signify India's continuing weakness. Whether China would be open to making such concessions, however, is questionable at a time when Beijing itself has been reasserting its claims in the eastern sector,[33] perhaps as a bargaining tactic to get India to acquiesce to the status quo all along the frontier, or because its more secure position internally and externally has left the regime with little incentive and urgency to pursue a more benign reputation through the swift and generous resolution of territorial issues.

In any case, what is clear is that the reputational imperative will feature increasingly in the thinking of leaders in both India and China in the years to come. This will become more likely as both countries rise to greater regional and global prominence and develop expanding commitments and interests around the world, rivaling each other in a growing number of arenas beyond the territorial domain. While such developments may make compromise on contentious issues such as the territorial dispute increasingly problematic, in part for reasons of reputation, the rise of the two countries also poses the intriguing possibility that their quest for growing influence and responsibility will also require both to more actively cultivate more benign reputations, including one for being generous with weaker countries. That the idea of soft power has increasingly entered the lexicon of leaders in China and India in recent years arguably suggests exactly such a recognition.[34] If these things are true, not only will we see the reputational imperative becoming more prominent in the decision-making calculus of these states, but we will also likely witness in increasingly sharper relief the tension that has been a central theme of this book: that involved in the simultaneous pursuit of a reputation of generosity and that of resolve.

# Notes

NOTES TO CHAPTER 1

1. As one scholar encapsulates this thinking, "Nehru has been blamed for leaving behind a legacy of conflict with Pakistan (as well as China). On that last count alone, some examiners might want to mark him with a failing grade in his chosen vocation of making a foreign policy of peace for India!" Surjit Mansingh, "Nehru and Pakistan," in *Legacy of Nehru: A Centennial Celebration*, ed. D. R. SarDesai and Anand Mohan (Springfield, VA: Nataraj Books, 1992), 310.

2. Prithwis Chandra Chakravarti, *India's China Policy* (Bloomington: Indiana University Press, 1962). Jaswant Singh speaks of Nehru's "idealistic romanticism" in his *Defending India* (Basingstoke: Macmillan, 1999), 34; Shashi Tharoor has similarly characterized Nehru's policy as a "messianic utopianism" in his *Reasons of State: Political Development and India's Foreign Policy Under Indira Gandhi, 1966–1977* (New Delhi: Vikas Publishing House, 1982), 26. See also David Malone, *Does the Elephant Dance? Contemporary Indian Foreign Policy* (London: Oxford University Press, 2011), 154–156.

3. The finest recent exposition of such an argument can be found in Srinath Raghavan, *War and Peace in Modern India* (New York: Palgrave Macmillan, 2010). Another work that points to elements of realpolitik in Indian foreign and security policy under Nehru is Bharat Karnad, *Nuclear Weapons and Indian Security: The Realist Foundations of Strategy* (New Delhi: Macmillan, 2002).

4. Neville Maxwell, *India's China War* (London: Cape, 1972). In the context of Pakistan, Burke similarly described Nehru as unreasonable, "making it difficult to negotiate any concrete dispute with him on a give and take basis." S. M. Burke, *Mainsprings of Indian and Pakistani Foreign Policies* (Minneapolis: University of Minnesota Press, 1974), 81.

5. Raghavan, *War and Peace*, 14.

6. Steven A. Hoffmann, *India and the China Crisis* (Berkeley: University of California Press, 1990), 7. For Hoffman's discussion of the roots of Indian nationalism with regard to the border dispute, see pp. 25–28.

7. Victoria Schofield, *Kashmir in Conflict: India, Pakistan and the Unfinished War* (New York: I. B. Tauris, 2000), 10.

8. Sumit Ganguly, *The Origins of War in South Asia: The Indo-Pakistani Conflicts Since 1947* (Boulder, CO: Westview Press, 1994); Ashutosh Varshney, "India, Pakistan, and Kashmir: Antinomies of Nationalism," *Asian Survey* 31, no. 11 (1991): 997–1007.

9. Ganguly, *The Origins of War,* 19.

10. Devin T. Hagerty, *The Consequences of Nuclear Proliferation: Lessons from South Asia* (Cambridge: MIT Press, 1998), 67.

11. Hoffmann, *India and the China Crisis*; Manjari Chatterjee Miller, *Wronged by Empire: Post-Imperial Ideology and Foreign Policy in India and China* (Stanford: Stanford University Press, 2013)

12. John W. Garver, *Protracted Contest: Sino-Indian Rivalry in the Twentieth Century* (Seattle: University of Washington Press, 2001), 91–100.

13. Report by Lt. Gen. T. B. Henderson Brooks and Brigadier Premindra Singh Bhagat (Brooks-Bhagat Report), part I, accessed August 1, 2017, at http://www.indiandefencereview.com/wp-content/uploads/2014/03/TopSecretdocuments2.pdf.

14. The list of publications dealing with reputation in international relations is long, and indeed the concept can be traced as far back as Thucydides' treatment of the Peloponnesian War: Thucydides, *History of the Peloponnesian War,* trans. Rex Warner and M. I. Finley (Baltimore: Penguin Books, 1972). A few of the more prominent contemporary books include Robert Jervis, Richard Ned Lebow, and Janice Gross Stein, *Psychology and Deterrence* (Baltimore: Johns Hopkins University Press, 1985); Robert Powell, *Nuclear Deterrence Theory: The Search for Credibility* (Cambridge: Cambridge University Press, 1990); Robert Jervis, *The Logic of Images in International Relations* (New York: Columbia University Press, 1989); Jonathan Mercer, *Reputation and International Politics* (Ithaca, NY: Cornell University Press, 1996); Daryl G. Press, *Calculating Credibility: How Leaders Assess Military Threats* (Ithaca, NY: Cornell University Press, 2005); Joshua D. Kertzer, *Resolve in International Politics* (Princeton: Princeton University Press, 2016); Frank P. Harvey and John Mitton, *Fighting for Credibility: US Reputation and International Politics* (Toronto: University of Toronto Press, 2017). Prominent journal articles engaged with the issue have been even more numerous.

15. Barbara F. Walter, *Reputation and Civil War: Why Separatist Conflicts Are So Violent* (Cambridge: Cambridge University Press, 2009), "Building Reputation: Why Governments Fight Some Separatists But Not Others," *American Journal of Political Science* 50, no. 2 (2006): 313–330, and "Explaining the Intractability of Territorial Conflict," *International Studies Review* 4, no. 4 (2003): 137–153; Monica Duffy Toft, *The Geography of Ethnic Violence: Identity, Interests, and the Indivisibility of Territory* (Princeton: Princeton University Press, 2003), and "Indivisible Territory, Geographic Concentration, and Ethnic War," *Security Studies* 12, no. 2 (2002): 82–119.

16. Thomas C. Schelling, *Arms and Influence* (New Haven: Yale University Press, 1966), 124.

17. Raghavan's *War and Peace* is the most recent one.

NOTES TO CHAPTER 2

1. There is a voluminous literature on territorial disputes as a cause of war. This literature includes Paul F. Diehl, ed., *A Road Map to War: Territorial Dimensions of International Conflict* (Nashville, TN: Vanderbilt University Press, 1999); Paul K. Huth, *Standing Your Ground: Territorial Disputes and International Conflict* (Ann Arbor: University of Michigan

Press, 1996); Paul Domenic Senese and John A. Vasquez, *The Steps to War: An Empirical Study* (Princeton: Princeton University Press, 2008); John A. Vasquez, *The War Puzzle* (Cambridge: Cambridge University Press, 1993); John A. Vasquez, ed., *What Do We Know About War?* (Lanham, MD: Rowman & Littlefield, 2000); John A. Vasquez and Marie T. Henehan, *Territory, War, and Peace* (New York: Routledge, 2011).

2. Hein E. Goemans, *War and Punishment: The Causes of War Termination and the First World War* (Princeton: Princeton University Press, 2000), 19–52.

3. Stephen D. Krasner, *Defending the National Interest: Raw Materials Investments and U.S. Foreign Policy* (Princeton: Princeton University Press, 1978), 5–34.

4. On structural/international sources of security policy, see John J. Mearsheimer, *The Tragedy of Great Power Politics* (New York: Norton, 2001); Kenneth N. Waltz, *Theory of International Politics* (Reading, MA: Addison-Wesley, 1979). On domestic sources, see Steven R. David, *Choosing Sides: Alignment and Realignment in the Third World* (Baltimore: Johns Hopkins University Press, 1991); Mohammed Ayoob, *The Third World Security Predicament: State Making, Regional Conflict, and the International System* (Boulder, CO: Lynne Reinner, 1995).

5. This reflects the insights of neoclassical realist theory. See Steven E. Lobell, Norrin M. Ripsman, and Jeffrey W. Taliaferro, eds., *Neoclassical Realism, the State, and Foreign Policy* (Cambridge: Cambridge University Press, 2009); Gideon Rose, "Review: Neoclassical Realism and Theories of Foreign Policy," *World Politics* 51, no. 1 (1998): 144–172.

6. Frank C. Zagare, "Rationality and Deterrence," *World Politics* 42, no. 2 (1990): 270–273.

7. Mearsheimer, *Tragedy*, 31. States indeed have strong incentives to mask their motives, intentions, and interests, which is said to generate informational asymmetries. James D. Fearon, "Rationalist Explanations for War," *International Organization* 49, no. 3 (1995): 390–401.

8. Fearon, "Rationalist Explanations," 401–409; Robert Powell, "War as a Commitment Problem," *International Organization* 60, no. 1 (2006): 169–203.

9. For discussions of state assessments of long-term power dynamics in regard to potential adversaries, see Dale C. Copeland, *The Origins of Major War* (Ithaca, NY: Cornell University Press, 2000); A. F. K. Organski and Jacek Kugler, *The War Ledger* (Chicago: University of Chicago Press, 1980).

10. On the security dilemma, see John H. Herz, "Idealist Internationalism and the Security Dilemma," *World Politics* 2, no. 2 (1950): 157–180; Robert Jervis, *Perception and Misperception in International Politics* (Princeton: Princeton University Press, 1976), 58–113; Andrew H. Kydd, *Trust and Mistrust in International Relations* (Princeton: Princeton University Press, 2005); Robert Jervis, "Cooperation under the Security Dilemma," *World Politics* 30, no. 2 (1978): 167–214; Charles L. Glaser, "The Security Dilemma Revisited," *World Politics* 50, no. 1 (1997): 171–201. On the opportunity costs of conflict and forgone cooperation, also see Robert M. Axelrod, *The Evolution of Cooperation* (New York: Basic Books, 1984).

11. Joseph M. Grieco, "Anarchy and the Limits of Cooperation: A Realist Critique of the Newest Liberal Institutionalism," *International Organization* 42, no. 3 (1988): 485–507; Robert Powell, "Absolute and Relative Gains in International Relations Theory," *American Political Science Review* 85, no. 4 (1991): 1303–1320.

12. Mearsheimer, *Tragedy*, 35–40.

13. Robert J. Art, "The Fungibility of Force," in *The Use of Force: Military Power and International Politics*, ed. Robert J. Art and Kenneth Neal Waltz (Lanham, MD: Rowman & Littlefield, 2004), 6–14.

14. Powell, "War as a Commitment Problem," 176–178; Fearon, "Rationalist Explanations," 408–409.

15. Jervis, *The Logic of Images*, 3.

16. Glenn Herald Snyder and Paul Diesing, *Conflict Among Nations: Bargaining, Decision Making, and System Structure in International Crises* (Princeton: Princeton University Press, 1977), 185.

17. Jonathan Mercer, *Reputation and International Politics* (Ithaca, NY: Cornell University Press, 1996), 6–7.

18. Allan Dafoe, Jonathan Renshon, and Paul Huth, "Reputation and Status as Motives for War," *Annual Review of Political Science* 17:372; Dale C. Copeland, "Do Reputations Matter?" *Security Studies* 7, no. 1 (1997): 33–71.

19. Snyder and Diesing, *Conflict Among Nations*, 183.

20. In the past few decades, this has become the conventional wisdom on the question of reputation formation. See, for instance, Daryl G. Press, *Calculating Credibility: How Leaders Assess Military Threats* (Ithaca, NY: Cornell University Press, 2005); Mercer, *Reputation*; Ted Hopf, *Peripheral Vision: Deterrence Theory and American Foreign Policy in the Third World, 1965–1990* (Ann Arbor: University of Michigan Press, 1994). New research, however, has resuscitated the idea of reputational attributions by others being made on the basis of past behavior, through empirical findings that suggest that states that yield in disputes are more likely to be challenged in the future, and that those that stay firm are less likely to be challenged. Alex Weisiger and Keren Yarhi-Milo, "Revisiting Reputation: How Past Actions Matter in International Politics," *International Organization* 69, no. 2 (2015): 473–495. Other works that engage with this matter include Shiping Tang, "Reputation, Cult of Reputation, and International Conflict," *Security Studies* 14, no. 1 (2005): 34–62; Paul K. Huth, "Reputations and Deterrence: A Theoretical and Empirical Assessment," *Security Studies* 7, no. 1 (1997): 72–99; Paul K. Huth and Bruce Russett, "What Makes Deterrence Work? Cases from 1900 to 1980," *World Politics* 36, no. 4 (1984): 496–526; Mark J. C. Crescenzi, "Reputation and Interstate Conflict," *American Journal of Political Science* 51, no. 2 (2007): 382–396.

21. Snyder and Diesing, *Conflict Among Nations*, 187.

22. Dafoe et al., "Reputation and Status," 381.

23. Thomas C. Schelling, *Arms and Influence* (New Haven: Yale University Press, 1966), 124–125.

24. Robert Jervis, "Security Regimes," *International Organization* 36, no. 2 (1982): 367.

25. Jervis, *The Logic of Images*, 8.

26. Jonathan Renshon, Allan Dafoe, and Paul Huth, "Leader Influence and Reputation Formation in World Politics," *American Journal of Political Science* (2018), accessed February 11, 2018, at doi:10.1111/ajps.12335.

27. Snyder and Diesing, *Conflict Among Nations*, 186.

28. Jervis, "Security Regimes," 367.

29. Joe Clare and Vesna Danilovic, "Multiple Audiences and Reputation Building in International Conflict," *Journal of Conflict Resolution* 54, no. 6: 860–882.

30. Barbara F. Walter, *Reputation and Civil War: Why Separatist Conflicts Are So Violent* (Cambridge: Cambridge University Press, 2009), 20–38; Monica Duffy Toft, *The Geography of Ethnic Violence: Identity, Interests, and the Indivisibility of Territory* (Princeton: Princeton University Press, 2003), 17–33.

31. Weisiger and Yarhi-Milo, "Revisiting Reputation," 492.

32. George W. Downs and Michael A Jones, "Reputation, Compliance, and International

Law," *Journal of Legal Studies* 31, no. 1 (2002): 96. See also Beth A. Simmons, "International Law and State Behavior: Commitment and Compliance in International Monetary Affairs," *American Political Science Review* 94, no. 4 (2000): 819–835.

33. Douglas M. Gibler, "The Costs of Reneging: Reputation and Alliance Formation," *Journal of Conflict Resolution* 52, no. 3: 426–454; Mark J. C. Crescenzi et al., "Reliability, Reputation, and Alliance Formation," *International Studies Quarterly* 56, no. 2 (2012): 259–274.

34. Michael Tomz, *Reputation and International Cooperation: Sovereign Debt Across Three Centuries* (Princeton: Princeton University Press, 2007)

35. Deborah W. Larson, "Trust and Missed Opportunities in International Relations," *Political Psychology* 18, no. 3 (1997): 701–734.

36. Anne E. Sartori, *Deterrence by Diplomacy* (Princeton: Princeton University Press, 2005); Alexandra Guisinger and Alastair Smith, "Honest Threats: The Interaction of Reputation and Political Institutions in International Crises," *Journal of Conflict Resolution* 46, no. 2: 175–200.

37. Paul K. Huth, "Why Are Territorial Disputes Between States a Central Cause of International Conflict?" in *What Do We Know About War?*, ed. John A. Vasquez (Lanham, MD: Rowman & Littlefield, 2000), 104–105. See also Beth A. Simmons, "See You in Court? The Appeal to Quasi-Judicial Legal Processes in the Settlement of Territorial Disputes," in *A Road Map to War: Territorial Dimensions of International Conflict*, ed. Paul F. Diehl (Nashville, TN: Vanderbilt University Press, 1999), 205–237.

38. Snyder and Diesing identified this problem in their 1977 work, noting that the problem for states lies in the fact that "successful coercion while minimizing risk also requires avoiding provocativeness in one's threats and declarations." *Conflict Among Nations*, 218. Recent work has engaged with the phenomenon of provocation in a more rigorous theoretical manner. They include Allan Dafoe, Sophia Hatz, and Baobao Zhang, "Coercion and Provocation," unpublished manuscript, accessed August 1, 2017, at http://www.allandafoe.com/provocation.pdf; Todd Hall, "On Provocation: Outrage, International Relations, and the Franco-Prussian War," *Security Studies* 26, no. 1 (2017): 1–29; David B. Carter, "Provocation and the Strategy of Terrorist and Guerrilla Attacks," *International Organization* 70, no. 1 (Winter 2016): 133–173; Hyun-Binn Cho, "Tying the Adversary's Hands: A Model of Provocation and the Sino-India War of 1962," unpublished manuscript (March 2016).

39. For discussions of the role of reputation in the institutional fostering of cooperation, see Robert O. Keohane, *After Hegemony: Cooperation and Discord in the World Political Economy* (Princeton: Princeton University Press, 1984), 105–108.

40. Snyder and Diesing, *Conflict Among Nations*, 254.

41. This is in keeping with, for instance, Paul's finding that nuclear weapons states seek both a reputation for resolve as well as a more positive one of abiding by the tradition of nonuse. T.V. Paul, *The Tradition of Non-Use of Nuclear Weapons* (Stanford: Stanford University Press, 2009)

42. Jervis, *Perception*, 90.

43. For a discussion of these issues, see the literature on the offense-defense balance, including Stephen Van Evera, "Offense, Defense, and the Causes of War," *International Security* 22, no. 4 (Spring 1998): 5–43.

44. This is in keeping with the discussion by M. Taylor Fravel, *Strong Borders, Secure Nation: Cooperation and Conflict in China's Territorial Disputes* (Princeton: Princeton University Press, 2008), 28.

45. Huth, *Standing Your Ground*, 53–54.

46. Snyder and Diesing, *Conflict Among Nations*, 193, 248, 256–262.

47. Paul K. Huth and Bruce Russett, "Deterrence Failure and Crisis Escalation," *International Studies Quarterly* 32, no. 1 (1988): 29–45; Paul Huth, Scott Bennett, and Christopher Gelpi, "Systemic Uncertainty, Risk Propensity, and International Conflict Among the Great Powers," *Journal of Conflict Resolution* 36, no. 3 (1992): 478–517; Paul Huth, Christopher Gelpi, and Scott Bennett, "The Escalation of Great Power Militarized Disputes," *American Political Science Review* 87, no. 3 (1993): 609–623.

48. Quoted in Jervis, *Perception*, 81.

49. David Reynolds, *From World War to Cold War: Churchill, Roosevelt, and the International History of the 1940s* (London: Oxford University Press, 2006), 78.

50. Quoted in Dan Reiter, *How Wars End* (Princeton: Princeton University Press, 2009), 100.

51. Quoted in ibid., 101.

52. For a discussion of delaying strategies in territorial disputes, see Fravel, *Strong Borders*, 12–13.

53. Huth, *Standing Your Ground*, 86.

54. I. William Zartman and Jeffrey Z. Rubin, "The Study of Power and the Practice of Negotiation," in *Power and Negotiation*, ed. I. William Zartman and Jeffrey Z. Rubin (Ann Arbor: University of Michigan Press, 2000), 3. This may also tie into research on how small states sometimes prevail in wars with big adversaries. Andrew Mack, "Why Big Nations Lose Small Wars: The Politics of Asymmetric Conflict," *World Politics* 27, no. 2 (1975): 175–200.

55. I. William Zartman and Jeffrey Z. Rubin, "Symmetry and Asymmetry in Negotiation," in *Power and Negotiation*, ed. I. William Zartman and Jeffrey Z. Rubin (Ann Arbor: University of Michigan Press, 2000), 271–272.

56. Dafoe et al., "Coercion and Provocation," 1.

57. Snyder and Diesing, *Conflict Among Nations*, 195. For more discussion, see Schelling, *Arms and Influence*, 79–80; Thomas C. Schelling, *The Strategy of Conflict* (Cambridge: Harvard University Press, 1960), 21–52; Robert J. Art, "To What Ends Military Power?" *International Security* 4, no. 4 (1980): 3–35.

58. Jervis, *Perception*, 90.

59. Snyder and Diesing, *Conflict Among Nations*, 279.

60. Dafoe et al., "Coercion and Provocation," 2.

61. Jervis's seminal work, for instance, is titled *The Logic of Images*.

62. I thank Amitav Acharya for encouraging me to clarify this crucial distinction.

63. Mercer (*Reputation*, 20), for instance, argues that Morgan's contention that other states seem to care less about reputation than the United States does might be explained by the country's extended deterrence commitments. For Morgan's argument, see Patrick M. Morgan, "Saving Face for the Sake of Deterrence," in *Psychology and Deterrence*, ed. Robert Jervis, Richard Ned Lebow, and Janice Gross Stein (Baltimore: Johns Hopkins University Press, 1985), 125–152.

64. Mercer, *Reputation*, 21.

65. Barbara F. Walter, "Explaining the Intractability of Territorial Conflict," *International Studies Review* 5, no. 4 (2003): 137–153.

66. Manjari Chatterjee Miller, *Wronged by Empire: Post-Imperial Ideology and Foreign Policy in India and China* (Stanford: Stanford University Press, 2013), 25.

67. For a useful discussion, see Huth, *Standing Your Ground*, 33–68. Also see Gary Goertz

and Paul F. Diehl, *Territorial Changes and International Conflict* (London: Routledge, 1992), 132–133.

68. Scholars have identified geography as one element in determining the offense-defense balance, that is, whether offense or defense is more or less costly in particular contexts. Robert Jervis, "Cooperation," 194–199; Stephen M. Walt, *The Origins of Alliances* (Ithaca, NY: Cornell University Press, 1987), 23–25.

69. Fearon, "Rationalist Explanations," 408; Powell, "War as a Commitment Problem," 185.

70. Toft, *The Geography of Ethnic Violence*, 17–33. Mansbach and Vasquez speak similarly of "symbolic" or "transcendent" stakes associated with territory. Richard W. Mansbach and John A. Vasquez, *In Search of Theory: A New Paradigm for Global Politics* (New York: Columbia University Press, 1981), 61–67. For a general discussion of the linkages between nationalism and war, see Stephen Van Evera, "Hypotheses on Nationalism and War," *International Security* 18, no. 4 (1994): 577–592.

71. Toft, *The Geography of Ethnic Violence*, 20. Also see Ron E. Hassner, *War on Sacred Grounds* (Ithaca, NY: Cornell University Press, 2009).

72. For more on this theoretical logic, see James D. Fearon, "Domestic Political Audiences and the Escalation of International Disputes," *American Political Science Review* 88, no. 3 (1994): 577–592; Kenneth A. Schultz, "Looking for Audience Costs," *Journal of Conflict Resolution* 45, no. 1 (2001): 32–60; Stacie E. Goddard, *Indivisible Territory and the Politics of Legitimacy: Jerusalem and Northern Ireland* (Cambridge: Cambridge University Press, 2010), 15–20. On the domestic political roots of strategy in general, also see, for instance, Paul K. Huth and Todd L. Allee, *The Democratic Peace and Territorial Conflict in the Twentieth Century* (Cambridge: Cambridge University Press, 2002); Robert D. Putnam, "Diplomacy and Domestic Politics: The Logic of Two-Level Games," *International Organization* 42, no. 3 (1988): 427–460; A. Bikash Roy, "Intervention Across Bisecting Borders," *Journal of Peace Research* 34, no. 3 (1997): 300–314; Stephen M. Saideman, *The Ties That Divide: Ethnic Politics, Foreign Policy, and International Conflict* (New York: Columbia University Press, 2001).

73. For such an argument, see Taylor Fravel's explanation, which he terms a "diversionary peace" argument, for China's compromises in its territorial disputes in the 1960s and 1990s. Fravel, *Strong Borders*.

74. For a more specific argument on the diversionary motives behind war, see Jack S. Levy's discussion in "The Diversionary Theory of War: A Critique," in *Handbook of War Studies*, ed. Manus Midlarsky (Boston: Unwin Hyman, 1989), 259–288.


NOTES TO CHAPTER 3

1. V. P. Menon, *The Story of the Integration of the Indian States* (Calcutta: Orient Longmans, 1956). Also see Ramachandra Guha, *India After Gandhi: The History of the World's Largest Democracy* (New York: HarperCollins, 2007), 51–73.

2. In keeping with the general practice in the scholarship on the issue, I adopt the shorthand "Kashmir" to refer to what is technically the state of Jammu and Kashmir.

3. President Bill Clinton first used the phrase "most dangerous place on earth" for Kashmir in the aftermath of 1998 nuclear tests by India and Pakistan and the soon-to-follow Kargil War, which began after Pakistani troops and militants infiltrated into the Kargil area of Indian Kashmir. Since then, commentators such as Salman Rushdie and Pankaj Mishra have used similar terms to describe the dispute. Salman Rushdie, "The Most Dangerous Place in the World," *New York Times*, May 30, 2002, accessed August 1, 2017, at http://

www.nytimes.com/2002/05/30/opinion/the-most-dangerous-place-in-the-world.html; Pankaj Mishra, "Kashmir: 'The World's Most Dangerous Place,'" *New York Review of Books*, March 4, 2010, accessed August 1, 2017, at http://www.nybooks.com/daily/2010/03/04/kashmir-the-worlds-most-dangerous-place.

4. Some of the scholarship detailing the history and salience of Kashmir for India and Pakistan includes Sumantra Bose, *Kashmir: Roots of Conflict, Paths to Peace* (Cambridge, MA: Harvard University Press, 2003); Michael Brecher, *The Struggle for Kashmir* (New York: Oxford University Press, 1953); Sumit Ganguly, *The Origins of War in South Asia: The Indo-Pakistani Conflicts since 1947* (Boulder, CO: Westview Press, 1994); Sisir Gupta, *Kashmir: A Study in India-Pakistan Relations* (Bombay: Indian Council of World Affairs, 1967); Josef Korbel, *Danger in Kashmir* (Princeton: Princeton University Press, 1966); Alastair Lamb, *Incomplete Partition: The Genesis of the Kashmir Dispute, 1947–1948* (Karachi: Oxford University Press, 2002); T. V. Paul, *The India-Pakistan Conflict: An Enduring Rivalry* (New York: Cambridge University Press, 2005); Victoria Schofield, *Kashmir in Conflict: India, Pakistan and the Unfinished War* (New York: I. B. Tauris, 2000); Robert Wirsing, *India, Pakistan, and the Kashmir Dispute: On Regional Conflict and Its Resolution* (New York: St. Martin's Press, 1994).

5. Ganguly, *The Origins of War;* Ashutosh Varshney, "India, Pakistan, and Kashmir: Antinomies of Nationalism," *Asian Survey* 31, no. 11 (1991): 997–1019; Vali Nasr, "National Identities and the India-Pakistan Conflict," in *The India-Pakistan Conflict: An Enduring Rivalry*, ed. T. V. Paul (New York: Cambridge University Press, 2005), 178–201.

6. Nehru to Stafford Cripps (December 17/18, 1948), in *Selected Works of Jawaharlal Nehru*, Second Series [*SWJN-SS*], ed. Sarvepalli Gopal et al. (New Delhi: Jawaharlal Nehru Memorial Fund and Oxford University Press, 1984–), 8:338.

7. Nehru to Sri Prakasa (November 25, 1947), *SWJN-SS*, 4:346.

8. Brecher, *The Struggle for Kashmir*, 46.

9. Schofield, *Kashmir in Conflict*, 10.

10. Nehru to Clement Atlee (October 25, 1947), *SWJN-SS*, 4:274–275. A similar case was made at the UN by the Indian representative there, Gopalaswami Ayyangar. *Documents on Kashmir Problem,* ed. M. S. Deora and R. Grover (New Delhi: Discovery Publishing House, 1991), 1:82–83.

11. Nehru to Sheikh Abdullah (October 10, 1947), *SWJN-SS*, 4:270.

12. "Impracticability of an Independent Kashmir" (August 25, 1952), *SWJN-SS*, 19:326.

13. V. P. Menon, *The Story of the Integration of the Indian States* (Calcutta: Orient Longmans, 1956), 81.

14. Sir Reginald Coupland, quoted in Brecher, *The Struggle for Kashmir*, 20.

15. Brecher, *The Struggle for Kashmir*, 20.

16. Quoted in Sisir Gupta, *Kashmir: A Study in India-Pakistan Relations* (Bombay: Indian Council of World Affairs, 1967), 77.

17. Nehru to the Maharaja (July 4, 1947), *SWJN-SS*, 3:253.

18. See H. V. Hodson, *The Great Divide: Britain-India-Pakistan* (Karachi: Oxford University Press, 1985), 443.

19. Nehru to Patel (September, 27 1947), *SWJN-SS*, 4:264. Dwarkanath Kachru, of the All-India States People's Conference, similarly suggested that unless the Congress was able to get the Maharaja to accede to India, Kashmir would be "doomed and there will be nothing to prevent the conquest of Kashmir by the Muslim League leaders and private armies." Quoted in Schofield, *Kashmir in Conflict*, 44.

20. Lord Mountbatten, Oral History Transcript [OHT] (July 26, 1967), Nehru Memorial Museum and Library, 43.

21. Menon, *The Story of the Integration*, 394.

22. Gen. Sir Roy Bucher, OHT (May 11, 1970), 3. This is corroborated by Alan Campbell-Johnson, *Mission with Mountbatten* (London: Hale, 1951), 223. Campbell-Johnson states that the States Ministry, under Patel, had sought to ensure that nothing was done that could be seen as forcing Kashmir to accede to India and "to give assurances that accession to Pakistan would not be taken amiss by India."

23. Russell Brines, *The Indo-Pakistani Conflict* (London: Pall Mall Press, 1968), 80.

24. Brecher, *The Struggle for Kashmir*, 20.

25. Gupta, *Kashmir*, 92.

26. Ibid., 91, 97.

27. Prem Shankar Jha, *Origins of a Dispute: Kashmir 1947* (New Delhi: Oxford University Press, 2003), 45–51.

28. Nehru to Patel (September 27, 1947), *SWJN-SS*, 44:264.

29. "Solution by Referendum" (October 1, 1947), *SWJN-SS*, 44:427.

30. There is some consensus in the scholarship that the Pakistani leadership actively encouraged and supported the invaders, even though it did not do so in an official capacity. For discussions, see Ayesha Jalal, *The State of Martial Rule: The Origins of Pakistan's Political Economy of Defence* (Cambridge: Cambridge University Press, 1990), 58; Shuja Nawaz, *Crossed Swords: Pakistan, Its Army, and the Wars Within* (Karachi: Oxford University Press, 2008), 43–53. For a firsthand account, see Akbar Khan, *Raiders in Kashmir* (Islamabad: National Book Foundation, 1975).

31. Sumit Ganguly, *The Crisis in Kashmir: Portents of War, Hopes of Peace* (Cambridge Cambridge University Press, 1997), 9–10; Srinath Raghavan, *War and Peace in Modern India* (New York: Palgrave Macmillan, 2010), 107.

32. M. C. Mahajan, *Looking Back* (London: Asia Publishing House, 1963), 126–127; Schofield, *Kashmir in Conflict*, 52–53.

33. Jha, *Origins of a Dispute*, 49.

34. Mountbatten to the Maharaja (October 27, 1947), *Documents on Kashmir*, 1:16.

35. Nehru to Liaquat Ali Khan (October 28, 1947), *SWJN-SS*, 1:21; Nehru to Liaquat Ali Khan (November 8, 1947), *SWJN-SS*, 1:39.

36. Nehru to Liaquat Ali Khan (November 8, 1947), *SWJN-SS*, 4:320.

37. Raghavan, *War and Peace*, 116–117; Andrew Bingham Kennedy, *The International Ambitions of Mao and Nehru: National Efficacy Beliefs and the Making of Foreign Policy* (Cambridge: Cambridge University Press, 2011), 177.

38. Nehru to Sheikh Abdullah (October 31, 1947), *SWJN-SS*, 4:295.

39. Pakistan, and especially Jinnah, was seemingly unenthusiastic about a plebiscite as long as there was some hope of delivering a military fait accompli in Kashmir. Raghavan, *War and Peace*, 111–112.

40. "Representative of India's Address to the President of the UNSC" (January 1, 1948), *SWJN-SS*, 1:82–83, 103.

41. UN Security Council Resolution 47, "The India-Pakistan Questions" (April 21, 1948), accessed August 1, 2017, at http://www.un.org/en/ga/search/view_doc.asp?symbol = S/RES/47.

42. "Resolution Adopted by the United Nations Commission for India and Pakistan"

(August 13, 1948), accessed August 1, 2017, at https://www.mtholyoke.edu/acad/intrel/uncom1.htm.

43. Ibid. (January 9, 1949), accessed August 1, 2017, at https://www.mtholyoke.edu/acad/intrel/uncom2.htm.

44. Raghavan, *War and Peace*, 130–137.

45. Liaquat Ali Khan to Clement Atlee (November 4, 1947), *Documents on Kashmir*, 1:32.

46. Nehru to Sheikh Abdullah (August 25, 1952), *SWJN-SS*, 19:322–330. See also A. G. Noorani, "Review: How and Why Nehru and Abdullah Fell Out," *Economic and Political Weekly* 34, no. 5 (1999): 269.

47. Raghavan, *War and Peace*, 103.

48. "A Note on Kashmir" (June 17, 1947), *SWJN-SS*, 3:229.

49. Nehru to Patel (September 27, 1947), *SWJN-SS*, 4:265.

50. Sarvepalli Gopal, *Jawaharlal Nehru: A Biography* (Cambridge, MA: Harvard University Press, 1976), 2:117–127; Schofield, *Kashmir in Conflict*, 77–93.

51. Raghavan, *War and Peace*, 219–226.

52. G. S. Bajpai to V. Pandit (May 17, 1950), Vijayalakshmi Pandit Papers, first installment, subject file 56, Nehru Memorial Museum and Library [NMML]; G. S. Bajpai to V. Pandit (July 20, 1950), Vijayalakshmi Pandit Papers, first installment, subject file 56.

53. Nehru to Abdul Kalam Azad (April 25, 1952), *SWJN-SS*, 18:389.

54. Nehru to Abdul Kalam Azad. (July 19, 1953), *SWJN-SS*, 23:290.

55. "Kashmir and Other Issues" (November 3, 1951), *SWJN-SS*, 17:424.

56. Guha, *India After Gandhi*, 86.

57. Raghavan, *War and Peace*, 117.

58. Ibid., 190.

59. Nehru to Sheikh Abdullah (August 25, 1952), *SWJN-SS*, 19:323, 326.

60. Gopal, *Nehru* 2:130.

61. Nehru to B. C. Roy (June 29, 1953), *SWJN-SS*, 22:203.

62. Nehru to J. P. Narayan (July 29, 1953), *SWJN-SS*, 23:300.

63. Noorani, "Review," 270.

64. Footnote in Nehru to Rajendra Prasad (July 15, 1953), *SWJN-SS*, 23:288.

65. Nehru to Rajendra Prasad (August 9, 1953), *SWJN-SS*, 23:316.

66. Nehru to Bakshi Ghulam Mohammad (July 30, 1953), *SWJN-SS*, 23:303.

67. Nehru to Bakshi Ghulam Mohammad (August 15, 1953), *SWJN-SS*, 23:329.

68. "Conversations with Mohammad Ali" (August 17, 1953), *SWJN-SS*, 23:333, 337.

69. Nehru to Bakshi Ghulam Mohammad (August 18, 1953), *SWJN-SS*, 23:341.

70. "Conversations with Mohammad Ali" (August 20, 1953), *SWJN-SS*, 23:343.

71. Gopal, *Jawaharlal Nehru*, 2:182.

72. Nehru to Mohammad Ali (September 3, 1953), *SWJN-SS*, 23:367.

73. "The War of Ideologies in Kashmir" (November 14, 1948), *SWJN-SS*, 8:83.

74. Nehru to M. C. Mahajan (October 21, 1947 ), *SWJN-SS*, 4:273.

75. "Solution by Referendum" (October 1, 1947), *SWJN-SS*, 4:427.

76. "Nationalization of the Armed Forces" (September 16, 1947), *SWJN-SS*, 4:484.

77. Surjit Mansingh, "Nehru and Pakistan," in *Legacy of Nehru: A Centennial Celebration*, edited by D. R. SarDesai and Anand Mohan, 307–321. (Springfield, VA: Nataraj Books), 310.

78. Nehru to Sheikh Abdullah (October 10, 1947), *SWJN-SS*, 4:269. Also see Judith M. Brown, *Nehru: A Political Life* (New Haven: Yale University Press, 2003), 266.

79. Jalal, *The State of Martial Rule*, 25–48. In Pakistan, such fears were exacerbated by the

belief that India was intent on exploiting these advantages and would eventually nullify partition. Hasan Askari Rizvi, *Pakistan and the Geostrategic Environment: A Study of Foreign Policy* (London: Macmillan, 1993), 9–10; S. M. Burke, *Pakistan's Foreign Policy: An Historical Analysis* (London: Oxford University Press, 1973), 8–10; Mohammad Ayub Khan, *Friends Not Masters: A Political Autobiography* (London: Oxford University Press, 1967), 115–116.

80. Stephen P. Cohen, *The Pakistan Army* (Karachi: Oxford University Press, 1998), 6–7. For a more recent and detailed account, see C. Christine Fair, *Fighting to the End: The Pakistan Army's Way of War* (New York: Oxford University Press, 2014), 54–59.

81. From an ideological perspective too, the logic for this thinking is not difficult to fathom. Even without Kashmir, India would be home to a massive Muslim population, meaning that the loss of state was, in logical terms, much less fatal for India's secular nationalism that it would have been for Pakistan's foundational religious nationalism.

82. Gupta, *Kashmir*, 79–82.

83. Nehru to Liaquat Ali Khan (October 31, 1947), *SWJN-SS*, 4:297.

84. "Record of a Meeting Convened by Lord Mountbatten" (December 8, 1947), *SWJN-SS*, 4:365.

85. In May 1948, Raghavan reveals, Nehru had even acknowledged that while additional troops were needed in Kashmir, they could not be spared so long as there was "danger of warlike developments in Hyderabad with other consequences in other parts of the country." Nehru also believed that it would be of "tremendous advantage to us if we could satisfactorily settle with Hyderabad." Raghavan, *War and Peace*, 88. Also see Kennedy, *The International Ambitions of Mao and Nehru*, 186–196.

86. Nehru to Krishna Menon (February 16, 1948), *SWJN-SS*, 5:219.

87. Nehru to Sheikh Abdullah (August 25, 1952), *SWJN-SS*, 19:326.

88. More details on these grievances follow in the next chapter, which explains the intransigent elements of Indian policy.

89. Raghavan, *War and Peace*, 140.

90. Nehru to Patel (October 27, 1948), *SWJN-SS*, 8:285.

91. Raghavan, *War and Peace*, 190.

92. "Status of Kashmir Constituent Assembly" (September 18, 1951), *SWJN-SS*, 16, part II:296.

93. Nehru to Syama Prasad Mookerjee (January 10, 1953), *SWJN-SS*, 21:179.

94. Raghavan, *War and Peace*, 190.

95. Sunil Khilnani, *The Idea of India* (New York: Farrar, Straus and Giroux, 1997), 178.

96. Kennedy, *The International Ambitions of Mao and Nehru*, 180.

97. "Mahatma Gandhi" (October 2, 1948), *SWJN-SS*, 7:149.


NOTES TO CHAPTER 4

1. Michael Brecher, *The Struggle for Kashmir* (New York: Oxford University Press, 1953), 53–66, 89–146.

2. Nehru to Josef Korbel (August 20, 1948), in *Selected Works of Jawaharlal Nehru*, Second Series [*SWJN-SS*], ed. Sarvepalli Gopal et al. (New Delhi: Jawaharlal Nehru Memorial Fund and Oxford University Press, 1984–), 7:303; Michael Brecher, "Kashmir: A Case Study in United Nations Mediation," *Pacific Affairs* 26, no. 3 (1953): 204–207.

3. Nehru to the Indian Delegation, New York (January 9, 1953), *SWJN-SS*, 21:230.

4. Nehru to V. Pandit (November 10, 1952), *SWJN-SS*, 20:381.

5. Nehru to Gopalaswami Ayyangar (January 10, 1948), *SWJN-SS*, 5:194.

6. "General Assembly Meeting 269" (March 18, 1948), in *Documents on Kashmir Problem*, ed. M. S. Deora and R. Grover (New Delhi: Discovery Publishing House, 1991), 2:339.

7. Nehru to Patel (October 30, 1948), *SWJN-SS*, 5:43.

8. The distinction T. V. Paul makes between global superiority and local superiority is useful here in that it points to the possibility that while a country may be militarily dominant in aggregate terms, such advantages may not necessarily translate neatly into the local context. So even while a country possesses greater bargaining strength in a dispute, this may be somewhat diminished by local factors. In this view, "a challenger and a status quo power need not be relatively equal in all aspects of national power. Even if the parties do not possess parity in aggregate power terms, they may be equal in one or two crucial measures of power. For instance, the party with the weaker aggregate power may be stronger in the theater of conflict, or it may have some other logistical advantage. This may be referred to as the stronger power's global superiority but local inferiority or equality." See T. V. Paul, "Why Has the India-Pakistan Rivalry Been So Enduring? Power Asymmetry and an Intractable Conflict," *Security Studies* 15, no. 4 (October–December 2006): 606.

9. Sumit Ganguly, *The Origins of War in South Asia: The Indo-Pakistani Conflicts Since 1947* (Boulder, CO: Westview Press, 1994), 66–67; Shuja Nawaz, *Crossed Swords: Pakistan, Its Army, and the Wars Within* (Karachi: Oxford University Press, 2008), 37.

10. Nehru to Patel (September 27, 1947), *SWJN-SS*, 4:264.

11. Nehru to M. C. Setalvad (December 20, 1947), *SWJN-SS*, 4:379.

12. In the Indian subcontinental numbering system, a *lakh* refers to 100,000, whereas a *crore* refers to 10 million. "Lord Mountbatten's Record of Interview with Nehru" (March 30, 1948), *SWJN-SS*, 5:261.

13. Nehru to G. S. Bajpai (December 5, 1948), *SWJN-SS*, 8:69.

14. Nehru to Liaquat Ali Khan (October 31, 1947), *Documents on Kashmir*, 1:20; Brecher, *The Struggle for Kashmir*, 30.

15. Speech by Indian Representative at SC meeting 285 (April 19, 1948), *Documents on Kashmir*, 3:7.

16. G. S. Bajpai to V. Pandit (March 9, 1951), Vijayalakshmi Pandit Papers, first installment, subject file 56.

17. Nehru to the Maharaja (December 1, 1947), *SWJN-SS*, 4:350.

18. Nehru to Gopalaswami Ayyangar (January 25, 1948), *SWJN-SS*, 5:202; Nehru to Roy Bucher (December 23, 1948), P. N. Haksar Papers, third installment, subject file 422, NMML.

19. Nehru to Krishna Menon (August 18, 1948), *SWJN-SS*, 7:299.

20. Notes on Nehru's meeting with Dixon (August 20, 1950), *SWJN-SS*, 15, part I:214.

21. "Owen Dixon's Report" (September 30, 1950), *SWJN-SS*, 15, part I:236.

22. Srinath Raghavan, *War and Peace in Modern India* (New York: Palgrave Macmillan, 2010), 191–196.

23. At around the same time, Liaquat had told Ayub Khan, his army chief, that he was tired of Indian threats and was prepared for war with the country. Pervaiz Iqbal Cheema, *Pakistan's Defense Policy* (New York: Palgrave Macmillan, 1990), 102–103.

24. Raghavan, *War and Peace*, 212.

25. Nehru to Krishna Menon (July 22, 1951), *SWJN-SS*, 16, part II:323.

26. Raghavan, *War and Peace*, 216–217.

27. "Impracticability of an Independent Kashmir" (August 25, 1952), *SWJN-SS*, 19:325.

28. Nehru to G. S. Bajpai (February 9, 1953), *SWJN-SS*, 21:238.

29. Raghavan, *War and Peace*, 146.

30. Quoted in Brecher, *The Struggle for Kashmir*, 102.

31. Nehru to G. S. Bajpai, "Assessment of Military Situation" (February 8, 1953), *SWJN-SS*, 21:237.

32. "Foreign Policy" (March 28, 1951), *SWJN-SS*, 16, part I:518; "Kashmir—Integral Part of India" (March 28, 1951), in *Kashmir 1947–56: Excerpts from Prime Minister Nehru's Speeches* (New Delhi: Information Service of India, 1956), 25.

33. Nehru to G. S. Bajpai (February 16, 1953), *SWJN-SS*, 21:241.

34. Statement by Gopalaswami Ayyangar in SC meeting 285 (April 19, 1948), *Documents on Kashmir*, 3:17.

35. "Mediation by Owen Dixon" (August 24, 1950), *SWJN-SS*, 15, part I:227.

36. Nehru to V. Pandit (May 17, 1949), Vijayalakshmi Pandit Papers, first installment, subject file 60.

37. "Lord Mountbatten's Record of Interview with Nehru" (March 30, 1948), *SWJN-SS*, 5:261.

38. Junagadh was one of three princely states where the religion of the ruler (in this case, a Muslim) was different from that of the majority (Hindu) population. It also, in contrast to Kashmir, shared no borders with Pakistan. In keeping with Indian policy, the nawab (ruler) was offered the option of conducting a plebiscite of his people so as to determine the future of the state. The nawab, however, unilaterally declared accession to Pakistan soon after independence, which Jinnah accepted a month later. After the nawab refused to reverse the accession and agree to a plebiscite, India eventually forcibly took over the state and carried out a plebiscite in December 1947, a vote that went overwhelmingly in favor of India. For a comprehensive discussion of the case see Raghavan, *War and Peace*, 26–64.

39. Ibid., 48. Patel had similarly contended that "if India did not now support the popular demand of the people of Junagadh, there was a danger that Hyderabad would decide to accede to Pakistan" (44).

40. Nehru to Liaquat Ali Khan (October 31, 1947), *SWJN-SS*, 4:297.

41. "Record of a Meeting Convened by Lord Mountbatten" (December 8, 1947), *SWJN-SS*, 4:365.

42. Russell Brines, *The Indo-Pakistani Conflict* (London: Pall Mall Press, 1968), 92.

43. Nehru to Krishna Menon (September 8, 1949), *SWJN-SS*, 13:218.

44. Nehru to Mountbatten (December 26, 1947), *SWJN-SS*, 4:400–401 (emphasis added).

45. Ibid., 401.

46. Raghavan, *War and Peace*, 120.

47. Nehru to V. Pandit (July 2, 1949), *SWJN-SS*, 12:330.

48. "Integration of Kashmir" (May 21, 1949), *SWJN-SS*, 11:124.

49. "Foreign Policy Regarding Pakistan and Afghanistan" (June 15, 1949), *SWJN-SS*, 11:370.

50. Nehru to Krishna Menon (September 11, 1949), *SWJN-SS*, 13:226.

51. Nehru to Liaquat Ali Khan (August 4, 1951), *SWJN-SS*, 16, part II:351.

52. Nehru to M. S. Mehta (September 20, 1952), *SWJN-SS*, 19:604.

53. "Mediation by Owen Dixon" (August 24, 1950), *SWJN-SS*, 15, part I:220.

54. Ibid., 224.

55. G. S. Bajpai to V. Pandit (March 22, 1950), Vijayalakshmi Pandit Papers, first installment, subject file 56.

56. Sarvepalli Gopal, *Jawaharlal Nehru: A Biography* (Cambridge: Harvard University Press, 1976), 2:90; Raghavan, *War and Peace*, 130–138.

57. The proposal was rejected by Liaquat, who suggested that the Muslim Conference leader could not possibly be subservient to Abdullah, India's "quisling." Raghavan, *War and Peace*, 127.

58. "Message to Owen Dixon" (August 16, 1950), *SWJN-SS*, 15, part I:213.

59. Raghavan, *War and Peace*, 127.

60. Ibid., 126, 131.

61. For details on this aspect, see Andrew Bingham Kennedy, *The International Ambitions of Mao and Nehru: National Efficacy Beliefs and the Making of Foreign Policy* (Cambridge: Cambridge University Press, 2011), 188–190.

62. Ibid., 189.

63. "Impracticability of an Independent Kashmir" (August 25, 1952), *SWJN-SS*, 19:323.

64. "Kashmir and the United States" (August 10, 1949), *SWJN-SS*, 12:340–342.

65. V. Pandit to G. S. Bajpai (May 24, 1951), Vijayalakshmi Pandit Papers, first installment, subject file 56.

66. Nehru to Krishna Menon (February 20, 1948), *SWJN-SS*, 5:224.

67. Nehru to Mountbatten (July 30, 1951), *SWJN-SS*, 16, part II:340.

68. Nehru to C. C. Desai (February 27, 1955), *SWJN-SS*, 28:235.

69. Nehru to C. C. Desai (March 8, 1955), *SWJN-SS*, 28:238.

70. "Talks with Mohammad Ali and Iskander Mirza—I" (May 14, 1955), *SWJN-SS*, 28:252.

71. "Talks with Mohammad Ali and Iskander Mirza—II" (May 15, 1955), *SWJN-SS*, 28:253–254; "Talks with Mohammad Ali and Iskander Mirza—IV" (May 17, 1955), *SWJN-SS*, 28:260–262.

72. "Talks with Mohammad Ali and Iskander Mirza—IV" (May 17, 1955), *SWJN-SS*, 28:261.

73. G. B. Pant in Srinagar (July 8, 1955), T. N. Kaul Papers, I-III installment, subject file 12, NMML.

74. "Indo-Pakistan Relations" (March 24– April 3, 1956), *SWJN-SS*, 32:432.

75. Nehru to Bakshi Ghulam Mohammed (July 12, 1956), *SWJN-SS*, 34:213; Record of Nehru's talks with Mohammad Ali (July 5, 1956), *SWJN-SS*, 34:376–77.

76. "Instructions to Indian Missions Abroad" (February 27, 1957), *SWJN-SS*, 37:402; Nehru to Bakshi Ghulam Mohammad (March 13, 1957), *SWJN-SS*, 37:411

77. Nehru to J. P. Narayan (May 3, 1956), *SWJN-SS*, 33:377.

78. Robert J. McMahon, "United States Cold War Strategy in South Asia: Making a Military Commitment to Pakistan, 1947–1954," *Journal of American History* 75, no. 3 (December 1988): 812.

79. Robert J. McMahon, *The Cold War on the Periphery: The United States, India, and Pakistan* (New York: Columbia University Press, 1994), 195. The agreement brought to fruition an arrangement that Pakistan had arguably been seeking since as early as October 1947, when Karachi had requested US military aid to the tune of $170 million in a bid to bolster its defense capabilities. Anita Inder Singh, *The Limits of British Influence: South Asia and the Anglo-American Relationship, 1947–1956* (London: Pinter, 1993), 57.

80. Nehru to V. Pandit (November 13, 1952), *SWJN-SS*, 20:348; "Pakistan and MEDO" (January 15, 1953), *SWJN-SS*, 21:491.

81. Raghavan, *War and Peace*, 217–218.

82. V. Pandit to Nehru (December 1, 1953),Vijayalakshmi Pandit Papers, first installment, subject file 48.

83. Gopal, *Nehru,* 2:184.

84. Nehru to Mohammad Ali (December 18, 1953), *SWJN-SS,* 24:409.

85. "Major Issues of Foreign Policy" (December 23, 1953), *SWJN-SS,* 24:567.

86. Nehru to Mohammad Ali (November 10, 1953), *SWJN-SS,* 24:416.

87. Nehru to Mohammad Ali (March 5, 1954), *SWJN-SS,* 25:321.

88. Gopal, *Nehru,* 2:186.

89. Nehru to Bakshi Ghulam Mohammad (February 14, 1954), *SWJN-SS,* 25:313.

90. Nehru to Ali Yavar Jung (May 15, 1954), *SWJN-SS,* 25:328.

91. Record of Nehru's talks with Mohammad Ali (July 5, 1956), *SWJN-SS,* 34:377.

92. Whether the pact actually led to such an outcome is a separate question. The Pakistanis, as it turns out, were far from satisfied with both the extent of the support that Washington was offering, as well as the speed with which the promised aid was being delivered. Nevertheless, the fact that the pact did shift the balance of power somewhat over time is indisputable. What is even more important for this discussion is that Nehru and his officials perceived such a shift to be in the offing. For more on Pakistan's complaints, see McMahon, *The Cold War on the Periphery,* 189–231

93. "US Military Aid to Pakistan" (March 1, 1954), *Kashmir 1947–56,* 38–42.

94. "Practical Solution" (April 13, 1956), *Kashmir 1947,* 45–46.

95. Nehru to Mohammad Ali (December 9, 1953), *SWJN-SS,* 24:436.

96. Nehru to Mohammad Ali (March 5, 1954), *SWJN-SS,* 25:320.

97. V. Pandit to Nehru (March 22, 1956),Vijayalakshmi Pandit Papers, first installment, subject file 59.

98. Footnote in Nehru's note to Mohammad Ali (September 29, 1954), *SWJN-SS,* 26:475.

99. Judith M. Brown, *Nehru: A Political Life* (New Haven: Yale University Press, 2003), 267.

100. Nehru to Mohammad Ali (March 5, 1954), *SWJN-SS,* 25:320.

101. "India and Military Aid" (March 1, 1954), *SWJN-SS,* 25:341.

102. Chester Bowles, OHT (March 9, 1971), 15.

103. "Manufacture and Purchase of Aircrafts" (February 21, 1954), *SWJN-SS,* 25:295.

104. Nehru to Anthony Eden (March 23, 1956), *SWJN-SS,* 32:290. Despite Pakistani complaints, over time the pact did result in Pakistan receiving some $730 million worth of offensive military items, including M–47/48 Patton tanks, F–86 and F–104 fighter aircraft, and an additional $1.3 billion in logistical support systems and training programs. Raju G. C. Thomas, "Security Relationships in Southern Asia: Differences in the Indian and American Perspectives," *Asian Survey* 21, no. 7 (July 1981): 699.

105. Nehru to Krishna Menon (January 30, 1957), *SWJN-SS,* 36:358.

106. Nehru to Ghanshyamdas Birla (April 2, 1957), *SWJN-SS,* 37:391.

107. "Conversation with Christian Paul Francis Pineau" (March 11, 1956), *SWJN-SS,* 32:394.

108. Nehru to Anthony Eden (December 2, 1955), *SWJN-SS,* 31:386.

109. Gopal, *Nehru,* 2:185. For a discussion of Nehru's general opposition to entry of great powers into Asia via such collective defense pacts, see Amitav Acharya, *Whose Ideas Matter? Agency and Power in Asian Regionalism* (Ithaca, NY: Cornell University Press, 2009), 45–49.

110. "Conversation with Christian Paul Francis Pineau" (March 11, 1956), *SWJN-SS*, 32:394

111. "Need for Non-Violent Defense Techniques" (May 4, 1957), *SWJN-SS*, 38:434.

112. "World Scenario and National Security" (March 13, 1956), *SWJN-SS*, 32:497.

113. "Practical Solution" (April 13, 1956), *Kashmir 1947–56*, 46.

114. Nehru to Lady Mountbatten (December 5, 1955), *SWJN-SS*, 31:333.

115. "Talks with Mohammad Ali and Iskander Mirza—IV" (May 17, 1955), *SWJN-SS*, 28:262.

116. Nehru to Krishna Menon (December 2, 1955), *SWJN-SS*, 31:373.

117. Quoted in "Talk with Gunnar Jarring—II" (March 27, 1957), *SWJN-SS*, 37:432.

118. Nehru to Mountbatten (April 2, 1957), *SWJN-SS*, 37:563.

119. "Conversation with Selwyn Lloyd—II" (March 4, 1956), *SWJN-SS*, 32:372.

120. "A Survey of Foreign Affairs" (March 20, 1956), *SWJN-SS*, 32:506.

121. Nehru to Subhadra Joshi (May 27, 1956), *SWJN-SS*, 33:384.

122. "A 'Holding' Resolution on Kashmir" (February 16, 1957), *SWJN-SS*, 36:400.

123. Nehru to Krishna Menon (February 21, 1957), *SWJN-SS*, 36:406.

124. "K. M. Cariappa's Visit to Pakistan" (September 8, 1957), *SWJN-SS*, 39:642.

125. Nehru to V. Pandit (February 8, 1957), *SWJN-SS*, 36:367.

126. Nehru to Mountbatten (February 11, 1957), Vijayalakshmi Pandit Papers, first installment, subject file 61.

127. Nehru to Mountbatten (February 11, 1957), *SWJN-SS*, 36:383–384.

128. "On Discussions in the Security Council" (March 20, 1957), *SWJN-SS*, 37:422.

129. Nehru to V. Pandit (February 11, 1957), *SWJN-SS*, 36:385.

130. Nehru to V. Pandit (February 12, 1957), *SWJN-SS*, 36:390.

131. Ibid., 392; V. Pandit to Nehru (December 9, 1955), Vijayalakshmi Pandit Papers, first installment, subject file 59.

132. "Talk with Gunnar Jarring—III" (March 27, 957), *SWJN-SS*, 37:434.

133. Nehru to Krishna Menon (February 4, 1957), *SWJN-SS*, 36:364; V. Pandit to Nehru (March 28, 1957), Vijayalakshmi Pandit Papers, first installment, subject file 59.

134. "On International Situation—I" (March 25, 1957), *SWJN-SS*, 37:489.

135. "On International Situation—II" (March 27, 1957), *SWJN-SS*, 37:490–491.

136. Nehru to Krishna Menon (September 15, 1957), *SWJN-SS*, 39:689.

137. Gupta, *Kashmir*, 338.

138. Robert Wirsing, *Kashmir in the Shadow of War: Regional Rivalries in a Nuclear Age* (Armonk, NY: M. E. Sharpe, 2003), 203.

139. Sarvepalli Gopal, *Jawaharlal Nehru: A Biography* (Cambridge, MA: Harvard University Press, 1976), 3:84.

140. Ganguly, *The Origins of War*, 74; Gopal, *Nehru*, 3:86–87.

141. Quoted in Gopal, *Nehru*, 3:143.

142. M. J. Desai to R. Dayal (December 31, 1961), B. K. Nehru Papers, subject file 17, NMML; M. J. Desai to B. K. Nehru (January 3, 1962), B. K. Nehru Papers, subject file 17.

143. Y. D. Gundevia to Nehru (March 9, 1962), B. K. Nehru Papers, subject file 17.

144. Y. D. Gundevia to B. K. Nehru (April 11, 1962), B. K. Nehru Papers, subject file 17.

145. For in-depth looks at the origins and evolution of the Sino-Pakistani "all-weather" relationship, see Answer Hussain Syed, *China and Pakistan: Diplomacy of an Entente Cordiale* (Amherst: University of Massachusetts Press, 1974). On more recent developments, see

Andrew Small, *The China-Pakistan Axis: Asia's New Geopolitics* (New York: Oxford University Press, 2015)

146. M. J. Desai to Nehru (May 19, 1962), B. K. Nehru Papers, subject file 17.

147. Jawaharlal Nehru, *Pakistan Seeks to Profit from Chinese Aggression* (New Delhi: Government of India, Ministry of Information and Broadcasting, July 1963), 10–15, 102.

148. For the most comprehensive account of these talks to date, see Rudra Chaudhuri, *Forged in Crisis: India and the United States Since 1947* (New York: Oxford University Press, 2014), 115–148. Also see Michael Brecher, "Non-Alignment Under Stress: The West and the India-China Border War," *Pacific Affairs* 52, no. 4 (1979): 622–625.

149. Y. D. Gundevia, *Outside the Archives* (Hyderabad: Sangam Books, 1984), 260–261.

150. Gopal, *Nehru*, 3:255–258.

151. Quoted in Chaudhuri, *Forged in Crisis*, 141.


NOTES TO CHAPTER 5

1. The origins of the McMahon Line have been extensively discussed in this literature. Suffice it to say that its origins lay in a conference between representatives of British India, China, and Tibet in 1913–1914 in Shimla with the purpose of determining the frontier between Tibet and India, on the one hand, and Tibet and China, on the other. Henry McMahon, the British representative, proposed a frontier along the upper crest of the Assam Himalayas, which led to an agreement initialed by the three representatives. The agreement was immediately repudiated by the Chinese government on their representative's return, and China continued to maintain that the McMahon Line had no legal validity. For extensive discussions of the history of the Sino-Indian frontier, see, among others, Alastair Lamb, *The China-India Border: The Origins of the Disputed Boundaries* (New York: Oxford University Press, 1964), and *The McMahon Line: A Study in the Relations Between India, China, and Tibet, 1904 to 1914* (London: Routledge, 1966); and A. G. Noorani, *India-China Boundary Problem 1846–1947: History and Diplomacy* (New Delhi: Oxford University Press, 2011).

2. Steven A. Hoffmann, "Rethinking the Linkage Between Tibet and the China-India Border Conflict: A Realist Approach," *Journal of Cold War Studies* 8, no. 3 (2006): 168–170.

3. John W. Garver, *Protracted Contest: Sino-Indian Rivalry in the Twentieth Century* (Seattle: University of Washington Press, 2001), 91–100.

4. Patel to Nehru (November 7, 1950), in *Sardar Patel's Correspondence, 1945–50*, ed. Durga Das, (Ahmedabad: Navajivan Publishing House, 1971), 10:338.

5. Neville Maxwell, *India's China War* (London: Cape, 1972), 31–36.

6. Hoffmann, *India and the China Crisis*, 15.

7. Ibid., 9–12.

8. Garver, *Protracted Contest*, 88.

9. Prithwis Chandra Chakravarti, *India's China Policy* (Bloomington: Indiana University Press, 1962); Margaret W. Fisher, Leo E. Rose, and Robert A. Huttenback, *Himalayan Battleground: Sino-Indian Rivalry in Ladakh* (New York: Praeger, 1963). A more recent such account can be found in Sarvepalli Gopal, *Jawaharlal Nehru: A Biography* (Cambridge, MA: Harvard University Press, 1976), vol. 2.

10. Chakravarti, *India's China Policy*, 52–74; Ashok Kapur, *India: From Regional to World Power* (London: Routledge, 2006), 41–44; Paul F. Power, "Indian Foreign Policy: The Age of Nehru," *Review of Politics* 26, no. 2 (1964): 80–81.

11. Quoted in Gopal, *Nehru* 3:223.

12. Maxwell, *India's China War*; Neville Maxwell, "Sino-Indian Border Dispute Reconsidered," *Economic and Political Weekly* 34, no. 15 (1999): 905–918. Also see Noorani, *India-China Boundary Problem*.

13. Srinath Raghavan, *War and Peace in Modern India* (New York: Palgrave Macmillan, 2010), and "Sino-Indian Boundary Dispute, 1948–60: A Reappraisal," *Economic and Political Weekly* 41, no. 36 (2006): 3882–3892; K. Subrahmanyam, "Nehru and the India-China Conflict of 1962," in *Indian Foreign Policy: The Nehru Years*, ed. B. R. Nanda (New Delhi: Vikas, 1975), 102–130.

14. Hoffmann, *India and the China Crisis*, 25–28; Manjari Chatterjee Miller, *Wronged by Empire: Post-Imperial Ideology and Foreign Policy in India and China* (Stanford: Stanford University Press, 2013).

15. Miller, *Wronged by Empire*, 30.

16. For an overview of the debates in the Indian parliament on the issue, see Nancy Jetly, *India China Relations, 1947–1977: A Study of Parliament's Role in the Making of Foreign Policy* (New Delhi: Radiant Publishers, 1979).

17. It is worth noting that in the eastern sector, British policy at the time of decolonization was that "the Government of India stand by the McMahon Line and will not tolerate incursion into India. . . . They would however at all times be prepared to discuss in a friendly way with China and Tibet any rectification of the frontier that might be urged on reasonable grounds by any of the parties to the abortive Simla Conference of 1914." Raghavan, *War and Peace*, 230.

18. Quoted in Chakravarti, *India's China Policy*, 12.

19. Noorani, *India-China Boundary Problem,* 210–218; Raghavan, *War and Peace*, 228–235.

20. Nehru to John Matthai (September, 10, 1949), in *Selected Works of Jawaharlal Nehru, Second Series* [*SWJN-SS*], ed. Sarvepalli Gopal et al. (New Delhi: Jawaharlal Nehru Memorial Fund and Oxford University Press, 1984–), 13:260.

21. "The Indian Mission in Lhasa" (July 9, 1949), *SWJN-SS*, 12:410. Nehru was responding to notes by K. P. S. Menon and Bajpai, the former suggesting continued military and moral support for any Tibetan resistance and the latter precautionary measures on the frontier.

22. Nehru to C. P. N. Singh (September 10, 1949), *SWJN-SS*, 13:258; Nehru to Krishna Menon (August 18, 1950), *SWJN-SS*, 15, part I:429.

23. "India's Policies" (December 6, 1950), *SWJN-SS*, 15, part II:433.

24. Patel to Nehru (November 7, 1950), in *Sardar Patel's Correspondence*, 10:336.

25. Quoted in Raghavan, *War and Peace*, 237.

26. Quoted in ibid., 230–231.

27. G. S. Bajpai to V. Pandit (September 10, 1950), Vijayalakshmi Pandit Papers, first installment, subject file 56.

28. "Policy Regarding Tibet and China" (November 18, 1950), *SWJN-SS*, 15, part II:344.

29. G. S. Bajpai to V. Pandit (August 21, 1950), Vijayalakshmi Pandit Papers, first installment, subject file 56.

30. "Recent Developments in East and Southeast Asia" (November 8, 1950), *SWJN-SS*, 15, part II:409. Also, Maxwell, *India's China War*, 69; Hugh E. Richardson, *Tibet and Its History* (London: Oxford University Press, 1962), 114.

31. Nehru to Panikkar (October 25, 1950), *SWJN-SS*, 15, part I:442.

32. Quoted in Andrew Bingham Kennedy, *The International Ambitions of Mao and Nehru: National Efficacy Beliefs and the Making of Foreign Policy* (Cambridge: Cambridge University Press, 2011), 221.

33. "The Indo-Tibetan Boundary" (November 22, 1950), *SWJN-SS*, 15, part II:348.

34. "Recent Developments in East and Southeast Asia" (November 8, 1950), *SWJN-SS*, 15, part II:409.

35. Raghavan, *War and Peace*, 235–236.

36. "North-Eastern Frontier Situation" (March 5, 1953), *SWJN-SS*, 21:555–558; Nehru to B. Medhi (July 20, 1953), *SWJN-SS*, 23:228; Nehru to Durgabai Deshmukh (September 16, 1953), *SWJN-SS*, 23:234; "Friendly Policy towards China" (October 25, 1953), *SWJN-SS*, 24:597.

37. Hoffmann, *India and the China Crisis*, 24–31.

38. Raghavan, *War and Peace*, 235; Maxwell, *India's China War*, 42, 73.

39. Nehru to K. M. Panikkar (April 12, 1952), *SWJN-SS*, 18:471 and (May 24, 1952), *SWJN-SS*, 18:473.

40. Hoffmann, *India and the China Crisis*, 32.

41. Nehru to Thakin Nu (February 8, 1951), *SWJN-SS*, 15, part II:549. Nu was known honorifically as U Nu or Thakin Nu.

42. "Relations with China and Tibet" (November 3, 1951), *SWJN-SS*, 17:507.

43. Note from Panikkar of September 28, 1951, quoted in Gopal, *Nehru*, 2:177.

44. Nehru to K. M. Panikkar (April 12, 1952), *SWJN-SS*, 18:471. K. P. S. Menon, similarly believed China was being "cunning" and suggested that the government "firmly adhere to our decision that any such proposal . . . can only be considered as part of a general settlement on Tibet." Quoted in Raghavan, *War and Peace*, 236–237.

45. Nehru to K. M. Panikkar (May 24, 1952), *SWJN-SS*, 18:473.

46. Nehru to K. M. Panikkar (June 16, 1952), *SWJN-SS*, 18:474–475.

47. Nehru to K. M. Panikkar (June 18, 1952), *SWJN-SS*, 18:475.

48. "On the Truce Talks" (July 25, 1952), *SWJN-SS*, 19:585.

49. "Border Issue with China" (July 29, 1952), *SWJN-SS*, 19:651.

50. "A Realistic Approach to Problems" (December 24, 1953), *SWJN-SS*, 24:577.

51. "The Beijing Conference" (December 3, 1953), *SWJN-SS*, 24:598–599; Nehru to B. K. Gokhale (December 21, 1953), *SWJN-SS*, 24:589.

52. "Coordination between India and Bhutan" (January 30, 1954), *SWJN-SS*, 24:593; "Future Negotiations with China" (May 12, 1954), *SWJN-SS*, 25:470.

53. Kennedy, *The International Ambitions of Mao and Nehru*, 223.

54. Gopal, *Nehru*, 2:181.

55. "Tibet and the Frontier with China" (July 1, 1954), *SWJN-SS*, 26:482–483; Gopal, *Nehru*, 3:33.

56. "Foreign Policies of America and China" (October 20, 1954), *SWJN-SS*, 27:20.

57. Hoffmann, *India and the China Crisis*, 35; Noorani, *India-China Boundary*, 224–225.

58. Raghavan, *War and Peace*, 239.

59. B. N. Mullik, *My Years with Nehru: The Chinese Betrayal* (New Delhi: Allied Publishers, 1971), 196–199.

60. Noorani, *India-China Boundary*, 220–221.

61. Subrahmanyam, "Nehru and the India–China Conflict," 112.

62. "The Indian Mission in Lhasa" (July 9, 1949), *SWJN-SS*, 12, 410.

63. "The Threat from Tibet" (October 5, 1951), *SWJN-SS*, 16, part 2:560.

64. "The Indo-Tibetan Frontier Issue" (December 24, 1953), *SWJN-SS*, 24:581–583.

65. "Talks with John Foster Dulles" (May 22, 1953), *SWJN-SS*, 22:511. On the KMT

intervention in Burma, see Robert H. Taylor, *Foreign and Domestic Consequences of the KMT Intervention in Burma* (Ithaca, NY: Southeast Asia Program, Cornell University, 1973).

66. "War and Peace" (October 23, 1954), *SWJN-SS*, 27:40.

67. The Chinese, Nehru noted, were "realists." "India and Indonesia" (June 28, 1949), *SWJN-SS*, 12:371. See also "The Asian Situation" (December 14, 1948), *SWJN-SS*, 7:329; Nehru to V. Pandit (July 19, 1949), *SWJN-SS*, 12:389; "Letters to Premiers of Provinces" (April 1, 1949), *SWJN-SS*, 12:307.

68. Nehru to B. N. Rau (September 25, 1949 ), *SWJN-SS*, 13:269; "Record of Conversation with US delegation to the UN" (October 19, 1949), *SWJN-SS*, 13:308–309.

69. "Preventing the Drift to Disaster" (December 7, 1950), *SWJN-SS*, 15, part II:438.

70. Nehru to M. S. Mehta (September 20, 1952), *SWJN-SS*, 19, part I:603.

71. "North-Eastern Frontier Situation" (March 5, 1953), *SWJN-SS*, 21, 558.

72. "Closer Indo-US Relations" (September 15, 1951), *SWJN-SS*, 16, part II:628. For a detailed discussion of Nehru's strategy of engaging China in hopes of making it a "responsible Asian power and player," see Amitav Acharya, *East of India, South of China: Sino-Indian Encounters in Southeast Asia* (New Delhi: Oxford University Press, 2017), 96–105. For an early account of Bandung, also see George McTurnan Kahin, *The Asian-African Conference, Bandung, Indonesia, April 1955* (Ithaca, NY: Cornell University Press, 1956).

73. Quoted in Chester Bowles, OHT, 2–3. Also see "Talks with the American Ambassador" (May 5, 1955), *SWJN-SS*, 28:283; "Conversation with Amir Faisal" (May 5, 1955), *SWJN-SS*, 28:225.

74. "India and the World Situation" (May 4, 1956), *SWJN-SS*, 33:8.

75. Raghavan, *War and Peace*, 239.

76. Bajpai, on the other hand, was of the opinion that it was clear that the Chinese, having never accepted the boundary, would raise the issue only when it served their convenience. Therefore, India ought to simply inform China that it regarded the McMahon Line as the border. Maxwell, *India's China War*, 77–78.

77. As early as 1949, Nehru had acknowledged to colleagues that regardless of what they might desire, there was little India could practically do to resist Chinese entry into Tibet. Nehru to John Matthai (September 10, 1949), *SWJN-SS*, 13:260. For Nehru, this meant that a nonhostile approach on the issue was best, both to preserve India's interests in, and to ensure maximal autonomy for, the region. "Policy Regarding China and Tibet" (November 18, 1950), *SWJN-SS*, 15, part II:342–347.

78. Speech in Rajya Sabha (December 8, 1959), *Prime Minister on Sino-Indian Relations: In Parliament* (New Delhi: External Publicity Division of Ministry of External Affairs, Government of India, 1962), 250.

79. Subimal Dutt to Nehru (November 24, 1959), Subimal Dutt Papers, subject file 39, NMML.

80. R. K. Nehru, OHT, 17–18.

81. Apa Pant, quoted in Raghavan, *War and Peace*, 244.

82. Gopal, *Nehru*, 2:227.

83. Kennedy, *The International Ambitions of Mao and Nehru*, 217.

84. Nehru to Thakin Nu (January 7, 1950), *SWJN-SS*, 14, part I:504.

85. Nehru to C. Rajagopalachari (November 1, 1950), *SWJN-SS*, 15, part II:336.

86. Nehru to B. C. Roy (November 15, 1950), *SWJN-SS*, 15, part II:341.

87. Nehru to V. Pandit (November 1, 1950), Vijayalakshmi Pandit Papers, first installment, subject file 60.

88. "Changing Situation in Afro-Asian Countries" (January 3, 1953), *SWJN-SS*, 21:469–471.

89. Gopal, *Nehru*, 2:230.

90. "Prime Minister's Secretariat" (September 15, 1951), Vijayalakshmi Pandit Papers, first installment, subject file 56.

91. "Dynamics of India's International Relations" (June 17, 1953), *SWJN-SS*, 22:519.

92. Mullik, *My Years with Nehru*, 78. Also see B. R. Nanda, "Introduction," in *Indian Foreign Policy: The Nehru Years*, ed. B. R. Nanda (New Delhi: Radiant, 1990), 16–17.

93. Furthermore, while he had sought to be sympathetic to China, Nehru conceded that "latterly I have been unable to appreciate it fully." Nehru to K. M. Panikkar (October 25, 1950), *SWJN-SS*, 15, part I:439–442.

94. "Cable to Indian Mission—Lhasa" (September 6, 1952), *SWJN-SS*, 19, part I:652.

95. Quoted in Raghavan, *War and Peace*, 233.

96. "A World Overburdened with Fear, Anger and Hatred" (March 17, 1953), *SWJN-SS*, 21:484.

97. Nehru to N. Raghavan (December 10, 1952), *SWJN-SS*, 20:488. Emphasis added.

98. Ibid.

99. Quoted in Gopal, *Nehru*, 2:148.

100. Quoted in Subrahmanyam, "Nehru and the India-China Conflict," 107.

101. Nehru to Thakin Nu (March 6, 1953), *SWJN-SS*, 21:535.

102. The five principles of peaceful coexistence agreed to by India and China at the end of their talks over Tibet in 1954 were mutual respect for each other's territorial integrity and sovereignty, mutual nonaggression, mutual noninterference in each other's internal affairs, equality and mutual benefit, and peaceful coexistence. Michael Arndt, *India's Foreign Policy and Regional Multilateralism* (Basingstoke: Palgrave Macmillan, 2013), 33.

103. Nehru to K. K. Chettur (May 9, 1954), *SWJN-SS*, 25:479.

104. Quoted in Raghavan, *War and Peace*, 241.

105. Nehru to K. K. Chettur (May 9, 1954).

106. Nehru to U Nu (May 29, 1954), *SWJN-SS*, 25:480.

107. "Tibet and China" (June 18, 1954), *SWJN-SS*, 26:477–478.

108. Interestingly, even the Americans seemed to have formed an impression during this period, as Dulles would convey in a note to his president, that a friendly approach to India was in order since Nehru had become increasingly more disconcerted about China's growing strength and its policies. John Foster Dulles—Memorandum to the President (November 30, 1954), T. N. Kaul Papers, I–III installment, subject file 13.

NOTES TO CHAPTER 6

1. Sarvepalli Gopal, *Jawaharlal Nehru: A Biography* (Cambridge, MA: Harvard University Press, 1976), 3:39.

2. "Chinese Maps of the Frontier with India" (May 6, 1956), in *Selected Works of Jawaharlal Nehru*, Second Series [*SWJN-SS*], ed. Sarvepalli Gopal et al. (New Delhi: Jawaharlal Nehru Memorial Fund and Oxford University Press, 1984–), 33:476.

3. Apa Pant to T. N. Kaul (May 1, 1956), Apa Pant Papers, subject file 3, NMML.

4. "Countering Chinese Moves on the Frontier" (May 12, 1956), *SWJN-SS*, 33:477–478.

5. "Chinese Incursions into Myanmar" (August 26, 1956), *SWJN-SS*, 34:385–386; "China-Myanmar Border Dispute" (September 1, 1956), *SWJN-SS*, 35:506.

6. Nehru to R. K. Nehru (September 16, 1956), *SWJN-SS*, 35:513.

7. "India-China Boundary Question" (September 7, 1956), *SWJN-SS*, 35:514. Nehru's exact words were that making the issue public could "come in the way of our taking this matter up more formally later with the Chinese government."

8. "Talks with Zhou Enlai—I" (December 31, 1956), *SWJN-SS*, 36:600. To U Nu, Nehru again noted that Zhou had indeed confirmed that China accepted the McMahon Line, though he did not agree with the justness of the Indian claim or with the name attached to the line. In order to satisfy himself of what had been said, Nehru had asked Zhou the question again, and the premier had repeated the Chinese position explicitly. Nehru to U Nu (April 22, 1957), *SWJN-SS*, 37:507–508.

9. Nehru to U Nu (April 22, 1957), *SWJN-SS*, 37:507–508.

10. Steven A. Hoffmann, *India and the China Crisis* (Berkeley: University of California Press, 1990), 35–36. That India had little interest or presence in the area until this point is apparent from the fact that New Delhi only learned about the highway from Indian embassy officials in China who had read about its impending opening to traffic in a Chinese newspaper. Subimal Dutt, *With Nehru in the Foreign Office* (Calcutta: Minerva Associates, 1977), 117.

11. Indian note (October 18, 1958), in *Notes, Memoranda and Letters Exchanged and Agreements Signed between the Governments of India and China* (New Delhi: Ministry of External Affairs, Government of India, 1959–1968), White Paper (hereafter cited as White Paper), 1:26–27.

12. Indian note (December 14, 1958), White Paper, 1:51.

13. Chinese note (January 23, 1959), White Paper, 1:53–54. In response, Nehru tried to demonstrate and assert the validity of the frontiers as they had been shown in Indian maps. Indian note (March 22, 1959), White Paper, 1:55–57.

14. Hoffmann, *India and the China Crisis*, 59–70.

15. Chinese note (September 8, 1959), White Paper, 2:27–33.

16. Gopal, *Nehru*, 3:206; Hoffmann, *India and the China Crisis*, 71.

17. Maxwell, *India's China War*, 122.

18. Chakravarti, *India's China Policy* (Bloomington: Indiana University Press, 1962), 94–95.

19. Raghavan, *War and Peace*, 252.

20. Indian note (February 5, 1960), White Paper, 3:80–81, and (February 12, 1960), White Paper, 3:82–95.

21. Chinese note (November 7, 1959), White Paper, 3:44–45.

22. Indian note (November 16, 1959), White Paper, 3:49.

23. Hoffmann, *India and the China Crisis*, 81; Raghavan, *War and Peace*, 260.

24. Indian note (November 16, 1959), White Paper, 3:48–50.

25. Gopal, *Nehru*, 3:96; Hoffmann, *India and the China Crisis*, 73.

26. Chinese note (December 17, 1959), White Paper, 3:52–53.

27. Hoffmann, *India and the China Crisis*, 85.

28. S. Dutt, address to conference of governors (October 28, 1959), Subimal Dutt Papers, subject file 109.

29. G. Parthasarathy to S. Dutt (April 5, 1960), P. N. Haksar Papers, I–II installment, subject file 25.

30. S. Dutt to Indian Missions (April 27, 1960), P. N. Haksar Papers, I–II installment, subject file 25.

31. Ibid.

32. R. K. Nehru, OHT, 30.

33. A. G. Noorani, *India-China Boundary Problem, 1846–1947: History and Diplomacy* (New Delhi: Oxford University Press, 2011), 227–228.

34. Speech in Rajya Sabha (February 20, 1961), *in Prime Minister on Sino-Indian Relations in Parliament* (New Delhi: External Publicity Division of External Affairs, Government of India, 1962), 1:383.

35. Indian note (March 13, 1962), White Paper, 6:17–19, and (April 30, 1962), White Paper, 6:32–36.

36. Indian note (May 14, 1962), White Paper, 6:43.

37. Raghavan, *War and Peace*, 283–284.

38. Ibid., 290–292; Allen Suess Whiting, *The Chinese Calculus of Deterrence: India and Indochina* (Ann Arbor: University of Michigan Press, 1975), 84–91.

39. Speech in Lok Sabha (February 23, 1961), *PM on Sino-Indian Relations*, 385–386.

40. S. Dutt to Nehru (February 3, 1958), Subimal Dutt Papers, subject file 31.

41. B. N. Mullik, *My Years with Nehru: The Chinese Betrayal* (New Delhi: Allied Publishers, 1971), 240.

42. S. Dutt to Joint Secretary (E) (September 23, 1958), Subimal Dutt Papers, subject file 33.

43. S. Dutt to Nehru (November 18, 1958), Subimal Dutt Papers, subject file 34.

44. The Macartney-McDonald compromise line was the only one that was ever formally offered to the Chinese by the British, in 1899. Maxwell, *India's China War*, 31–35, 85.

45. Mullik, *My Years with Nehru*, 203–206.

46. Ibid., 201.

47. Quoted in Raghavan, *War and Peace*, 240.

48. Indian note (November 8, 1958), White Paper, 1:29.

49. Speech in Rajya Sabha (September 10, 1959), *PM on Sino-Indian Relations*, 134.

50. Speech in Lok Sabha (August 18, 1959), in *PM on Sino-Indian Relations*, 80, and (November 19, 1959), in *PM on Sino-Indian Relations*, 153.

51. Speech in Rajya Sabha (August 31, 1959), in *PM on Sino-Indian Relations*, 98.

52. Speech in Rajya Sabha (September 4, 1959), in *PM on Sino-Indian Relations*, 119.

53. Speech in Rajya Sabha (September 12, 1959), in *PM on Sino-Indian Relations*, 148–149.

54. Speech in Rajya Sabha (April 29, 1960), in *PM on Sino-Indian Relations*, 342.

55. R. K. Nehru, OHT, 29–30.

56. Quoted in Raghavan, *War and Peace*, 261.

57. Judith M. Brown, *Nehru: A Political Life* (New Haven: Yale University Press, 2003), 270.

58. "The Position of China" (July 2, 1956), *SWJN-SS*, 34:250; "India and the World Situation" (May 4, 1956), *SWJN-SS*, 33:8.

59. Nehru to K. N. Katju (July 28, 1956), *SWJN-SS*, 34:203.

60. "Recent Developments in Tibet and Their Effects on the Security of India and Her Border States and on Their Trade with Tibet" (n.d.), Apa Pant Papers, subject file 3.

61. "China, Tibet and South-East Asia" (June 28, 1957), *SWJN-SS*, 38:612.

62. Nehru to Sampurnanand (May 14, 1957), *SWJN-SS*, 38:689–690.

63. Nehru to U Nu (April 22, 1957), *SWJN-SS*, 37:507–508; Nehru to R. K. Nehru (July 15, 1957), *SWJN-SS*, 38:693.

64. S. Dutt to Nehru (February 24, 1955), Subimal Dutt Papers, subject file 31.

65. Dutt, *With Nehru*, 117.

66. Dawa Norbu, "Tibet in Sino-Indian Relations: The Centrality of Marginality," *Asian Survey* 37, no. 11 (1997): 1080–1082.

67. Quoted in Chakravarti, *India's China Policy*, 105.

68. Record of meeting between Nehru and Zhou (April 20, 1960), P. N. Haksar Papers, I–II installment, subject file 24. India's home minister at the time similarly asserted during his talks with Zhou and Chen Yi that the "1954 agreement clearly implies that there was no border problem between India and China." Record of meeting of G. B. Pant with Zhou and Chen Yi (April 21, 1960), P. N. Haksar Papers, I-II installment, subject file 26.

69. Indian note (November 4, 1959), White Paper, 2:20.

70. Maxwell, *India's China War*, 100.

71. Ali Yavar Jung, note on interview with President Tito at Brioni, June 9, 1958, Subimal Dutt Papers, subject file 32.

72. Nehru to S. Dutt (June 15, 1958), Subimal Dutt Papers, subject file 32.

73. Dutt revealed that the Sikkim royal family was receiving clear overtures from the Chinese to shift their allegiance away from India to Tibet (and thereby China), with which Sikkim had more in common culturally. S. Dutt to Secretary, Ministry of Commerce and Industry (June 25, 1958), Subimal Dutt Papers, subject file 32.

74. According to Apa Pant, the Chinese had reportedly told the Dalai Lama that "though India and China were friends American and British imperialists were 'influencing Pandit Nehru' and that they could not be too careful when they are dealing with India as they were afraid that 'Nehru may side with the imperialist.'" Apa Pant report on visit to Tibet (November 28, 1957), Apa Pant Papers, subject file 5.

75. Speech in Lok Sabha (March 23, 1959), in *PM on Sino-Indian Relations*, 33.

76. Speech in Rajya Sabha (September 10, 1959), in *PM on Sino-Indian Relations*, 139–141.

77. Speech in Rajya Sabha (December 8, 1959), in *PM on Sino-Indian Relations*, 240.

78. Speech in Lok Sabha (March 17, 1960), in *PM on Sino-Indian Relations*, 323.

79. Speech in Lok Sabha (November 27, 1959), in *PM on Sino-Indian Relations*, 214.

80. Speech in Lok Sabha (November 25, 1959), in *PM on Sino-Indian Relations*, 188.

81. Nehru to V. Pandit (April 15, 1959), Vijayalakshmi Pandit Papers, first installment, subject file 61.

82. Speech in Rajya Sabha (September 12, 1959), in *PM on Sino-Indian Relations*, 153.

83. Quoted in Raghavan, *War and Peace*, 257.

84. Speech in Lok Sabha (September 4, 1959), in *PM on Sino-Indian Relations*, 117.

85. Gopal, *Nehru*, 3:91.

86. Speech in Rajya Sabha (December 8, 1959), in *PM on Sino-Indian Relations*, 244–246.

87. Speech in Rajya Sabha, 244.

88. Speech in Lok Sabha (November 23, 1960), in *PM on Sino-Indian Relations*, 369.

89. Mullik, *My Years with Nehru*, 187.

90. Speech in Rajya Sabha (September 12, 1959), in *PM on Sino-Indian Relations*, 147–148.

91. Gopal, *Nehru*, 3:98.

92. S. Dutt address to Conference of Governors (October 28, 1959), Subimal Dutt Papers, subject file 109.

93. Yaacov Vertzberger, *Misperceptions in Foreign Policymaking: The Sino-Indian Conflict, 1959–1962* (Boulder, CO: Westview Press, 1984), 151–156. According to Vertzberger, with regard to the McMahon Line, India also drew the opposite conclusions to what China in-

tended from its territorial agreements with Burma and Nepal by construing such concessions as further validating India's legal position.

94. Maxwell, *India's China War*, 119–120.

95. S. Dutt to Joint Secretary (E) (October 7, 1959), Subimal Dutt Papers, subject file 38.

96. Hoffmann, *India and the China Crisis*, 83.

97. Gopal, *Nehru*, 3:134.

98. The Indian officials' report later in 1960 added to Nehru's conviction about India's case, leading him to conclude that he could not "conceive of their [China] having read this and not having felt that their position was a weak one." Quoted in Maxwell, *India's China War*, 218.

99. S. Dutt to R. Dayal (April 26, 1960), P. N. Haksar Papers, I–II installment, subject file 25.

100. S. Dutt to Nehru (June 12, 1958), P. N. Haksar Papers, I–II installment, subject file 32.

101. S. Dutt to Nehru (October 8, 1958), P. N. Haksar Papers, I–II installment, subject file 33.

102. S. Dutt to Nehru (June 3, 1958), P. N. Haksar Papers, I–II installment, subject file 25.

103. Dutt, *With Nehru in the Foreign Office*, 131.

104. Quoted in Raghavan, *War and Peace*, 263.

105. Dutt, *With Nehru in the Foreign Office*, 131–132. Such fears were exacerbated later in 1960 when in the meetings of officials over the boundary issue, the Chinese delegation claimed territory in Ladakh beyond claim lines presented by Zhou in 1956. See Dutt, *With Nehru in the Foreign Office*, and also Nehru's statement in Rajya Sabha (February 20, 1961), in *PM on Sino-Indian Relations*, 381.

106. Speech in Lok Sabha (April 1, 1961), in *PM on Sino-Indian Relations*, 390.

107. Quoted in Raghavan, *War and Peace*, 264.

108. G. Parthasarathy to S. Dutt (March 27, 1960), P. N. Haksar Papers, I–II installment, subject file 25.

109. R. K. Nehru, OHT, 28–30. Additionally, Dutt would let it be known that if the Chinese did not relent in the face of Indian arguments, "our officials will also have to take a more or less similar attitude." S. Dutt to Nehru (April 29, 1960), Subimal Dutt Papers, subject file 42.

110. Raghavan, *War and Peace*, 262–264.

111. S. Dutt to Nehru (May 27, 1960), Subimal Dutt Papers, subject file 42.

112. S. Dutt to Director (N) (May 29, 1960), Subimal Dutt Papers, subject file 43.

113. Hoffmann, *India and the China Crisis*, 97.

114. Minutes and details of meeting from Maxwell, *India's China War*, 221.

115. Russell Brines, *The Indo-Pakistani Conflict* (London: Pall Mall Press, 1968), 190–191.

116. Maxwell, *India's China War*, 292.

117. Hoffmann, *India and the China Crisis*, 104–106.

118. Whiting, *The Chinese Calculus*, 77–78.

119. Bruce Riedel, *JFK's Forgotten Crisis: Tibet, the CIA, and the Sino-Indian War* (Washington, DC: Brookings Institution, 2015), 122–123.

120. Raghavan, *War and Peace*, 270–271.

121. For a detailed discussion, see D. K. Palit, *War in the High Himalaya: Indian Army in Crisis, 1962* (London: Hurst, 1991), 79–83.

122. Hoffmann, *India and the China Crisis*, 98.

123. Quoted in Maxwell, *India's China War*, 254.

124. Quoted in Raghavan, *War and Peace*, 269.

125. Report by Lieutenant General T.B. Henderson Brooks and Brigadier Premindra Singh Bhagat (Brooks-Bhagat Report), part I, 15, accessed August 1, 2017, at http://www .indiandefencereview.com/wp-content/uploads/2014/03/TopSecretdocuments2.pdf. Emphasis added.

126. Maxwell, *India's China War*, 129.

127. Ibid., 174.

128. J. P. Dalvi, *Himalayan Blunder* (Bombay: Thacker and Co., 1966), 68.

129. Raghavan, *War and Peace*, 276; Whiting, *The Chinese Calculus*, 40.

130. Lt. Gen. B. M. Kaul, OHT (January 13, 1972), 144–145.

131. Quoted in Maxwell, *India's China War*, 254.

132. Raghavan, *War and Peace*, 257.

133. Quoted in Hoffmann, *India and the China Crisis*, 96.

134. Palit, *War the High Himalaya*, 97.

135. Raghavan, *War and Peace*, 276.

136. For details of both cases, see Palit, *War in the High Himalaya*, 173–179; Raghavan, *War and Peace*, 286–287.

137. Gopal, *Nehru*, 3:211.

138. Kaul, OHT, 146.

139. Quoted in Gopal, *Nehru*, 3:202.

140. Palit, *War in High Himalaya*, 188–191.

141. Raghavan, *War and Peace*, 294–295.

142. Palit, *War in the High Himalaya*, 213.

143. Lt. Gen. Brij Mohan Kaul, *The Untold Story* (Bombay: Allied Publishers, 1967), 367–368. Emphasis in original.

144. Riedel, *JFK's Forgotten Crisis*, 113.

145. Quoted in Raghavan, *War and Peace*, 278.

146. Mullik, *My Years with Nehru*, 186–188.

147. Kaul, *Untold Story*, 339.

148. John Kenneth Galbraith, *Ambassador's Journal: A Personal Account of the Kennedy Years* (London: Hamish Hamilton, 1969), 376–403.

149. Quoted in Andrew Bingham Kennedy, *The International Ambitions of Mao and Nehru: National Efficacy Beliefs and the Making of Foreign Policy* (Cambridge: Cambridge University Press, 2011), 231–232.

150. Quoted in Raghavan, *War and Peace*, 280.

151. Brooks-Bhagat Report, part 1, 42–43.

152. Xu Yan, cited in Thomas J. Christensen, "Windows and War: Trend Analysis and Beijing's Use of Force," in *New Directions in the Study of China's Foreign Policy*, ed. Alastair I. Johnston and Robert S. Ross (Stanford: Stanford University Press, 2006), 64.

153. For an official Indian history of the war, see P. B. Sinha and A. A. Athale, *History of the Conflict with China, 1962* (New Delhi: Government of India, Ministry of Defense, 1992). On the initiation of the Chinese offensive, see pp. 101–104.

154. Quoted in Maxwell, *India's China War*, 374.

155. Ramachandra Guha, *India After Gandhi: The History of the World's Largest Democracy* (New York: HarperCollins, 2007), 339.

156. Quoted in Sankar Ghose, *Jawaharlal Nehru: A Biography* (New Delhi: Allied Publishers, 1993), 298.

157. Brown, *Nehru*, 260–261; Kingsley Martin and Dorothy Woodman, OHT (August 8, 1967), 32–33.

158. Hoffmann, *India and the China Crisis*, 67–68; Maxwell, *India's China War*, 115–116; Vertzberger, *Misperceptions*, 65–68, 138–147.

159. Raghavan, *War and Peace*, 253.

160. Quoted in Michael Brecher, *India and World Politics: Krishna Menon's View of the World* (London: Oxford University Press, 1968), 40. R. K. Nehru has similarly pointed to Nehru's belief that "public opinion would not accept a settlement at present." R. K. Nehru, OHT, 38. For K. P. S. Menon, "It is possible that a solution might have been reached on these lines [Zhou's package deal]. . . . But Jawaharlal Nehru did not assert himself vis-a-vis Parliament and vis-a-vis what we regard as public opinion." K.P.S. Menon, OHT (September 30, 1981), 21–22.

161. Quoted in Hoffmann, *India and the China Crisis*, 86.

162. According to Hoffmann, any tendencies that the India leadership had toward compromising on claims in the Aksai Chin were lost by China's "failing to recognize a moment of opportunity, and by occupying the Western Sector territory pre-emptively." Hoffmann, *India and the China Crisis*, 112. Maxwell similarly suggests that if Zhou had brought up the Aksai Chin issue during talks in 1956, Nehru might have been prepared to compromise, "which was definitely not possible once China had built a road and committed a perceived aggression." Maxwell, *India's China War*, 93.

163. Maxwell, *India's China War*, 134.

164. Noorani, *India-China Boundary*, 230.

165. While the Congress itself held massive majorities in parliament, none of the opposition parties could garner enough seats (50 out of 518 in the fifth Lok Sabha) to count as the official opposition. Of these opposition parties, the largest was often the Communist Party, which remained the most sympathetic to the Chinese viewpoint in parliamentary debates. Nancy Jetly, *India China Relations, 1947–1977: A Study of Parliament's Role in the Making of Foreign Policy* (New Delhi: Radiant Publishers, 1979), 8. Garver postulates that "had Nehru accepted Zhou's 1960 offer . . . he [Nehru] could very probably have carried Indian public opinion with him—and avoided war." John W. Garver, "China's Decision for War with India in 1962," in *New Directions in the Study of China's Foreign Policy*, ed. Alastair I. Johnston and Robert S. Ross (Stanford: Stanford University Press, 2006), 105. Maxwell suggests similarly that while public pressures were immense, they only cemented a position that Nehru had already adopted, and that he could have carried parliament with him if he had really chosen an alternative path. Maxwell, *India's China War*, 152–153.

166. Speech in Rajya Sabha (December 8, 1959), in *PM on Sino-Indian Relations*, 239.

167. Speech in Lok Sabha (November 27, 1959), in *PM on Sino-Indian Relations*, 213–216.

168. Nehru to U Nu (September 4, 1956), *SWJN-SS*, 35:509.

169. Walter R. Crocker, *Nehru: A Contemporary's Estimate* (London: Allen & Unwin, 1966), 105.

170. Indian note (August 28, 1959), White Paper, 1:44.

171. Quoted in Maxwell, *India's China War*, 127.

172. Nehru now also floated the idea of sending the dispute to arbitration at the International Court of Justice, provided that the Chinese withdraw to positions as they existed before 8 September. Jetly, *India China Relations*, 191–197.

173. Gopal, *Nehru*, 3:234.

174. Jawaharlal Nehru, *Pakistan Seeks to Profit from Chinese Aggression* (New Delhi: Government of India, Ministry of Information and Broadcasting, July 1963), 4.

175. Quoted in Brines, *The Indo-Pakistani Conflict*, 196.

NOTES TO CHAPTER 7

1. M. Taylor Fravel, *Strong Borders, Secure Nation: Cooperation and Conflict in China's Territorial Disputes* (Princeton: Princeton University Press, 2008); Eric A. Hyer, *The Pragmatic Dragon: China's Grand Strategy and Boundary Settlements* (Vancouver: University of British Columbia Press, 2015).

2. Hyer, *The Pragmatic Dragon*, 4.

3. Fravel, *Strong Borders*, 41–51; John W. Garver, *Protracted Contest: Sino-Indian Rivalry in the Twentieth Century* (Seattle: University of Washington Press, 2001), 80–88. China's frontier disputes in general average 4.5 on a 12–point salience scale. Paul Hensel and Sara Mitchell, "Issue Indivisibility and Territorial Claims," *GeoJournal* 64, no. 4 (2005): 278.

4. The fact that, as Hyer notes, the Chinese did not publicize some of these settlements "for fear of undermining the Communist Party's role as an uncompromising defender of Chinese sovereignty against imperial encroachment" suggests some salience to the disputed territory. Hyer, *The Pragmatic Dragon*, 7; see pp. 24–30 for detailed discussion of these claims. For discussions of the importance of history to Chinese foreign policy, also see Michael H. Hunt, "Chinese Foreign Relations in Historical Perspective," in *China's Foreign Relations in the 1980s*, ed. Harry Harding (New Haven: Yale University Press, 1984), 1–42; John K. Fairbank, "China's Foreign Policy in Historical Perspective," *Foreign Affairs* 47, no. 3 (April 1969): 449–463.

5. Quoted in Allen S. Whiting, *The Chinese Calculus of Deterrence: India and Indochina* (Ann Arbor: University of Michigan Press, 1975), 7.

6. John Rowland, *A History of Sino-Indian Relations: Hostile Co-Existence* (Princeton: Van Nostrand, 1967), 53.

7. Chinese note (September 8, 1959), in *Notes, Memoranda and Letters Exchanged and Agreements Signed between the Governments of India and China* (New Delhi: Ministry of External Affairs, Government of India, 1959–1968), White Paper, 2:27 (hereafter cited as White Paper).

8. Record of meeting between Nehru and Zhou (April 22, 1960), P. N. Haksar Papers, I–II installment, subject file 24.

9. Manjari Chatterjee Miller, *Wronged by Empire: Post-Imperial Ideology and Foreign Policy in India and China* (Stanford: Stanford University Press, 2013), 63.

10. For a discussion of this belief in the efficacy of the military instrument, see Andrew Bingham Kennedy, *The International Ambitions of Mao and Nehru: National Efficacy Beliefs and the Making of Foreign Policy* (Cambridge: Cambridge University Press, 2011). Also see the chapter on the Korean War in T. V. Paul, *Asymmetric Conflicts: War Initiation by Weaker Powers* (Cambridge: Cambridge University Press, 1994), 86–106. For the cultural roots of such beliefs, see Alastair Johnston's classic work, *Cultural Realism: Strategic Culture and Grand Strategy in Chinese History* (Princeton: Princeton University Press, 1998).

11. For more on this, see the later discussion of the important works by Fravel and Hyer on China's territorial concessions during this period.

12. On the Sino-Soviet split, see Lorenz M. Lüthi, *The Sino-Soviet Split: Cold War in the Communist World* (Princeton: Princeton University Press, 2008).

13. This was in keeping with Chinese policy in all of its frontier disputes during this period, choosing to defer opening up the territorial question even when others had sought to bring it up. Fravel, *Strong Borders*, 71.

14. Quoted in Sarvepalli Gopal, *Jawaharlal Nehru: A Biography* (Cambridge, MA: Harvard University Press, 1976), 2:177.

15. Nehru to K. M. Panikkar (June 16, 1952), in *Selected Works of Jawaharlal Nehru*, Second Series [*SWJN-SS*], ed. Sarvepalli Gopal et al. (New Delhi: Jawaharlal Nehru Memorial Fund and Oxford University Press, 1984–), 18:474–475.

16. "Relations with China and Tibet" (November 3, 1951), *SWJN-SS*, 17:507.

17. "Foreign Policies of America and China" (October 20, 1954), *SWJN-SS*, 27:14–20.

18. "Tibet and the Frontier with China" (July 1, 1954), *SWJN-SS*, 26:482–483. Also see Steven A. Hoffmann, *India and the China Crisis* (Berkeley: University of California Press, 1990), 35; A. G. Noorani, *India-China Boundary Problem, 1846–1947: History and Diplomacy* (New Delhi: Oxford University Press, 2011), 223–224.

19. Fravel, *Strong Borders*, 48–50, 72–75.

20. Garver, *Protracted Contest*, 85–86.

21. Whiting, *The Chinese Calculus*, 8–9.

22. Garver, *Protracted Contest*, 46–47; Nancy Jetly, *India China Relations, 1947–1977: A Study of Parliament's Role in the Making of Foreign Policy* (New Delhi: Radiant Publishers, 1979), 15–17. For an account for foreign activities in Tibet over the first decade of Chinese Communist rule, see A. Tom Grunfeld, *The Making of Modern Tibet* (Armonk, NY: M. E. Sharpe, 1996), 82–106, 151–165.

23. For a detailed discussion of this period, see Shakya Tsering, *The Dragon in the Land of Snows: A History of Modern Tibet Since 1947* (New York: Penguin Compass, 2000), 33–130.

24. Jetly, *India China Relations,* 38.

25. Garver, *Protracted Contest*, 28.

26. Chinese note (January 23, 1959), White Paper, 1:53.

27. Neville Maxwell, *India's China War* (London: Cape, 1972), 81–82.

28. Ibid., 81–82, 92–93.

29. "Talks with Zhou Enlai—I" (December 31, 1956, and January 1, 1957), *SWJN-SS*, 36:600.

30. "Talks with Zhou Enlai—III" (December 31, 1956, and January 1, 1957), *SWJN-SS*, 36:614–616.

31. Dawa Norbu, "Tibet in Sino-Indian Relations: The Centrality of Marginality," *Asian Survey* 37, no. 11 (1997): 1080–1082.

32. Chinese note (January 23, 1959), White Paper, 1:53.

33. Chinese note (September 8, 1959), White Paper, 2:27.

34. Chinese note (November 7, 1959), White Paper, 3:46.

35. Chinese note (December 17, 1959), White Paper, 3:52–57.

36. Noorani, *India-China Boundary*, 227–228.

37. Quoted in Eric Hyer, "The Strategic and Regional Contexts of the Sino-Indian Border Conflict," in *The Sino-Indian War of 1962: New Perspectives*, ed. Amit Das Gupta and Lorenz M. Lüthi (London: Routledge, 2017), 90.

38. Quoted in Fravel, *Strong Borders*, 85.

39. Fravel, *Strong Borders*, 95–96, 100–101.

40. Arthur S. Lall, *The Emergence of Modern India* (New York: Columbia University Press, 1981), 156.

41. For the most detailed account on the domestic dimensions, see Fravel's work cited previously. For article length treatments, see M. Taylor Fravel, "Regime Security and International Cooperation: Explaining China's Compromises in Territorial Disputes," *International Security* 30, no. 2 (2005): 46–83, and "Power Shifts and Escalation: Explaining China's Use of Force in Territorial Disputes," *International Security* 32, no. 3 (2008): 44–83. Also see Chien-Peng Chung, *Domestic Politics, International Bargaining and China's Territorial Disputes* (London: Routledge, 2004); Dai Chaowu, "From 'Hindi-Chini Bhai Bhai' to 'International Class Struggle' Against Nehru: China's India Policy and the Frontier Dispute, 1950–62," in *The Sino-Indian War of 1962: New Perspectives*, ed. Amit Das Gupta and Lorenz M. Lüthi (London: Routledge, 2017), 68–84. For an argument emphasizing the international context see Eric Hyer's work cited previously.

42. Shakya Tsering, *The Dragon in the Land of Snows: A History of Modern Tibet Since 1947* (New York: Penguin Compass, 2000), 201–203.

43. Maxwell, *India's China War*, 104.

44. Nehru to Apa Pant (July 11, 1958), Apa Pant Papers, subject file 6.

45. John W. Garver, "China's Decision for War with India in 1962." In *New Directions in the Study of China's Foreign Policy*, edited by Alastair I. Johnston and Robert S. Ross (Stanford: Stanford University Press, 2006), 94–95.

46. Quoted in Garver, *Protracted Contest*, 62.

47. Chaowu, "From 'Hindi-Chini Bhai-Bhai,'" 72, 76.

48. Chinese note (8 September 1959), White Paper, 2:27–33.

49. Record of meeting between Nehru and Zhou (April 20, 1960), P. N. Haksar Papers, I–II installment, subject file 24. In the same discussion, Zhou complained that "the activities of Dalai Lama and his followers have far exceeded the limits of political asylum."

50. Record of meeting between R. K. Nehru and Zhou (April 20, 1960), P. N. Haksar Papers, I–II installment, subject file 26.

51. Quoted in Garver, *Protracted Contest*, 59.

52. Hyer, "The Strategic and Regional Contexts," 85–86.

53. Bruce Riedel, *JFK's Forgotten Crisis: Tibet, the CIA, and the Sino-Indian War* (Washington, DC: Brookings Institution Press, 2015), 100–101.

54. Allen S. Whiting, "Chinese Behavior Towards India: 1962," *First Sino-American Conference on Mainland China* 22 (1971): 15.

55. Fravel, *Strong Borders*, 70–125, provides details of Chinese thinking along these lines in all of its border disputes in the 1960s.

56. Hyer "The Strategic and Regional Contexts," 86.

57. Fravel, *Strong Borders*, 84.

58. Garver, *Protracted Contest*, 116.

59. Prithwis Chandra Chakravarti, *India's China Policy* (Bloomington: Indiana University Press, 1962), 154–155.

60. Kennedy, *The International Ambitions of Mao and Nehru*, 43–67.

61. Fravel, *Strong Borders*, 85–86; also see 71–72.

62. Record of meeting between Sardar Swaran Singh and Marshal Chen Yi (April 23, 1960), P. N. Haksar Papers, I–II installment, subject file 26.

63. Indian Embassy in Beijing to S. Dutt (April 27, 1960), P. N. Haksar Papers, I–II installment, subject file 25.

64. For details of these compromises, see Fravel, *Strong Borders*. For more on the Sino-Pak border negotiations, see Nasim Ahmed, "China's Himalayan Frontiers: Pakistan's At-

titude," *International Affairs* 38, no. 4 (1962): 478–484; Alastair Lamb, "The Sino-Pakistani Boundary Agreement of 2 March 1963," *Australian Outlook* 18, no. 3 (1964): 299–312; and Rudra Chaudhuri, "The Making of an 'All Weather Friendship': Pakistan, China and the History of a Border Agreement: 1949–1963," *International History Review* (March 2017): 1–24, accessed August 1, 2017, at doi:10.1080/07075332.2017.1298529. On the nature of the Sino-Burmese dispute, also see Harold C. Hinton, *China's Relations with Burma and Vietnam: A Brief Survey* (New York: Institute of Pacific Relations, 1958), 40–45; J. R. V. Prescott, *Map of Mainland Asia by Treaty* (Carlton: Melbourne University Press, 1975), 347–353; Richard J. Kozicki, "The Sino-Burmese Frontier Problem," *Far Eastern Survey* 26, no. 3 (1957): 33–38. Such a policy also tied into the Chinese government's broader efforts after the Bandung conference in 1955 to use generous foreign aid to build up relations in the African and Asian developing world. Between 1956–1965, China promised $942 million in foreign aid to eighteen countries, a startling amount considering that the Chinese themselves were hugely dependent on support from the Soviet Union. See Miller, *Wronged by Empire*, 71.

65. Arthur S. Lall, *How Communist China Negotiates* (New York: Columbia University Press, 1968), 188.

66. Neville Maxwell, "China and India: The Un-Negotiated Dispute," *China Quarterly* 43 (1970): 53, and "Sino-Indian Border Dispute Reconsidered," *Economic and Political Weekly* 34, no. 15 (1999): 905–906.

67. Daphne E. Whittam, "The Sino-Burmese Boundary Treaty," *Pacific Affairs* 34, no. 2 (1961): 182.

68. Lall, *How Communist China Negotiates*, 186

69. The other two principles involved acknowledging that the border disputes were a consequence of imperialism and that negotiations should proceed on the basis of existing boundary agreements, even if they had been imposed on China in the past. Hyer, "The Strategic and Regional Contexts," 91.

70. Lall, *How Communist China Negotiates*, 199.

71. Quoted in Russell Brines, *The Indo-Pakistani Conflict* (London: Pall Mall Press, 1968), 198.

72. Quoted in Fravel, *Strong Border*, 88.

73. Record of meeting between Nehru and Zhou (April 20, 1960), P. N. Haksar Papers, I–II installment, subject file 24.

74. Record of meeting between Sardar Swaran Singh and Marshal Chen Yi (April 23, 1960), P. N. Haksar Papers, I–II installment, subject file 26.

75. Record of meeting between Sardar Swaran Singh and Marshal Chen Yi (April 22, 1960), P. N. Haksar Papers, I–II installment, subject file 26.

76. Chinese note (May 31, 962), White Paper, 6:101.

77. Quoted in Hyer, "The Strategic and Regional Contexts," 92.

78. Record of meeting between Nehru and Zhou (April 20, 1960), P. N. Haksar Papers, I–II installment, subject file 26.

79. Record of Indian Vice President's discussion with Zhou and Chen Yi (April 21, 1960), P. N. Haksar Papers, I–II installment, subject file 26.

80. Chinese note (December 17, 1959), White Paper, 3:52–53.

81. Chinese note (May 4, 1961), White Paper, 6:57.

82. Chinese note (May 11, 1962), White Paper, 6:200.

83. Garver, *Protracted Contest*, 91.

84. Record of meeting between Sardar Swaran Singh and Marshal Chen Yi (April 22, 1960), P. N. Haksar Papers, I–II installment, subject file 26.

85. All of this Indian nibbling was happening as internal troubles in China were being compounded as the failure of the Great Leap Forward became apparent, and unrest was brewing in Xinjiang while Beijing was still engaged in ending the rebellion in Tibet. External actors, moreover, were seemingly intent on exploiting China's misfortunes, with the Taiwanese and Americans strongly suspected of planning an assault on the mainland. Relations with Moscow seemed to be deteriorating rapidly as well, all of which reinforced China's sense of growing encirclement. In the frontier region itself, the economic travails, and especially food shortages affecting the troops and their families in other parts of China, were directly manifesting themselves on the PLA troops' morale and efficiency. Fravel, *Strong Borders*, 176–177; Whiting, *The Chinese Calculus*, 12–41.

86. Quoted in Fravel, *Strong Borders*, 175.

87. Chinese note (November 2, 1961), White Paper, 6:1–2.

88. Chinese note (November 30, 1961), White Paper, 6:4.

89. Chinese note (March 1, 1962), White Paper, 6:14.

90. Fravel, *Strong Borders*, 184–185.

91. Chinese note (July 16, 1962), White Paper, 6:91.

92. Chinese note (September 13, 1962), White Paper, 7:73.

93. Ibid., 68.

94. Hoffmann, *India and the China Crisis*, 130–141; Maxwell, *India's China War*, 294–300.

95. Quoted in Raghavan, *War and Peace*, 301.

96. Quoted in Garver, "China's Decision," 39.

97. Quotes in Fravel, *Strong Borders*, 190–197.

98. For an extended discussion of this aspect, see Whiting, *The Chinese Calculus*, 114–169.

99. Quoted in Hyun-Binn Cho, "Tying the Adversary's Hands: A Model of Provocation and the Sino-India War of 1962" (unpublished manuscript, March 2016), 29.

100. Quoted in ibid., 29–30.

101. Quoted in ibid., 31.

102. Chinese note (October 3, 1962), White Paper, 7:97.

103. Whiting, *The Chinese Calculus*, 116–117.

104. Indian note (October 27, 1962), White Paper, 7:4–5.

105. Chinese note (November 7, 1962), White Paper 8:7–11.

106. Whiting, *The Chinese Calculus*, 142–143.

107. The Washington-Moscow face-off in previous months had diverted much of the international attention from the Sino-Indian conflict and also forced the Soviets to reassess earlier moves at getting closer to India and to reiterate their commitment to their Communist brethren, thereby allowing an opening for Beijing to exploit in initiating war. Khrushchev had also consequently decided to delay the previously promised shipment of MiG-21s to India. Raghavan, *War and Peace*, 302–303.

108. For a detailed look at diplomatic moves in India-US relations during this crisis, see Chaudhuri, *Forged in Crisis*, 81–113.

109. Margaret Macmillan, *Nixon and Mao: The Week That Changed the World* (New York: Random House, 2008), 238.

110. Dai, "From 'Hindi-Chini Bhai-Bhai,'" 79.

NOTES TO CHAPTER 8

1. For the classic exposition of this logic, see James D. Fearon, "Signaling Foreign Policy Interests: Tying Hands Versus Sinking Costs," *Journal of Conflict Resolution* 41, no. 1 (February 1997): 68–90.

2. On rivalries, see among others, Paul F. Diehl and Gary Goertz, *War and Peace in International Rivalry* (Ann Arbor: University of Michigan Press, 2000); Michael P. Colaresi, *Scare Tactics: The Politics of International Rivalry* (Syracuse: Syracuse University Press, 2005); and Karen A. Rasler and William R. Thompson, "Contested Territory, Strategic Rivalries, and Conflict Escalation," *International Studies Quarterly* 50, no. 1 (2006): 145–168.

3. This is akin to Jervis's "security dilemma" or "spiral" model of the descent to conflict. See Robert Jervis, *Perception and Misperception in International Politics* (Princeton: Princeton University Press, 1976), 58–113.

4. Dorothy Woodman, *The Making of Burma* (London: Cresset Press, 1962), 534–535. Even the concession that Burma was willing to make (three villages in the Hpimaw area) was based on an acceptance that the Chinese claims there were strong. This was confirmed by the Indian Historical Division, which attested that even the British had conceded Chinese claims to the territory. Nehru to U Nu (May 14, 1957), in *Selected Works of Jawaharlal Nehru*, Second Series [*SWJN-SS*], ed. Sarvepalli Gopal et al. (New Delhi: Jawaharlal Nehru Memorial Fund and Oxford University Press, 1984–) 38:728.

5. Quoted in Leo E. Rose, *Nepal: Strategy for Survival* (Berkeley: University of California Press, 1971), 225.

6. S. Dutt to Nehru (October 19, 1959), Subimal Dutt Papers, subject file 4.

7. Rose, *Nepal*, 238. Mahindra would state the hope that "there will be no chance for any unfriendly behavior calculated to spoil our good relations" on China's part. Quoted in S. D. Muni, *Foreign Policy of Nepal* (Delhi: National Publishing House, 1973), 120.

8. Quoted in Rose, *Nepal*, 238.

9. "India, Bangladesh Ratify Historic Land Deal, Narendra Modi Announces New $2 Billion Line of Credit to Dhaka," *Times of India*, June 6, 2015, accessed August 1, 2017, at http://timesofindia.indiatimes.com/india/India-Bangladesh-ratify-historic-land-deal-Narendra-Modi-announces-new-2-billion-line-of-credit-to-Dhaka/articleshow/47567164.cms.

10. Sourabh Gupta, "India and Bangladesh: Calculus of Territorial Dispute Settlement," *East Asia Forum*, October 20, 2011, accessed August 1, 2017, at http://www.eastasiaforum.org/2011/10/10/india-and-bangladesh-calculus-of-territorial-dispute-settlement/. For a discussion of the problems that have historically bedeviled India's relations with Bangladesh, see Harsh V. Pant, "India and Bangladesh: Will the Twain Ever Meet?" *Asian Survey* 47, no. 2 (2007): 231–249.

11. Named after I. K. Gujral who was first foreign minister and then prime minister of India between 1996–1998.

12. For the earliest exposition of the Gujral Doctrine, see Bhabani Sen Gupta, "India in the Twenty-First Century," *International Affairs* 73, no. 2: 307–311.

13. For more details on the history of Naga separatism and India's other troubles in the northeast see Subir Bhaumik, *Troubled Periphery: Crisis of India's North East* (New Delhi: Sage, 2009).

14. Nehru to Bisnuram Medhi (May 13, 1956), *SWJN-SS*, 33:172–173.

15. Nehru to Fazl Ali (September 9, 1956), *SWJN-SS*, 35:136.

16. "Military Aspect Essential at Present" (May 23, 1955), *SWJN-SS*, 33:183.

17. "The Naga Resistance and the Government Actions" (May 30, 1956), 33:189.

18. Nehru to G. B. Pant (December 13, 1956), *SWJN-SS*, 36:236.

19. Nehru to Fazl Ali (January 22, 1957), *SWJN-SS*, 36:242. See also Nehru to Fazl Ali (February 24, 1957), *SWJN-SS*, 37:246.

20. Nehru to Fazl Ali (March 3, 1957), *SWJN-SS*, 37:251.

21. "Necessity of Withdrawing the Army" (May 23, 1957), *SWJN-SS*, 38:259.

22. "Dealing with the Tribal Areas" (July 23, 1957), *SWJN-SS*, 38:267.

23. In Pakistan, for instance, educational curricula have been used to serve the purpose of myth creation. Stephen P. Cohen, *The Idea of Pakistan* (Washington, DC: Brookings Institution Press, 2004), 67–68, 101, 107. For a discussion on how the 1962 war is remembered in India, see Jabin T. Jacob, "Remembering 1962 in India, 50 Years On," in *The Sino-Indian War of 1962: New Perspectives*, ed. Amit Das Gupta and Lorenz M. Lüthi (London: Routledge, 2017), 233–252.

24. Such an argument for the Kashmir case is made, for instance, by Robert Wirsing, *Kashmir in the Shadow of War: Regional Rivalries in a Nuclear Age* (Armonk, NY: M. E. Sharpe, 2003), 219–223. Ganguly and Bajpai have similarly pointed to there being "no sign that any Indian leader or party today has the courage and persuasive powers to change the public's mind." Sumit Ganguly and Kanti Bajpai, "India and the Crisis in Kashmir," *Asian Survey* 34, no. 5 (1994): 413.

25. Such an argument is also in keeping with findings that hawkish political leaders in general find it easier to make peace. See Kenneth A. Schultz, "The Politics of Risking Peace: Do Hawks or Doves Deliver the Olive Branch?" *International Organization* 50, no. 1: 1–38.

26. Wirsing, *Kashmir in the Shadow of War*, 35.

27. These back-channel talks are recounted in detail in Steve Coll, "The Back Channel: India and Pakistan's Secret Kashmir Talks," *New Yorker*, March 2, 2009, accessed August 1, 2017, at http://www.newyorker.com/magazine/2009/03/02/the-back-channel.

28. The earliest explicit exploration of such an option arguably happened at American and British insistence as early as 1963. See Rudra Chaudhuri, *Forged in Crisis: India and the United States Since 1947* (New York: Oxford University Press, 201), 137–140.

29. For discussions of the varied dimensions of the enduring rivalry dynamics of the India-Pakistan conflict, see T. V. Paul, ed., *The India-Pakistan Conflict: An Enduring Rivalry* (New York: Cambridge University Press, 2005).

30. For the text of agreement, see "Agreement Between the Government of the Republic of India and the Government of the People's Republic of China on the Political Parameters and Guiding Principles for the Settlement of the India-China Boundary Question," April 11, 2005, accessed August 2, 2017, at http://www.mea.gov.in/bilateral-documents.htm?dtl/6534/Agreement+between+the+Government+of+the+Republic+of+India+and+the+Government+of+the+Peoples+Republic+of+China+on+the+Political+Parameters+and+Guiding+Principles+for+the+Settlement+of+the+IndiaChina+Boundary+Question.

31. One these developments, see Waheguru Pal Singh Sidhu and Jing-Dong Yuan, "Resolving the Sino-Indian Border Dispute: Building Confidence Through Cooperative Monitoring," *Asian Survey* 41, no. 2 (2001): 351–376.

32. For discussions of the contemporary sources of the rivalry, see, for instance, Harsh V. Pant, *The Rise of China: Implications for India* (New Delhi: Foundation Books, 2012); Jeff M. Smith, *Cold Peace: China-India Rivalry in the Twenty-First Century* (Lanham, MD: Lexington

Books, 2014); and C. Raja Mohan, *Samudra Manthan: Sino-Indian Rivalry in the Indo-Pacific* (Washington, DC: Carnegie Endowment for International Peace, 2012).

33. The most recent instance of this was former State Councilor Dai Bingguo's assertion that "the major reason the boundary question persists is that China's reasonable requests [in the east, specifically with regard to Tawang] have not been met." Mohan Guruswamy, "Sino-Indian Border Dispute: New Package Deal Floated by Former Chinese Negotiator Is No Deal at All," *Scroll.in*, March 15, 2017, accessed August 2, 2017, at https://scroll.in/article/830978/sino-indian-border-dispute-new-package-deal-floated-by-former-chinese-negotiator-is-no-deal-at-all.

34. David Shambaugh, *China Goes Global: The Partial Power* (New York: Oxford University Press, 2013); Patryk Kugiel, *India's Soft Power: A New Foreign Policy Strategy* (New York: Routledge, 2017). China's assertion in the early 2000s of its desire to rise peacefully similarly fit into this pattern. Zheng Bijian, "China's 'Peaceful Rise' to Great-Power Status," *Foreign Affairs* 84, no. 5 (2005): 18–24; Yong Deng, "Reputation and the Security Dilemma: China Reacts to the China Threat Theory," in *New Directions in the Study of China's Foreign Policy*, ed. Alastair I. Johnston and Robert S. Ross (Stanford: Stanford University Press, 2006), 186–216. China's recent assertiveness in the region has significantly undermined this narrative.

# Bibliography


UNPUBLISHED SOURCES

Bowles, Chester. Oral history transcript. Nehru Memorial Museum and Library, New Delhi.
Bucher, Gen. Sir Roy. Oral history transcript. Nehru Memorial Museum and Library, New Delhi.
Dutt, Subimal. Papers. Nehru Memorial Museum and Library, New Delhi.
Haksar, P. N. Papers. Nehru Memorial Museum and Library, New Delhi.
Kaul, Lt. Gen. B. M. Oral history transcript. Nehru Memorial Museum and Library, New Delhi.
Kaul, T. N. Papers. Nehru Memorial Museum and Library, New Delhi.
Martin, Kingsley, and Dorothy Woodman. Oral history transcript. Nehru Memorial Museum and Library, New Delhi.
Menon, K. P. S. Oral history transcript. Nehru Memorial Museum and Library, New Delhi.
Mountbatten, Lord. Oral history transcript. Nehru Memorial Museum and Library, New Delhi.
Nehru B. K. Papers. Nehru Memorial Museum and Library, New Delhi.
Nehru, R. K. Oral history transcript. Nehru Memorial Museum and Library, New Delhi.
Pandit, Vijayalakshmi. Papers. Nehru Memorial Museum and Library, New Delhi.
Pant, Apa. Papers. Nehru Memorial Museum and Library, New Delhi.

PUBLISHED SOURCES

Acharya, Amitav. *East of India, South of China: Sino-Indian Encounters in Southeast Asia*. New Delhi: Oxford University Press, 2017.
———. *Whose Ideas Matter? Agency and Power in Asian Regionalism*. Ithaca, NY: Cornell University Press, 2009.

"Agreement Between the Government of the Republic of India and the Government of the People's Republic of China on the Political Parameters and Guiding Principles for the Settlement of the India-China Boundary Question." April 11, 2005. Accessed August 2, 2017, at http://www.mea.gov.in/bilateral-documents.htm?dtl/6534/Agreement+between+the+Government+of+the+Republic+of+India+and+the+Government+of+the+Peoples+Republic+of+China+on+the+Political+Parameters+and+Guiding+Principles+for+the+Settlement+of+the+IndiaChina+Boundary+Question.

Ahmed, Nasim. "China's Himalayan Frontiers: Pakistan's Attitude." *International Affairs* 38, no. 4 (1962): 478–484.

Art, Robert J. "The Fungibility of Force." In *The Use of Force: Military Power and International Politics*, edited by Robert J. Art and Kenneth Neal Waltz, 3–22. Lanham, MD: Rowman & Littlefield, 2004.

———. "To What Ends Military Power?" *International Security* 4, no. 4 (1980): 3–35.

Art, Robert J., and Kenneth N. Waltz, eds. *The Use of Force: Military Power and International Politics*. Lanham, MD: Rowman & Littlefield, 2004.

Axelrod, Robert M. *The Evolution of Cooperation*. New York: Basic Books, 1984.

Ayoob, Mohammed. *The Third World Security Predicament: State Making, Regional Conflict, and the International System*. Boulder, CO: Lynne Rienner, 1995.

Bhaumik, Subir. *Troubled Periphery: Crisis of India's North East*. New Delhi: Sage, 2009.

Bijian, Zheng. "China's 'Peaceful Rise' to Great-Power Status." *Foreign Affairs* 84, no. 5 (2005): 18–24.

Bose, Sumantra. *Kashmir: Roots of Conflict, Paths to Peace*. Cambridge, MA: Harvard University Press, 2003.

Brecher, Michael. *India and World Politics: Krishna Menon's View of the World*. London: Oxford University Press, 1968.

———. "Kashmir: A Case Study in United Nations Mediation." *Pacific Affairs* 26, no. 3 (1953): 195–207.

———. "Non-Alignment Under Stress: The West and the India-China Border War." *Pacific Affairs* 52, no. 4 (1979): 612–630.

———. *The Struggle for Kashmir*. New York: Oxford University Press, 1953.

Brines, Russell. *The Indo-Pakistani Conflict*. London: Pall Mall Press, 1968.

Brown, Judith M. *Nehru: A Political Life*. New Haven: Yale University Press, 2003.

Burke, S. M. *Mainsprings of Indian and Pakistani Foreign Policies*. Minneapolis: University of Minnesota Press, 1974.

———. *Pakistan's Foreign Policy: An Historical Analysis*. London: Oxford University Press, 1973.

Campbell-Johnson, Alan. *Mission with Mountbatten*. London: Hale, 1951.

Carter, David B. "Provocation and the Strategy of Terrorist and Guerilla Attacks." *International Organization* 70, no. 1 (Winter 2016): 133–173

Chakravarti, Prithwis Chandra. *India's China Policy*. Bloomington: Indiana University Press, 1962.

Chaowu, Dai. "From 'Hindi-Chini Bhai Bhai' to 'International Class Struggle' Against Nehru: China's India Policy and the Frontier Dispute, 1950–62." In *The Sino-Indian War of 1962: New Perspectives*, edited by Amit Das Gupta and Lorenz M. Lüthi, 68–84. London: Routledge, 2017.

Chaudhuri, Rudra. *Forged in Crisis: India and the United States Since 1947*. New York: Oxford University Press, 2014.

———. "The Making of an 'All Weather Friendship': Pakistan, China and the History of a Border Agreement: 1949–1963." *International History Review* (March 2017), 1–24. Accessed August 1, 2017, at doi:10.1080/07075332.2017.1298529.

Cheema, Pervaiz Iqbal. *Pakistan's Defense Policy, 1947–58.* Basingstoke: Macmillan, 1990.

Cho, Hyun-Binn. "Tying the Adversary's Hands: A Model of Provocation and the Sino-India War of 1962." Unpublished manuscript, March 2016.

Christensen, Thomas J. "Windows and War: Trend Analysis and Beijing's Use of Force." In *New Directions in the Study of China's Foreign Policy*, edited by Alastair I. Johnston and Robert S. Ross, 50–85. Stanford: Stanford University Press, 2006.

Chung, Chien-Peng. *Domestic Politics, International Bargaining and China's Territorial Disputes.* London: Routledge, 2004.

Clare, Joe, and Vesna Danilovic. "Multiple Audiences and Reputation Building in International Conflict." *Journal of Conflict Resolution* 54, no. 6: 860–882.

Cohen, Stephen P. *The Idea of Pakistan.* Washington, DC: Brookings Institution Press, 2004.

———. *The Pakistan Army.* Karachi: Oxford University Press, 1998.

Colaresi, Michael P. *Scare Tactics: The Politics of International Rivalry.* Syracuse: Syracuse University Press, 2005.

Coll, Steve. "The Back Channel: India and Pakistan's Secret Kashmir Talks." *New Yorker*, March 2, 2009. Accessed August 1, 2017, at http://www.newyorker.com/magazine/2009/03/02/the-back-channel.

Copeland, Dale C. "Do Reputations Matter?" *Security Studies* 7, no. 1 (1997): 33–71.

———. *The Origins of Major War.* Ithaca, NY: Cornell University Press, 2000.

Crescenzi, Mark J. C. "Reputation and Interstate Conflict." *American Journal of Political Science* 51, no. 2 (2007): 382–396.

Crescenzi, Mark J., Jacob D. Kathman, Katja B. Kleinberg, and Reed M. Wood. "Reliability, Reputation, and Alliance Formation." *International Studies Quarterly* 56, no. 2 (2012): 259–274.

Crocker, Walter R. *Nehru: A Contemporary's Estimate.* London: Allen & Unwin, 1966.

Dafoe, Allan, Sophia Hatz, and Baobag Zhang. "Coercion and Provocation." Unpublished manuscript, February 21, 2017. Accessed August 1, 2017, at http://www.allandafoe.com/provocation.pdf.

Dafoe, Allan, Jonathan Renshon, and Paul Huth. "Reputation and Status as Motives for War." *Annual Review of Political Science* 17:371–393.

Dalvi, J. P. *Himalayan Blunder.* Bombay: Thacker and Co., 1966.

Das, Durga, ed. *Sardar Patel's Correspondence, 1945–50.* Ahmedabad: Navajivan Publishing House, 1971.

Das Gupta, Amit, and Lorenz Lüthi, eds. *The Sino-Indian War of 1962: New Perspectives.* London: Routledge, 2017.

David, Steven R. *Choosing Sides: Alignment and Realignment in the Third World.* Baltimore: Johns Hopkins University Press, 1991.

Deng, Yong. "Reputation and the Security Dilemma: China Reacts to the China Threat Theory." In *New Directions in the Study of China's Foreign Policy*, edited by Alastair I. Johnston and Robert S. Ross, 186–216. Stanford: Stanford University Press, 2006.

Diehl, Paul F., ed. *A Road Map to War: Territorial Dimensions of International Conflict.* Nashville, TN: Vanderbilt University Press, 1999.

Diehl, Paul F., and Gary Goertz. *War and Peace in International Rivalry.* Ann Arbor: University of Michigan Press, 2000.

Deora, M. S., and R. Grover, eds. *Documents on Kashmir Problem*, 3 vols. New Delhi: Discovery Publishing House, 1991.

Downs, George W., and Michael A. Jones. "Reputation, Compliance, and International Law." *Journal of Legal Studies* 31, no. S1 (2002): S95–S114.

Dutt, Subimal. *With Nehru in the Foreign Office.* Calcutta: Minerva Associates, 1977.

Fair, Christine C. *Fighting to the End: The Pakistan Army's Way of War.* New York: Oxford University Press, 2014.

Fairbank, John K. "China's Foreign Policy in Historical Perspective." *Foreign Affairs* 47, no. 3 (April 1969): 449–463.

Fearon, James D. "Domestic Political Audiences and the Escalation of International Disputes." *American Political Science Review* 88, no. 3 (1994): 577–592.

———. "Rationalist Explanations for War." *International Organization* 49, no. 3 (1995): 379–414.

———. "Signaling Foreign Policy Interests: Tying Hands Versus Sinking Costs." *Journal of Conflict Resolution* 41, no. 1 (1997): 68–90.

Fisher, Margaret W., Leo E. Rose, and Robert A. Huttenback. *Himalayan Battleground: Sino-Indian Rivalry in Ladakh.* New York: Praeger, 1963.

Fravel, M. Taylor. "Power Shifts and Escalation: Explaining China's Use of Force in Territorial Disputes." *International Security* 32, no. 3 (2008): 44–83.

———. "Regime Insecurity and International Cooperation: Explaining China's Compromises in Territorial Disputes." *International Security* 30, no. 2 (2005): 46–83.

———. *Strong Borders, Secure Nation: Cooperation and Conflict in China's Territorial Disputes.* Princeton: Princeton University Press, 2008.

Galbraith, John Kenneth. *Ambassador's Journal: A Personal Account of the Kennedy Year.* London: Hamish Hamilton, 1969.

Ganguly, Sumit. *The Crisis in Kashmir: Portents of War, Hopes of Peace.* Cambridge: Cambridge University Press, 1997.

———. *The Origins of War in South Asia: The Indo-Pakistani Conflicts Since 1947.* Boulder, CO: Westview Press, 1994.

Ganguly, Sumit, and Kanti Bajpai. "India and the Crisis in Kashmir." *Asian Survey* 34, no. 5 (1994): 401–416.

Garver, John W. "China's Decision for War with India in 1962." In *New Directions in the Study of China's Foreign Policy,* edited by Alastair I. Johnston and Robert S. Ross, 86–130. Stanford: Stanford University Press, 2006.

———. *Protracted Contest: Sino-Indian Rivalry in the Twentieth Century.* Seattle: University of Washington Press, 2001.

Ghose, Sankar. *Jawaharlal Nehru: A Biography.* New Delhi: Allied Publishers, 1993.

Gibler, Douglas M. "The Costs of Reneging: Reputation and Alliance Formation." *Journal of Conflict Resolution* 52, no. 3: 426–454.

Glaser, Charles L. "The Security Dilemma Revisited." *World Politics* 50, no. 1 (1997): 171–201.

Goddard, Stacie E. *Indivisible Territory and the Politics of Legitimacy: Jerusalem and Northern Ireland.* Cambridge: Cambridge University Press, 2010.

Goemans, Hein E. *War and Punishment: The Causes of War Termination and the First World War.* Princeton: Princeton University Press, 2000.

Goertz, Gary, and Paul F. Diehl. *Territorial Changes and International Conflict.* London: Routledge, 1992.

Gopal, Sarvepalli. *Jawaharlal Nehru: A Biography,* 3 vols. Cambridge, MA: Harvard University Press, 1976.

Gopal, Sarvepalli, Ravinder Kumar, H.Y. Sharada Prasad, A. K. Damodaran, and Mushirual

Hasan eds. *Selected Works of Jawaharlal Nehru: Second Series*. New Delhi: Jawaharlal Nehru Memorial Fund and Oxford University Press, 1984–.

Grieco, Joseph M. "Anarchy and the Limits of Cooperation: A Realist Critique of the Newest Liberal Institutionalism." *International Organization* 42, no. 3 (1988): 485–507.

Grunfeld, Tom A. *The Making of Modern Tibet*. Armonk, NY: M. E. Sharpe, 1996.

Guha, Ramachandra. *India After Gandhi: The History of the World's Largest Democracy*. New York: HarperCollins, 2007.

Guisinger, Alexandra, and Alastair Smith. "Honest Threats: The Interaction of Reputation and Political Institutions in International Crises." *Journal of Conflict Resolution* 46, no. 2: 175–200.

Gundevia, Y. D. *Outside the Archives*. Hyderabad: Sangam Books, 1984.

Gupta, Sisir. *Kashmir: A Study in India-Pakistan Relations*. Bombay: Indian Council of World Affairs, 1967.

Gupta, Sourabh. "India and Bangladesh: Calculus of Territorial Dispute Settlement." *East Asia Forum*, October 20, 2011. Accessed August 1, 2017, at *http://www.eastasiaforum. org/2011/10/10/india-and-bangladesh-calculus-of-territorial-dispute-settlement/*.

Guruswamy, Mohan. "Sino-Indian Border Dispute: New Package Deal Floated by Former Chinese Negotiator is No Deal at All." *Scroll.in*, March 15, 2017. Accessed August 2, 2017, at https://scroll.in/article/830978/sino-indian-border-dispute-new-package-deal -floated-by-former-chinese-negotiator-is-no-deal-at-all.

Hagerty, Devin T. *The Consequences of Nuclear Proliferation: Lessons from South Asia*. Cambridge, MA: MIT Press, 1998.

Hall, Todd. "On Provocation: Outrage, International Relations, and the Franco-Prussian War." *Security Studies* 26, no. 1 (2017): 1–29

Harding, Harry, ed. *China's Foreign Relations in the 1980s*. New Haven: Yale University Press, 1984.

Harvey, Frank P., and John Mitton. *Fighting for Credibility: US Reputation and International Politics*. Toronto: University of Toronto Press, 2017.

Hassner, Ron E. *War on Sacred Grounds*. Ithaca, NY: Cornell University Press, 2009.

Hensel, Paul, and Sara Mitchell. "Issue Indivisibility and Territorial Claims." *GeoJournal* 64, no. 4 (2005): 275–285.

Herz, John H. "Idealist Internationalism and the Security Dilemma." *World Politics* 2, no. 2 (1950): 157–180.

Hinton, Harold C. *China's Relations with Burma and Vietnam: A Brief Survey*. New York: Institute of Pacific Relations, 1958.

Hodson, H. V. *The Great Divide: Britain-India-Pakistan*. Karachi: Oxford University Press, 1985.

Hoffmann, Steven A. *India and the China Crisis*. Berkeley: University of California Press, 1990.

————. "Rethinking the Linkage Between Tibet and the China–India Border Conflict: A Realist Approach." *Journal of Cold War Studies* 8, no. 3 (2006): 165–194.

Hopf, Ted. *Peripheral Vision: Deterrence Theory and American Foreign Policy in the Third World, 1965–1990*. Ann Arbor: University of Michigan Press, 1994.

Hunt, Michael H. "Chinese Foreign Relations in Historical Perspective." In *China's Foreign Relations in the 1980s*, edited by Harry Harding, 1–42. New Haven: Yale University Press, 1984.

Huth, Paul K. "Reputations and Deterrence: A Theoretical and Empirical Assessment." *Security Studies* 7, no. 1 (1997): 72–99.

———. *Standing Your Ground: Territorial Disputes and International Conflict.* Ann Arbor: Univeristy of Michigan Press, 1996.

———. "Why Are Territorial Disputes Between States a Central Cause of International Conflict?" In *What Do We Know About War?* edited by John A. Vasquez, 85–110. Lanham, MD: Rowman & Littlefield, 2000.

Huth, Paul K., and Todd L. Allee. *The Democratic Peace and Territorial Conflict in the Twentieth Century.* Cambridge: Cambridge University Press, 2002.

Huth, Paul K., Scott Bennett, and Christopher Gelpi. "Systemic Uncertainty, Risk Propensity, and International Conflict Among the Great Powers." *Journal of Conflict Resolution* 36, no. 3 (1992): 478–517.

Huth, Paul K., Christopher Gelpi, and Scott Bennett. "The Escalation of Great Power Militarized Disputes." *American Political Science Review* 87, no. 3 (1993): 609–623.

Huth, Paul K., and Bruce Russett. "Deterrence Failure and Crisis Escalation." *International Studies Quarterly*, 32, no. 1 (1988): 29–45.

Huth, Paul K., and Bruce Russett. "What Makes Deterrence Work? Cases from 1900 to 1980." *World Politics* 36, no. 4 (1984): 496–526.

Hyer, Eric A. *The Pragmatic Dragon: China's Grand Strategy and Boundary Settlements.* Vancouver: University of British Columbia Press, 2015.

———. "The Strategic and Regional Contexts of the Sino-Indian Border Conflict." In *The Sino-Indian War of 1962: New Perspectives*, edited by Amit Das Gupta and Lorenz M. Lüthi, 85–102. London: Routledge, 2017.

"India, Bangladesh Ratify Historic Land Deal, Narendra Modi Announces New $2 Billion Line of Credit to Dhaka." *Times of India*, June 6, 2015. Accessed August 1, 2017, at http://timesofindia.indiatimes.com/india/India-Bangladesh-ratify-historic-land-deal-Narendra-Modi-announces-new-2-billion-line-of-credit-to-Dhaka/articleshow/47567164.cms.

Jacob, Jabin T. "Remembering 1962 in India, 50 Years On," In *The Sino-Indian War of 1962: New Perspectives*, edited by Amit Das Gupta and Lorenz M. Lüthi, 233–252. London: Routledge, 2017.

Jalal, Ayesha. *The State of Martial Rule: The Origins of Pakistan's Political Economy of Defense.* Cambridge: Cambridge University Press, 1990.

Jervis, Robert. "Cooperation under the Security Dilemma." *World Politics* 30, no. 2 (1978): 167–214.

———. *The Logic of Images in International Relations.* New York: Columbia University Press, 1970.

———. *Perception and Misperception in International Politics.* Princeton: Princeton University Press, 1976.

———. "Security Regimes." *International Organization* 36, no. 2 (1982): 357–378.

Jervis, Robert, Richard Ned Lebow, and Janice Gross Stein. *Psychology and Deterrence.* Baltimore: Johns Hopkins University Press, 1985.

Jetly, Nancy. *India China Relations, 1947–1977: A Study of Parliament's Role in the Making of Foreign Policy.* New Delhi: Radiant Publishers, 1979.

Jha, Prem Shankar. *Origins of a Dispute: Kashmir 1947.* New Delhi: Oxford University Press, 2003.

Johnston, Alastair I. *Cultural Realism: Strategic Culture and Grand Strategy in Chinese History.* Princeton: Princeton University Press, 1998.

Johnston, Alastair I., and Robert S. Ross, eds. *New Directions in the Study of China's Foreign Policy.* Stanford: Stranford University Press, 2006.

Kahin, George M. *The Asian-African Conference, Bandung, Indonesia, April 1955*. Ithaca, NY: Cornell University Press, 1956.

Kapur, Ashok. *India: From Regional to World Power*. London: Routledge, 2006.

*Kashmir 1947–56: Excerpts from Prime Minister Nehru's Speeches*. New Delhi: Information Service of India, 1956.

Kaul, Lt. Gen. Brij Mohan. *The Untold Story*. Bombay: Allied Publishers, 1967.

Kennedy, Andrew Bingham. *The International Ambitions of Mao and Nehru: National Efficacy Beliefs and the Making of Foreign Policy*. Cambridge: Cambridge University Press, 2011.

Keohane, Robert O. *After Hegemony: Cooperation and Discord in the World Political Economy*. Princeton: Princeton University Press, 1984.

Kertzer, Joshua D. *Resolve in International Politics*. Princeton: Princeton University Press, 2016.

Khan, Akbar. *Raiders in Kashmir*. Islamabad: National Book Foundation, 1975.

Khan, Ayub Mohammad. *Friends Not Masters: A Political Autobiography*. London: Oxford University Press, 1967.

Khilnani, Sunil. *The Idea of India*. New York: Farrar, Straus and Giroux, 1997.

Korbel, Josef. *Danger in Kashmir*. Princeton: Princeton University Press, 1966.

Kozicki, Richard J. "The Sino-Burmese Frontier Problem." *Far Eastern Survey* 26, no. 3 (1957): 33–38.

Krasner, Stephen D. *Defending the National Interest: Raw Materials Investments and U.S. Foreign Policy*. Princeton: Princeton University Press, 1978.

Kugiel, Patryk. *India's Soft Power: A New Foreign Policy Strategy*. New York: Routledge, 2017.

Kydd, Andrew H. *Trust and Mistrust in International Relations*. Princeton: Princeton University Press, 2005.

Lall, Arthur S. *The Emergence of Modern India*. New York: Columbia University Press, 1981.

———. *How Communist China Negotiates*. New York: Columbia University Press, 1968.

Lamb, Alastair. *The China-India Border: The Origins of the Disputed Boundaries*. New York: Oxford University Press, 1964.

———. *Incomplete Partition: The Genesis of the Kashmir Dispute, 1947–1948*. Karachi: Oxford University Press, 2002.

———. *The McMahon Line: A Study in the Relations Between India, China, and Tibet, 1904 to 1914*. London: Routledge, 1966.

———. "The Sino-Pakistani Boundary Agreement of 2 March 1963." *Australian Outlook* 18, no. 3 (1964): 299–312.

Larson, Deborah W. "Trust and Missed Opportunities in International Relations." *Political Psychology* 18, no. 3 (September 1997): 701–734.

Levy, Jack S. "The Diversionary Theory of War: A Critique." In *Handbook of War Studies*, edited by Manus I. Midlarsky, 259–288. Boston: Unwin Hyman, 1989.

Lobell, Steven E., Norrin M. Ripsman, and Jeffrey W. Taliaferro, eds. *Neoclassical Realism, the State, and Foreign Policy*. Cambridge: Cambridge University Press, 2009.

Lüthi, Lorenz M. *The Sino-Soviet Split: Cold War in the Communist World*. Princeton: Princeton University Press, 2008.

Mack, Andrew. "Why Big Nations Lose Small Wars: The Politics of Asymmetric Conflict." *World Politics* 27, no. 2 (1975): 175–200.

Macmillan, Margaret. *Nixon and Mao: The Week That Changed the World*. New York: Random House, 2008.

Mahajan, M. C. *Looking Back*. London: Asia Publishing House, 1963.

Malone, David. *Does the Elephant Dance? Contemporary Indian Foreign Policy*. London: Oxford University Press, 2011.

Mansbach, Richard W., and John A. Vasquez. *In Search of Theory: A New Paradigm for Global Politics*. New York: Columbia University Press, 1981.

Mansingh, Surjit. "Nehru and Pakistan." In *Legacy of Nehru: A Centennial Celebration*, edited by D. R. SarDesai and Anand Mohan, 307–321. Springfield, VA: Nataraj Books.

Maxwell, Neville. "China and India: The Un-Negotiated Dispute." *China Quarterly* 43 (1970): 47–80.

———. *India's China War*. London: Cape, 1972.

———. "Sino-Indian Border Dispute Reconsidered." *Economic and Political Weekly* 34, no. 15 (1999): 905–918.

McMahon, Robert J. *The Cold War on the Periphery: The United States, India, and Pakistan*. New York: Columbia University Press, 1994.

———. "United States Cold War Strategy in South Asia: Making a Military Commitment to Pakistan, 1947–1954." *Journal of American History* 75, no. 3 (December 1988): 812–840.

Mearsheimer, John J. *The Tragedy of Great Power Politics*. New York: Norton, 2001.

Menon, V. P. *The Story of the Integration of the Indian States*. Calcutta: Orient Longmans, 1956.

Mercer, Jonathan. *Reputation and International Politics*. Ithaca, NY: Cornell University Press, 1996.

Midlarsky, Manus I., ed. *Handbook of War Studies*. Boston: Unwin Hyman, 1989.

Miller, Manjari Chatterjee. *Wronged by Empire: Post-Imperial Ideology and Foreign Policy in India and China*. Stanford: Stanford University Press, 2013.

Mishra, Pankaj. "Kashmir: The World's Most Dangerous Place." *New York Review of Books*, March 4, 2010. Accessed August 1, 2017, at http://www.nybooks.com/daily/2010/03/04/kashmir-the-worlds-most-dangerous-place.

Morgan, Patrick M. "Saving Face for the Sake of Deterrence." In *Psychology and Deterrence*, edited by Robert Jervis, Richard Ned Lebow, and Janice Gross Stein, 125–152. Baltimore: Johns Hopkins University Press, 1985.

Mullik, B. N. *My Years with Nehru: The Chinese Betrayal*. New Delhi: Allied Publishers, 1971.

Muni, S. D. *Foreign Policy of Nepal*. Delhi: National Publishing House, 1973.

Nanda, B. R. "Introduction." In *Indian Foreign Policy: The Nehru Years*, edited by B. R. Nanda, 1–23. New Delhi: Radiant, 1990.

———, ed. *Indian Foreign Policy: The Nehru Years*. New Delhi: Radiant, 1990.

Nasr, Vali. "National Identities and the India-Pakistan Conflict." In *The India-Pakistan Conflict: An Enduring Rivalry*, edited by T. V. Paul, 178–201. New York: Cambridge University Press, 2005.

Nawaz, Shuja. *Crossed Swords: Pakistan, Its Army, and the Wars Within*. Karachi: Oxford University Press, 2008.

Nehru, Jawaharlal. *Pakistan Seeks to Profit from Chinese Aggression*. New Delhi: Government of India, Ministry of Information and Broadcasting, July 1963.

Noorani, A. G. "The Dixon Plan." *Frontline* 19, no. 21 (October 12–25, 2002). Accessed August 1, 2017, at http://www.frontline.in/static/html/fl1921/stories/20021025002508200.htm.

———. *India-China Boundary Problem, 1846–1947: History and Diplomacy*. New Delhi: Oxford University Press, 2011.

———. "Review: How and Why Nehru and Abdullah Fell Out." *Economic and Political Weekly* 34, no. 5 (1999): 268–272.

Norbu, Dawa. "Tibet in Sino-Indian Relations: The Centrality of Marginality." *Asian Survey* 37, no. 11 (1997): 1078–1095.

*Notes, Memoranda and Letters Exchanged and Agreements Signed Between the Governments of India and China.* New Delhi: Government of India, Ministry of External Affairs, 1959–1968.

Organski, A. F. K., and Jacek Kugler. *The War Ledger.* Chicago: University of Chicago Press, 1980.

Palit, D. K. *War in the High Himalaya: Indian Army in Crisis, 1962.* London: Hurst, 1991.

Pant, Harsh V. "India and Bangladesh: Will the Twain Ever Meet?" *Asian Survey* 47, no. 2 (2007): 231–249.

———. *The Rise of China: Implications for India.* New Delhi: Foundation Books, 2012.

Paul, T. V. *Asymmetric Conflicts: War Initiation by Weaker Powers.* Cambridge: Cambridge University Press, 1994.

———. *The Tradition of Non-Use of Nuclear Weapons.* Stanford: Stanford University Press, 2009.

———. "Why Has the India–Pakistan Rivalry Been So Enduring? Power Asymmetry and an Intractable Conflict." *Security Studies* 15, no. 4 (2006): 600–630.

———, ed. *The India-Pakistan Conflict: An Enduring Rivalry.* New York: Cambridge University Press, 2005.

Powell, Robert. "Absolute and Relative Gains in International Relations Theory." *American Political Science Review* 85, no. 4 (1991): 1303–1320.

———. *Nuclear Deterrence Theory: The Search for Credibility.* Cambridge: Cambridge University Press, 1990.

———. "War as a Commitment Problem." *International Organization* 60, no. 1 (2006): 169–203.

Power, Paul F. "Indian Foreign Policy: The Age of Nehru." *Review of Politics* 26, no. 2 (1964): 257–286.

Prescott, J. R. V. *Map of Mainland Asia by Treaty.* Carlton: Melbourne University Press, 1975.

Press, Daryl G. *Calculating Credibility: How Leaders Assess Military Threats.* Ithaca, NY: Cornell University Press, 2005.

*Prime Minister on Sino-Indian Relations: In Parliament,* vol. 1. New Delhi: External Publicity Division of Ministry of External Affairs, Government of India, 1962.

Putnam, Robert D. "Diplomacy and Domestic Politics: The Logic of Two-Level Games." *International Organization* 42, no. 3 (1988): 427–460.

Raghavan, Srinath. "Sino-Indian Boundary Dispute, 1948–60: A Reappraisal." *Economic and Political Weekly* 41, no. 36 (2006): 3882–3892.

———. *War and Peace in Modern India.* New York: Palgrave Macmillan, 2010.

Raja Mohan, C. *Samudra Manthan: Sino-Indian Rivalry in the Indo-Pacific.* Washington, DC: Carnegie Endowment for International Peace, 2012.

Rasler, Karen A., and William R. Thompson. "Contested Territory, Strategic Rivalries, and Conflict Escalation." *International Studies Quarterly* 50, no. 1 (2006): 145–168.

Reiter, Dan. *How Wars End.* Princeton: Princeton University Press, 2009.

Renshon, Jonathan, Allan Dafoe, and Paul Huth. "Leader Influence and Reputation Formation in World Policits." *American Journal of Political Science* (2018). Accessed February 11, 2018, at doi:10.1111/ajps.12335.

"Resolution Adopted by the United Nations Commission for India and Pakistan." August 13, 1948. Accessed August 1, 2017, at https://www.mtholyoke.edu/acad/intrel/un com1.htm.

"Resolution Adopted by the United Nations Commission for India and Pakistan." January 9, 1949. Accessed August 1, 2017, at https://www.mtholyoke.edu/acad/intrel/uncom 2.htm.

Reynolds, David. *From World War to Cold War: Churchill, Roosevelt, and the International History of the 1940s*. London: Oxford University Press, 2006.

Richardson, Hugh E. *Tibet and Its History*. London: Oxford University Press, 1962.

Riedel, Bruce. *JFK's Forgotten Crisis: Tibet, the CIA, and the Sino-Indian War*. Washington, DC: Brookings Institution Press, 2015.

Rizvi, Hasan Askari. *Pakistan and the Geostrategic Environment: A Study of Foreign Policy*. London: Macmillan, 1993.

Rose, Gideon. "Review: Neoclassical Realism and Theories of Foreign Policy." *World Politics* 51, no. 1 (1998): 144–172.

Rose, Leo E. *Nepal: Strategy for Survival*. Berkeley: University of California Press, 1971.

Rowland, John. *A History of Sino-Indian Relations: Hostile Co-Existence*. Princeton: Van Nostrand, 1967.

Roy, A. Bikash. "Intervention Across Bisecting Borders." *Journal of Peace Research* 34, no. 3 (1997): 303–314.

Rushdie, Salman. "The Most Dangerous Place in the World." *New York Times*, May 30, 2002. Accessed August 1, 2017, at http://www.nytimes.com/2002/05/30/opinion/the -most-dangerous-place-in-the-world.html.

Saideman, Stephen M. *The Ties That Divide: Ethnic Politics, Foreign Policy, and International Conflict*. New York: Columbia University Press, 2001.

SarDesai, D. R., and Anand Mohan, eds. *Legacy of Nehru: A Centennial Celebration*. Springfield, VA: Nataraj Books, 1992.

Sartori, Anne E. *Deterrence by Diplomacy*. Princeton: Princeton University Press, 2005.

Schelling, Thomas C. *Arms and Influence*. New Haven: Yale University Press, 1966.

———. *The Strategy of Conflict*. Cambridge: Harvard University Press, 1960.

Schofield, Victoria. *Kashmir in Conflict: India, Pakistan and the Unfinished War*. New York: I. B. Tauris, 2000.

Schultz, Kenneth A. "Looking for Audience Costs." *Journal of Conflict Resolution* 45, no. 1 (2001): 32–60.

———. "The Politics of Risking Peace: Do Hawks or Doves Deliver the Olive Branch?" *International Organization* 50, no. 1: 1–38.

Senese, Paul Domenic, and John A. Vasquez. *The Steps to War: An Empirical Study*. Princeton: Princeton University Press, 2008.

Sen Gupta, Bhabani. "India in the Twenty-First Century." *International Affairs* 73, no. 2: 297–314.

Shambaugh, David. *China Goes Global: The Partial Power*. New York: Oxford University Press, 2013.

Sidhu, Waheguru Pal Singh, and Jing-Dong Yuan. "Resolving the Sino-Indian Border Dispute: Building Confidence Through Cooperative Monitoring." *Asian Survey* 41, no. 2 (2001): 351–376.

Singh, Anita Inder. *The Limits of British Influence: South Asia and the Anglo-American Relationship, 1947–1956*. London: Pinter, 1993.

Singh, Jaswant. *Defending India*. Basingstoke: Macmillan, 1999.

Simmons, Beth A. "International Law and State Behavior: Commitment and Compliance in International Monetary Affairs." *American Political Science Review* 94, no. 4 (2000): 819–835.

————. "See You in Court? The Appeal to Quasi-Judicial Legal Processes in the Settlement of Territorial Disputes." In *A Road Map to War: Territorial Dimensions of International Conflict*, edited by Paul F. Diehl, 205–37. Nashville, TN: Vanderbilt University Press, 1999.

Sinha, P. B., and A. A. Athale. *History of the Conflict with China, 1962.* New Delhi: Government of India, Ministry of Defense, 1992.

Small, Andrew. *The China-Pakistan Axis: Asia's New Geopolitics.* New York: Oxford University Press, 2015.

Smith, Jeff M. *Cold Peace: China-India Rivalry in the Twenty-First* Century. Lanham, MD: Lexington Books, 2014.

Snyder, Glenn Herald, and Paul Diesing. *Conflict Among Nations: Bargaining, Decision Making, and System Structure in International Crises.* Princeton: Princeton University Press, 1977.

Subrahmanyam, K. "Nehru and the India-China Conflict of 1962." In *Indian Foreign Policy: The Nehru Years*, edited by B. R. Nanda, 102–130. New Delhi: Vikas, 1976.

Syed, Anwar Hussain. *China and Pakistan: Diplomacy of an Entente Cordiale.* Amherst: University of Massachusetts Press, 1974.

Tang, Shiping. "Reputation, Cult of Reputation, and International Conflict." *Security Studies* 14, no. 1 (2005): 34–62.

Taylor, Robert H. *Foreign and Domestic Consequences of the KMT Intervention in Burma.* Ithaca, NY: Southeast Asia Program, Cornell University, 1973.

Tharoor, Shashi. *Reasons of State: Political Development and India's Foreign Policy Under Indira Gandhi, 1966–1977.* New Delhi: Vikas Publishing House, 1982.

Thomas, Raju G. C. "Security Relationships in Southern Asia: Differences in the Indian and American Perspectives." *Asian Survey* 21, no. 7 (July 1981): 689–709.

Thucydides. *History of the Peloponnesian War.* Translated by Rex Warner. Baltimore: Penguin, 1972.

Toft, Monica Duffy. *The Geography of Ethnic Violence: Identity, Interests, and the Indivisibility of Territory.* Princeton: Princeton University Press, 2003.

————. "Indivisible Territory, Geographic Concentration, and Ethnic War." *Security Studies* 12, no. 2 (2002): 82–119.

Tomz, Michael, *Reputation and International Cooperation: Sovereign Debt Across Three Centuries.* Princeton: Princeton University Press, 2007.

Tsering, Shakya. *The Dragon in the Land of Snows: A History of Modern Tibet Since 1947.* New York: Penguin Compass, 2000.

Van Evera, Stephen. "Hypotheses on Nationalism and War." *International Security* 18, no. 4 (1994): 5–39.

————. "Offense, Defense, and the Causes of War." *International Security* 22, no. 4 (Spring 1998): 5–43.

Varshney, Ashutosh. "India, Pakistan, and Kashmir: Antinomies of Nationalism." *Asian Survey* 31, no. 11 (1991): 997–1019.

Vasquez, John A. *The War Puzzle.* Cambridge: Cambridge University Press, 1993.

————, ed. *What Do We Know About War?* Lanham, MD: Rowman & Littlefield, 2000.

Vasquez, John A., and Marie T. Henehan. *Territory, War, and Peace.* New York: Routledge, 2011.

Vertzberger, Yaacov. *Misperceptions in Foreign Policymaking: The Sino-Indian Conflict, 1959–1962.* Boulder, CO: Westview Press, 1984.

Walt, Stephen M. *The Origins of Alliances.* Ithaca, NY: Cornell University Press, 1987.

Walter, Barbara F. "Building Reputation: Why Governments Fight Some Separatists But Not Others." *American Journal of Political Science* 50, no. 2 (2006): 313–330.

———. "Explaining the Intractability of Territorial Conflict." *International Studies Review* 5, no. 4 (2003): 137–153.

———. *Reputation and Civil War: Why Separatist Conflicts Are So Violent.* Cambridge: Cambridge University Press, 2009.

Waltz, Kenneth N. *Theory of International Politics.* Reading, MA: Addison-Wesley, 1979.

Weisiger, Alex, and Keren Yarhi-Mili. "Revisiting Reputation: How Past Actions Matter in International Politics." *International Organization* 69, no. 2 (Spring 2016): 473–495.

Whiting, Allen S. "Chinese Behavior Towards India: 1962." *First Sino-American Conference on Mainland China* 22 (1971).

———. *The Chinese Calculus of Deterrence: India and Indochina.* Ann Arbor: University of Michigan Press, 1975.

Whittam, Daphne E. "The Sino-Burmese Boundary Treaty." *Pacific Affairs* 34, no. 2 (1961): 174–183.

Wirsing, Robert. *India, Pakistan, and the Kashmir Dispute: On Regional Conflict and Its Resolution.* New York: St. Martin's Press, 1994.

———. *Kashmir in the Shadow of War: Regional Rivalries in a Nuclear Age.* Armonk, NY: M. E. Sharpe, 2003.

Woodman, Dorothy. *The Making of Burma.* London: Cresset Press, 1962.

Zagare, Frank C. "Rationality and Deterrence." *World Politics* 42, no. 2 (1990): 238–260.

Zartman, I. William, and Jeffrey Z. Rubin. "The Study of Power and the Practice of Negotiation." In *Power and Negotiation*, edited by I. William Zartman and Jeffrey Z. Rubin, 3–28. Ann Arbor: University of Michigan Press, 2000.

———. "Symmetry and Asymmetry in Negotiation." In *Power and Negotiation*, edited by I. William Zartman and Jeffrey Z. Rubin, 271–294. Ann Arbor: University of Michigan Press, 2000.

———, eds. *Power and Negotiation.* Ann Arbor: University of Michigan Press, 2000.

# Index

Page references followed by *m* or *t* refer to maps or tables, respectively. Page numbers followed by "n" refer to endnotes.

*Political Conflict and Economic Interdependence Across the Taiwan Strait and Beyond.*
By Scott L. Kastner.
2009

*(Re)Negotiating East and Southeast Asia: Region, Regionalism,
and the Association of Southeast Asian Nations*
By Alice D. Ba.
2009

*Normalizing Japan: Politics, Identity, and the Evolution of Security Practice.*
By Andrew L. Oros.
2008

*Reluctant Restraint: The Evolution of China's Nonproliferation Policies and Practices,
1980–2004.*
By Evan S. Medeiros.
2007

*Why Taiwan? Geostrategic Rationales for China's Territorial Integrity.*
By Alan M. Wachman.
2007

*Beyond Compliance: China, International Organizations, and Global Security.*
By Ann Kent.
2007

*Dangerous Deterrent: Nuclear Weapons Proliferation and Conflict in South Asia.*
By S. Paul Kapur.
2007

*Minimum Deterrence and India's Nuclear Security.*
By Rajesh M. Basrur.
2006

*Rising to the Challenge: China's Grand Strategy and International Security.*
By Avery Goldstein.
2005

*Unifying China, Integrating with the World:
Securing Chinese Sovereignty in the Reform Era.*
By Allen Carlson.
2005

*Rethinking Security in East Asia: Identity, Power, and Efficiency.*
Edited by J. J. Suh, Peter J. Katzenstein, and Allen Carlson.
2004